Kid's Eye View
OF
Science

A Conceptual, Integrated Approach to Teaching Science, K-6

Susan J. Kovalik | Karen D. Olsen

CORWIN
A SAGE Company

For information:

Corwin
A SAGE Company
2455 Teller Road
Thousand Oaks, California 91320
(800) 233-9936
Fax: (800) 417-2466
www.corwin.com

SAGE Ltd.
1 Oliver's Yard
55 City Road
London EC1Y 1SP
United Kingdom

SAGE India Pvt. Ltd.
B 1/I 1 Mohan Cooperative Industrial Area
Mathura Road, New Delhi 110 044
India

SAGE Asia-Pacific Pte. Ltd.
33 Peking Street #02-01
Far East Square
Singapore 048763

Printed in the United States of America

Library of Congress Catalog-in-Publication Data

Kovalik, Susan.
Kid's eye view of science : a conceptual, integrated approach to teaching science, K–6 / Susan J. Kovalik, Karen D. Olsen.
      p. cm.
Includes bibliographical references and index.
ISBN 978-1-4129-9091-2 (pbk.)

  1. Science—Study and teaching (Elementary) 2. Science teachers—In-service training.
  I. Olsen, Karen (Karen D.) II. Title.

LB1585.K69 2010
372.3'5—dc22   2010021883

Earlier editions published by Books for Educators, Inc., 2007, 1994, 1991.

This book is printed on acid-free paper.

10 11 12 13 14 10 9 8 7 6 5 4 3 2 1

Acquisitions Editor:	Hudson Perigo
Associate Editor:	Joanna Coelho
Editorial Assistant:	Allison Scott
Graphic Design and Layout:	Lanitta Jaye Delk
Illustrations, Icons, and Charts:	Lanitta Jaye Delk
Frog Illustrations:	Virginia Hull Farnquist and Linea Frei
Editor:	Kathleen Wolgemuth
Proofreader:	Wendy Jo Dymond
Indexer:	Jean Casalegno
Cover Designer:	Rose Storey

TABLE OF CONTENTS

Welcome From the City Author

I grew up in San Francisco, California, the third generation of my family to be born there. I was surrounded by streetcars, buses attached to electric lines, elevators, escalators, tunnels, bridges, a grandfather who made wine in a huge vat in his basement and cured his own olives, and an uncle who had a car with a rumble seat. My experience with animals was limited to cats until the onset of World War II. When citizens were given permission to have chickens in their yards, I had my own chicken named Martha. She was a delight, followed me everywhere, and, without fail, each time she sat on her nest, she laid an egg. It was the most amazing occurrence. As my grandmother taught me how to collect eggs and carefully store them in the cooler, I literally began my science education.

My grandparents had a summer home on the Russian River 45 miles north of San Francisco. After this experience with chickens, I was on the lookout for other amazing animals. Along my route to the river, there were fields of cows, some of which were sitting. Based on my firsthand experience with chickens, I was sure they were laying eggs. And when those large eggs were cracked, milk would surely pour out. At the river house, I learned about crayfish, blackberry bushes, climbing trees, picking cherries, and the consequences of putting a leash on cats.

By the time I was five, I could create a fort in tall weeds in vacant lots, make dirt-clod bombs, slide down hills on cardboard boxes, and make kites from butcher paper. The day after the Fourth of July, I also knew how to find firecrackers that hadn't gone off and how to empty all the powder into a pile and create a minor explosion. I knew that horses belonged to policemen who rode through the neighborhood just as regularly as the fishman came with his fresh fish packed in ice. I surmised that the ice must have come from Wintergreen Arena where I went each year to see the Ice Follies.

I knew that margarine got its color from a little orange packet and that transfers allowed you to ride the buses and streetcars all day for a nickel. I knew that the 120 strawberry plants in our backyard created enough berries for pie, jam, ice cream topping, additions to our cereal, and food for the birds. I helped protect our two artichoke plants, being careful not to be punctured by the thorns, and I learned to love Best Foods Mayonnaise. I knew that Golden Gate Park was the largest park in the world and that the fish and flowers and tea gardens and stuffed animals in dioramas were something I could visit every week and still be dazzled.

I looked forward to the fall each year because of the incredible smell of burning leaves. I knew that all children had to order the flavor of ice cream that best matched what they were wearing, especially if it was Sunday and you were going to visit the "other" grandparents. I believed that the Emporium was the largest department store ever created—it had six floors, elevators and escalators, and a restaurant—and you could be there all day and nobody minded. I found out that a baby sister could be noisy and fun to play with and that the best thing about having your tonsils out was that you could have unlimited ice cream and green Jell-0.

On the eve of my fifth birthday, I was burned severely and had to spend the next six weeks in a military hospital across the bay surrounded by the range of injuries suffered by the men who had been at war—the results of technology gone astray. I was confronted with many realities there. Among them were that children were placed in cribs in the hallways because there were not enough rooms or beds. These hallways provided a seemingly endless parade of the horrors of war—men without limbs and some without faces. A painful reality was that my mother couldn't visit every day because the hospital was across the bay in Oakland and gas was rationed. Air raid sirens meant blackout curtains must cover each window, making the hospital a darkened, quiet pit of fear. In short, I was catapulted into an adult world maimed by war with scars yet to form.

I entered school as a five-year-old with an incredible range of firsthand experiences. At school I learned that warm milk and graham crackers were supposed to be good for you, that taking turns in the playhouse was expected, and that rest time on a small carpet was what kindergartners did whether they were tired or not. Little did I realize that this was a prelude for Dick and Jane and that my time at school would have little or nothing to do with my "real" life.

I remember science only vaguely once I started school; a fourth-grade teacher showed us how to make dioramas in a shoebox. We looked at pictures of animal families in our textbook and replicated them in the box, then put cellophane on top for sky.

In eighth grade, I saw my first science lab and all the requisite rules for the gas jets, the chemicals, and the animals in cages, and animals in jars of formaldehyde, and stuffed animals on the shelves. I don't remember any notable instruction—it was the room that fascinated me.

In high school, Miss Fauquet was the physiology teacher and what a year that was. We typed our blood, dissected rats, and recorded every muscle, bone, and organ that we found. We had a lab partner and an amazing three-ring binder where we kept records of everything that we did. It was the first time that I realized that science wasn't a subject—it was a gift waiting to be explored. Fifty years later, I still have that binder!

It wasn't until college that the magic of how science could be taught was demonstrated by Dr. Thaw. It was my last class for teacher preparation, a three-hour lab at night in the old science building, dark and smelly, filled with unknowns.

On the first night of our lab, he came in, climbed on the desk with an eraser and a dustpan and dropped both onto the floor.

"That, ladies, is science!" For the next semester, he acted as our tour director regaling the wonders of science by taking us throughout the campus during the day to show us that science is everywhere and our job was to see it, understand it, and realize how it effected our lives. Our lab assignment was to replicate the science in what we saw and see how it was connected to everything on campus. He truly was my inspiration for using science as my main course of instruction once I became a teacher.

I have grandchildren now, and as they have grown up I have shared the adventures of the world around them. On a dark winter morning at 6:30, I was having a candlelight breakfast with my oldest granddaughter who was four at that time. When we finished breakfast, I showed her how a candle flame would go out if you covered it with a glass. I know I said something about oxygen, and then she had a chance to make it happen herself. She asked how I knew how to do this and I responded that I had been a science teacher once. Her response to me was, "You'll always be a science teacher to me, Grandma."

Science is life and it is all around us. Use your LIFESKILL of Courage and go forth with the one subject that could forever change your students' ideas of learning, and in the process, create citizens who are knowledgeable and informed.

Welcome From the Country Author

"You can take the kid out of the country but you can't take the country out of the kid" is more true than anyone could ever guess; only a fellow country kid would truly understand. After short, city-habitat stays from coast-to-coast while traveling in the wake of a military-pilot father, my mother, brother, and I moved to the country when I was five. A brand spanking-new, one-room, first-through-eighth-grade schoolhouse and an old, drafty house with an earthquake-cracked chimney became my home in Parkfield, California, Earthquake Capital of the World.

As I recall, the country kids didn't immediately take to us transplants. As a result, my brother and I had plenty of time to hang out together—not at the malls we two, but in the hills, the scuz-entrusted reservoir, and, our favorite, the creek that ran behind the dozen buildings loosely referred to as "town." (The real town, where groceries and other necessities could be purchased, was an 80-mile round trip.)

Every day was an adventure. After five years of cramped city living, we had a lot to catch up on. In the summers, we chaffed under our mother's bedtime curfew; after all, it was still light outside and there were important things to do. Furthermore, why waste time taking a shower when we knew with certainty that we would only get dirty again? Besides, we hated drawing the short straw because the second shower invariably ended with cold water.

Our mother tried hard to bring us civilization, but we reveled in the ever-changing earth, the incredibly blue sky, the high hills all around us, the virtually endless list of things to do.

We explored firsthand the principles of simple machines through running about the countryside with purloined 78-speed records nailed to the end of a stick with a pop bottle top for an axle cap. The object was to see how many miles one could run before the record chipped (tensile strength, brittleness, force—all were factors carefully taken into account). Chipping lost you a point; crashing altogether meant you lost. That occupied us for most of a summer; I saw more of the hills that year than any time before or since.

Then there was the simple machine called the lever—the human arm. We were forever experimenting with how best to use the human body to make enormous things happen, such as a four-foot child attempting to saddle a five-foot horse.

We defied gravity and ran down steep hills as fast as our upper bodies could go, which was always faster than our feet. Headlong crashes were a mark of pride—speed and distance were the measures of success.

We made forts armed with freshly pulled grass rootballs, dug an underground house in a vacant lot, built our own toys—anything and everything we needed. Our only store-bought entertainment items were our baseball gloves with which we played not softball, as per regulations of the county schools office, but hard ball because it was smaller and thus more easily thrown and caught (a lecture on inertia, energy, and work was not needed; the point was obvious).

When our feisty school team, composed of the nine oldest kids in school, challenged the school down the road to a baseball duel, we were in for a shock. As the hosting team providing the equipment tossed out a legal, very large softball, I can still remember my total surprise. No lecture on the path of trajectories was needed to tell me that no one on our team would be able to adapt to the heft and size of the regulation softball for at least the first half of the game. We knew with certainty that we were on our way to defeat. Piffle on county rules!

Fresh with our annoyance at the foolish rules of the county schools office, we launched into serious, and illegal, roller skating on our school's basketball court, a small cement island in the midst of a large-rock gravel spill on the playground and rimmed by three feet of rough blacktop. We played crack the whip by the hour with as many as 12 of us (more wouldn't fit the radius of the court). Wonderful lessons in centrifugal force and skinless knees and elbows.

In short, our bodies became the simple machines a for our physical science lessons. Never mind "hands-on," our version was "bodies-in."

But my greatest love was the biological side of life and its earth science base. My stepfather was a superb farmer and a master diagnostician of anything that moved without benefit of a pumping heart. My questions of him were endless, his patience considerable. I used to drive about the countryside with him as he went out to "see his crops grow." He had a passion for it unequaled in the valley. His fence lines were readily identifiable: The crop on his side of the fence was always at least six inches taller and shades greener than the crop on the other side.

But nothing compared to my hours in the saddle, roaming for 10 to 15 miles in all directions. Out of sheer necessity, I learned to use the compass in my nose. To this day, I prefer my directions in term of north and south, not left and right. The wind in my face, the sun on my back, and all of nature spread out before me.

The seasons were a fascination and I loved to compare the goings on of one spring to another: Why did the woodpeckers suddenly seem to disappear from the valley? And while a sudden drop in the number of woodpeckers wouldn't have seemed significant to many in the valley, for my brother and I, who had two of the best bird-egg collections in the area, it set off an alarm

matched only by the publishing of *Silent Spring*. Not so surprisingly, the woodpeckers returned about the same time that the peregrine falcon and bald eagle started a come back and for the same reasons—DDT in paradise. We observed our world closely; little slipped by us.

I lived science, and I had a stepfather and mother who could and would answer any and all questions deemed well asked. I can remember, at age seven, asking my stepfather how internal combustion engines worked because I'd been thinking about it for a couple of weeks and couldn't figure it out. He burst out laughing. Indignant, and responding before I had time to monitor my words, I blurted out, "But if you really understood it, you could explain it in a way that I could understand." He stopped laughing, and I started to cringe because cheek like that wasn't allowed. He studied me soberly for a moment and then replied, "Well, I do understand it well. So, here's how they work." From that time on, I was in heaven. I got an accurate explanation for every question I asked. As I got older, the answers became, appropriately, increasingly complex.

But interestingly, I don't ever remember studying science in elementary school. I recall that my fourth through eighth grade was neither a mathematician (some days she taught percentages correctly, some days incorrectly) nor a scientist. We never touched the shiny new science kit that arrived one day via rural delivery. From time to time, she pointed at the science texts and, noticeably wincing, declared that we should read open it up and do a of couple assignments. However; they were never graded, never returned. While science was a rare event in those school days, we nevertheless readily absorbed her attitude toward "science." We avoided science books, all the while unaware that we were living science to the hilt.

This book is written in the hope that the science that children live in the real world can become the science that they study in school.

DEDICATION

To our parents who expected us to understand the world around us and who never
failed to answer our questions.
We owe them more than words can express.

To the courageous teachers throughout the United States who have found the power
of science-based, integrated curriculum.

To the associates for *Highly Effective Teaching*
(Susan Kovalik & Associates) who have coached
thousands of teachers on the road to meaningful content.

Thank you one and all.

PREFACE

Kid's Eye View of Science began as a training text for a K-6 science improvement program funded by the David and Lucile Packard Foundation, 1987-96. The primary goal was to help teachers use science to teach science—to use the emerging brain research about how the human brain learns to improve how science is taught. Three editions later, the goal is the same, but the brain research available is generations down the road, confirming the four principles from brain research introduced almost a quarter of a century ago as well as opening up wholly new areas of research, such as the stunning new discoveries about mirror neurons and the impact of aerobic exercise on brain chemistry and thus the brain's ability to learn. While more is yet to come, we already know enough to transform the teaching and learning of science for Grades K-6.

A Proven Track Record

The educational model described in this book, originally known as the Kovalik ITI (Integrated Thematic Instruction), emerged during the late 1970s. The 700 teachers who participated in the Mid-California Science Improvement Program (MCSIP), each for a minimum of three years, helped the authors hone the model. Working with that many teachers over a 10-year period provided the classroom reality needed to make an innovation successful. As you read these pages, you will be building upon the considerable experiences and successes of those teachers. The ITI model, now known as the Highly Effective Teaching (*HET*) model, was created by teachers for teachers.

Using science to teach science had far-reaching effects in the MCSIP schools. Not surprisingly, science achievement skyrocketed, but the outcomes in language, particularly for second-language learners, in reading, and for special education students were also impressive.

Whether working alone to implement the vision of science education described in this book or whether lucky enough to participate in a schoolwide team, the readers of this book will begin on the shoulders of thousands of teachers who have implemented this model in 37 states and in almost a dozen countries abroad over the past 25 years.

The ITI/*HET* model was one of 22 chosen for inclusion in the Comprehensive School Reform Program effort in 1999; a key criterion for such models was that improvement in student achievement, including personal and social growth, was predictable in all settings for all students. The ITI/*HET* model was also selected by Dr. Charles M. Reigeluth, Indiana University, as one of only a handful of models that met his stringent criteria for a curriculum-instruction model (see *Instructional-Design Theories and Models, Volume II: A New Paradigm of Instructional Theory*, edited by Charles M. Reigeluth, Indiana University). For a description of *HET* in an all-subject, fully integrated environment, see *Exceeding Expectations: A User's Guide to Implementing Brain Research in the Classroom*, 5th ed., by Susan J. Kovalik and Karen D. Olsen.

How to Use This Book

As with many books aimed at comprehensive reform, this is not a book to be read in one sitting. It's organized to provide the reader with a quick overview, Chapter 1, The Science of Teaching Science, and with immediate starting points—examples of bodybrain-compatible curriculum in Chapter 2.

Chapters 3 and 4 cut to the chase—how to make curriculum conceptual, how to localize it for your students (bridge the yawning gap between national and state standards and the prior experiences of your students), and how to make it action oriented and memorable.

Chapter 5, The Scientific Thinking Processes, examines these processes through the lens of the unfolding developmental processes of a young child's brain and what constitutes age-appropriate curriculum content, the subject of Chapter 7.

Chapter 8 compares assessment approaches to the brain research-based definition of learning as a two-step process. The authors recommend that teachers commit themselves to the goal of Effective First Teaching (EFT) and focus on formative assessment, mining information that can be used to improve student learning in the moment. The chapter describes how to design formative assessments using the curriculum development tools within the *HET* model.

Chapters 9 through 13 describe the brain research base for the *HET* model. Chapter 14 describes how to translate the four brain principles from Chapters 10–13 into practical, everyday approaches. While the authors well understand how precious time is, it's highly recommended that these chapters be read before reading Chapters 3–8.

Throughout the book runs a central theme: Science curriculum must be based in *being there* experiences, frequent visits to locations where students can experience science as it occurs in the real world. While these locations can be a simple as a corner of the school campus, they need to provide rich sensory input.

What's offered in these pages is a comprehensive strategy for teaching science, one that will ring true with each reader's learning journey into the world of science.

Getting the Most Out of This Book

As the reader will soon discover, the layout of this book differs from the traditional typographical layout typical of books over the past several hundred years. The new elements are not due to attempts at artistic flair. Rather, they are specifically designed to enhance the reader's ability to see patterns in content and make meaning of those patterns, thus speeding understanding and ability to apply what is encountered within these pages.

While discussion of pattern seeking may seem unusual or even foreign at this point in the book, the authors are hopeful that readers will soon grasp the power of the concept of pattern seeking as the brain's chief means of learning.

This being the case, you will find the following elements, each designed to enhance pattern seeking, meaning making, and memory retention.

A Built-In Outline for Navigation and Review. To aid in navigation through the book and to provide continuous review of contents, every page spread has a built-in outline.

- In the upper right-hand column of the odd-numbered pages, a mindmap outlines the major sections of the chapter, with page numbers. The section discussed on the page appears in dark ink; the others appear in gray.

- In the box at the bottom of the right-hand column of every odd-numbered page is an outline of the main ideas within the major section highlighted in the mindmap at the top of the page.

These thumbnail outlines serve both to guide one to the desired information and to provide a recurring review to assist in wiring information into one's long-term memory.

Pagination Within Each Chapter. Rather than the traditional pagination of 1 to 300, each chapter is numbered starting with the chapter number, then a decimal point, and finally, the number of the page in that chapter. For example, page 10.3 identifies the third page of Chapter 10. This is intended to assist in navigating to a particular chapter currently being studied. Such pagination helps group content into easily located study modules and readily lets one know when one has flipped short of or beyond the desired chapter or study module.

More Headers. The reader will find more headers within each chapter to help create a detailed outline of the chapter, a quick scaffolding upon which to add relevant details through the chapter.

ACKNOWLEDGMENTS

Dolly Sacks, Program Officer for the David and Lucile Packard Foundation, lent her unflagging support of the Integrated Thematic Instruction model (ITI) — our model for improving science in the Mid-California Science Improvement Program and pre-curser to the Highly Effective Teaching Model. We thank you for your belief in us and our model — its dream for kids and its reality in the classroom — and for your commitment to good things for students and teachers. Your personal courage in facing the tough issues of education, your unerring sense of what's important for children, and your perceptive yet gentle questioning helped shape a science improvement effort of national significance. The MCSIP program was as much your creation as ours.

We will be forever grateful to David Packard, a man of great vision and equally great ability to turn those visions into reality, for his faith in our enthusiasm and our commitment to improve science education. On behalf of the 500 teachers and their 30,000 students impacted by the MCSIP program during the 10 years of funding by the David and Lucile Packard Foundation, we thank you.

To all the MCSIP participants and their coaches, thank you for sharing your triumphs and tribulations as you strove to apply brain research to teaching science using the ITI model (now known as the Highly Effective Teaching Model). Your work, from 1987 through 1996, inspired this book. The thousands of teachers trained in the model since then continue to shape the model and our view of the importance of science as the starting point for integrating curriculum.

PUBLISHER'S ACKNOWLEDGMENTS

Corwin gratefully acknowledges the contributions of the following reviewers:

Regina Brinker
Science Teacher
Christensen Middle School
Livermore, CA

Sally Koczam
Science Teacher
Wydown Middle School
Clayton, MO

Linda Keteylan
Teacher of Science/Math Grade 5
National Board Certified
Priest Elementary School
Detroit, MI

Maria Mesires
Seventh-Grade Science Teacher
Case Middle School
Watertown, NY

INTRODUCTION

In an era of tightening budgets, it may seem a fool's errand to even propose improving science education. Staggering under all the usual pressures endured by public school teachers, heightened all the more by the testing juggernaut created by No Child Left Behind, and faced with increasing class sizes, where would one begin?

The authors believe that the only sane place to begin is with a commitment to using science to teach science—using what we now know about how the human brain learns to transform not only science but also the entire school. Although the *HET* model is a proven method of doing so, challenges remain, the biggest of which is time, or lack thereof.

The Clock—Making Time

Part of the solution can be solved by the clock—making more minutes and hours per week available for science. However, since it's unlikely that the current economy will support adding minutes to the day or days to the year, the only way to make more minutes for science is to steal time from other subjects. The only legitimate way to do so is through integrating subjects—studying two or more subjects simultaneously.

Integration—An Imperative. While integrating has been touted as a good idea over the past half century, it's now an imperative. There's simply no other feasible way to make time for science.

In theory, and in practice, integrating subjects, especially the basic skills, is far easier than most people believe. For example, practicing comprehension skills while reading a science book is still reading, minutes to be used to meet the required minutes per day/week for that subject. Likewise, when writing about a science observation, the skills and rules of writing are the same, be the topic nonfiction or fiction. And using numbers from a *being there* experience—how many, how big, how long, how heavy, how fast, how much, time, and so forth—deepens science understandings while giving relevance and a sense of numbers to math applications. Applying the basic skills through science is easy and seamless.

How We Use the Time We Do Have

The other part of the solution is how we use the clock—using effectively the time we do have. In other words, we must do the job right the first time. There is no time for remediation or do-overs. We must commit ourselves to the concept of Effective First Teaching (EFT) so that our students' memories of science and its place in their lives are greater than those left to us by our schooling.

Effective First Teaching. The goal and need for EFT is getting the job done right the first time. No re-teaching, no remediation, no RTI (Response to Intervention). Go straight from introduction to mastery and then to long-term memory in a straight line and do so as quickly as physiologically possible for the brain.

To accomplish this goal, we must use the best of brain research findings to guide how we

- Develop curriculum for the classroom.

- Select and implement instructional strategies to best teach that curriculum.

- Use formative assessment that is authentic, that assesses students' ability to use the concepts, significant knowledge, and skills of the curriculum in real-world applications.

Kid's Eye View of Science describes how to use the *HET* model to solve the problem of carving out time for science, to master how to teach effectively the first time, and, in so doing, create a world-class science education program and lay the foundation for a conceptual, fully integrated approach to all subject areas.

THE SCIENCE OF TEACHING SCIENCE

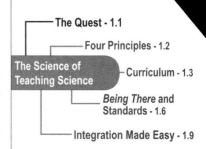

From a kid's eye view of science, learning is about experiencing the world. And it's also true that brain research confirms this perspective—learning is the result of real physiological growth in the brain spurred by massive sensory input. Such sensory input is not possible in the classroom, especially when study is based on textbooks and worksheets. When it comes to improving science education, kids and brain researchers share overlapping perspectives.

THE QUEST

In the quest to improve science education, would you not expect to utilize the results of scientific research about how the brain learns, research that has been accumulated and validated over the past 30 years? Would you not expect the prowess of 21st-century technology to reveal inner workings of the brain that have eluded us for centuries? We think so. And although the brain is admittedly complex and stubbornly mysterious, there is much we already know. Our challenge is to begin to apply this knowledge within our classrooms and schools in ways that make the learning environment compatible with how the human brain learns rather than an extension of tradition.

Science—when taught as a direct experience of the world around us—is a highly brain-compatible subject because learning from and about the natural world is as natural for the human brain as the sun's rising and setting (due, of course, to the Earth spinning). Our very existence as a species attests to this fact.

In contrast, other areas of the elementary school curriculum are comparatively recent human constructions, such as reading, writing, and mathematics. These newcomers in the evolution of the human brain bristle with abstractions which cannot be experienced by children firsthand through their senses; thus, students must learn how to learn about them before they can learn the content.

Science, when taught as a direct experience of the natural world, is easy for students to grasp and to apply in meaningful, inventive, and often highly complex ways. It should come as no surprise, for example, that many of our early astronauts were Midwestern farm boys who grew up doing science as an unavoidable aspect of growing up on the south forty. They had hours of practice, on a daily basis, with using the scientific thinking processes,[1] solving real problems, and inventing or producing useful products—from repairing farm equipment to strategies to improve profit margins.

Doing science in such real-life settings was natural and automatic, a kinder's garden for many of the best scientist this country has ever known. And while returning to our rural roots is not an option for most of us, we certainly can commit ourselves to making science experienceable, to using science to teach science.

In so many respects, current brain research findings come as no surprise and even as a validation of our personal experience as learners. It is this fit with the brain that we seek—the power to produce learning which remains vivid for a lifetime.

FOUR PRINCIPLES FROM BRAIN RESEARCH

Although the brain is enormously complex, descriptions of how the human brain learns can be expressed in relatively simple conceptual terms. And although we may not know as much as we will, we certainly know enough to get started.

The learning principles outlined here are, we believe, fundamental to establishing a working theory of human learning for the 21st century. Corroborated by researchers studying the human brain from many different avenues, they provide a powerful template for making decisions about curriculum, instruction, and other issues needed for systemic rethinking of American education.

The four principles from brain research are as follows[2]:

PRINCIPLE A — *Intelligence as a function of experience*[3]

Learning is the result of real, observable physiological growth in the brain that occurs as a result of sensory input and the processing, organizing, and pruning it promotes.[4] Genetics is not the immutable determiner of intelligence it was generally believed to be; although it sets parameters, experiences with high levels of sensory input can significantly increase development of one's capacity.

PRINCIPLE B — *Learning is an inseparable partnership between the brain and body.*[4]

- Emotion is the gatekeeper to learning and performance.

  Much of the information processed in the brain comes from information substances produced throughout the body, many of which are the "molecules of emotion"[5] that drive attention, which in turn drives learning, memory, and virtually everything else.[6]

MARY FROGGINS

Welcome. Meet your new guide-on-the-side, Mary Froggins.

The role of Mary Froggins in this book is to challenge and summarize by stating the obvious and not so obvious in a humorous and, hopefully, not to be forgotten way. At times she will be audacious as she attempts to make a point strongly enough to compete with our unexamined pictures of "schooling" as we have known it for the past 170 years.

So, from Mary Froggins and the authors, we wish you a healthy sense of humor as you read this book and go about the task of creating a kid's eye view of science.

- Movement enhances learning.[7]

  Movement is crucial to every brain function including planning and executing those plans, memory, emotion, language, and learning.

- Aerobic exercise kick-starts the chemicals for learning.

  Aerobic exercise of at least 35 minutes at 70 percent heart rate unleashes a cascade of neurotransmitters that prepare the brain to learn (create neurons in the hippocampus) and enhances learning processes).

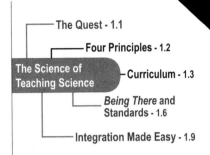

PRINCIPLE C — *There are multiple intelligences.*[8]

We have not one, generic intelligence but at least seven, each of which operates from a different part of our brain. As defined by Howard Gardner, intelligence is "a problem-solving and/or product-producing capability."[9] This applies both to learning and to demonstrating understanding of an idea/concept.

PRINCIPLE D — *Learning is a two-step process.*[10]

- Detecting and understanding patterns—processes through which our brain creates meaning

- Developing meaningful mental programs to use what is understood and to store it in long-term memory. Such capacity to use what's understood is developed first with assistance, then used independently and finally with near automaticity.

These four principles, their brain research sources, and their implications for curriculum and instruction are described in Chapters 9-14. Chapters 2-8 describe practical, day-to-day applications.

CURRICULUM AND THE BRAIN

All decisions about science curriculum should be made with brain research in mind, particularly the new, brain-based definition of learning and the necessity for high sensory experience in learning. Since the content has largely been established by your state standards, the most important question to solve is how to localized your state standards—how to bridge the gap between national expectations and your students' prior experiences by selecting *being there* location that will provide the best illustration of the concepts and skills you need to teach.

FOUR PRINCIPLES FROM BRAIN RESEARCH

Principle A: Intelligence and Experience

Principle B: Inseparable Partnership — Brain and Body

Principle C: Multiple Intelligences

Principle D: Learning as Two-Step Process

MARY FROGGINS

We have rearranged the deck chairs on the Titanic so many times, each reform era with its own special vocabulary, that we have lost sight of the common sense of it all.

The bottom line about curriculum can—and should— be boiled down to these two questions:

- WHAT DO I WANT MY STUDENTS TO **<u>UNDERSTAND</u>**?

- WHAT DO I WANT MY STUDENTS TO **<u>DO</u>** WITH WHAT THEY UNDERSTAND?

And, clearly, this means <u>do</u> in real-world applications, not on end-of-chapter questions, worksheets, or tests.

Anchoring Curriculum in Real-Life Locations

Anchoring curriculum in real-life locations makes key tasks easy. For example, making content meaningful and mentally and physically engaging while vastly increasing the amount of sensory input over that of the traditional tools of textbooks, worksheets, lectures, and an occasional video or Internet scan. Let two pivotal questions guide your thinking:

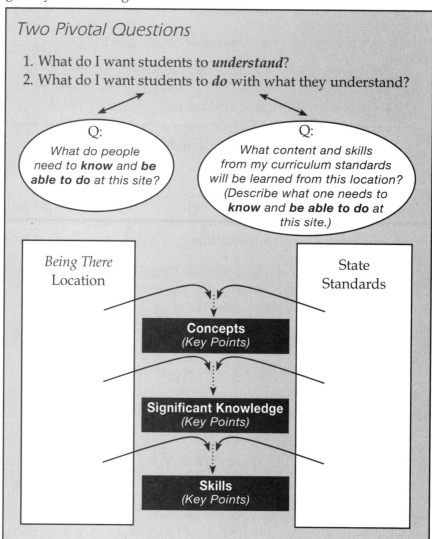

Figure 1A

Some readers may believe that their district doesn't allow money for field trips. We're not talking about field trips or end-of-year travel rewards. We are talking about study trips designed in accordance with brain research findings about how the human brain learns. Is there a difference? You bet! Is it doable? Affordable? Absolutely, if we choose locations near the school that we and our students can revisit frequently by walking or by taking a short ride on public transportation.

Are we talking about ignoring state standards? Absolutely not. Standards adopted by the district tell us what we as teachers are expected to teach our students. We owe our students a curriculum with no gaps and no repetitions as they progress from grade to grade. Curriculum standards, be they district adopted, state driven, or school generated, are an essential foundation for good curriculum planning at the classroom level.

Are we talking about throwing away textbooks? No. But we are suggesting that textbooks be used as one of many resources, not as the curriculum and paramount instructional tool.

Anchoring curriculum in real-life locations gives students clear pictures of what we want them to understand and what we want them to do with what they understand because they can see how and when people use such knowledge and skills. The richness of these pictures also allows students to make connections both to other locations and among other content areas.

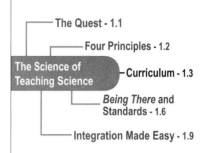

Examples of Engaging Being There *Locations*

Look for sites that are immediately accessible—a walking trip of 15 minutes or less. First, look for sites on campus, such as the playground, cafeteria, bus barn, or maintenance center. Next, branch out into the neighborhoods within walking distance. Then, look for sites that can be reached by inexpensive public transportation.

Be creative. The most intriguing study trips are often the ones to locations right under our noses—locations where we have gone innumerable times but never thought to take a behind-the-scenes look, such as grocery stores, malls, our own school cafeteria or bus system.

Examples of *being there* locations[11] include:

Kindergarten — Schoolyard, backyard of a nearby home (for examples of the natural world and relevant hobbies), nearby pond, creek, or man-made pond on the school grounds, nearby park or empty lot, pet store, and animals living in or visiting the classroom and so forth.

First Grade — Any of the above locations, especially underground aspects of those locations, local habitats that are rich in animal and plant life, farms, nearby gardens (school Lifelab or nearby backyard), larger bodies of water such as lakes, rivers, ocean, and a zoo or aquarium.

CURRICULUM AND THE BRAIN

Anchoring Curriculum in Real-Life Locations

Examples of Engaging *Being There* Locations

MARY FROGGINS

Participation in being there experiences activates many of our 20 senses, which in turn creates physical changes in the brain and allows for greater connections when studying the material.

There are at least 20 senses:
   Sight
   Hearing
   Touch
   Taste
   Smell
   Balance
   Vestibular
   Temperature
   Pain
   Eidetic imagery
   Magnetic
   Infrared
   Ultraviolet
   Ionic
   Vomeronasal
   Proximal
   Electrical
   Barometric
   Proprioception
   Geogravimetric

See page 10.6 for an example of the 20 senses activated by a being there experience.

Second Grade — Any of the above locations plus natural history museums, taxidermy shops, construction sites and repair shops where a variety of tools are used, local businesses, and city agencies and resources such as police, fire, hospitals, and medical clinics.

Third Grade — Any of the above locations plus nearby road cuts that expose changes in landscape, before and after a flood or earthquake, recycling operations from pick up to remanufacturing to resale, and lots of neighborhood illustrations of life cycles, machines, and so forth. Also, community landmarks, businesses (grocery stores, malls, mom-and-pop stores of any kind). And don't forget observation of daily weather and the nighttime sky.

Fourth Grade — Select four or five complex ecosystems such as a nearby creek, slough, marsh, tide pool, lake, forest, or biodiverse park or backyard garden. Also have **students create and maintain as many** habitats in the classroom and schoolyard as possible, e.g., the Salmanoid project hatching salmon, a pond with all its inhabitants. What is learned in-depth there can then be extended through numerous being there experiences in varying ecosystems. Also include a state historical site or its replication that parallels your state history curriculum.

Fifth Grade — Fortunately, systems are everywhere, so start with those right under your students' noses: school transportation systems, school food systems (including where food comes from and where the leftovers go), schoolyards, local gardens and parks, telephone company, television/radio stations, a nearby creek or river, water treatment plants, car repair shops, malls, city/county bus systems, and theme parks such as Sea World, Great America, Boardwalk, Disneyworld, and Epcot. Include sites of national historical significance that illustrate concepts from your state stanards.

Sixth Grade — Any of the above observed with change and constancy of systems in mind, such as yards in the neighborhood whose growth is old and diverse, biodiverse city and state parks, waste and water treatment plants, health clinics, locations of airplane and satellite photos that illustrate change and constancy, recent cuts in hillsides due to highway building or major real estate development, agricultural fields, local manufacturing plants, local engineering firms and biotech labs, human-made systems such as a school campus or a mall with its heat/air system, water and electrical systems, and so forth, plus family homes or condos (examples of energy efficient and inefficient systems).

BRINGING TOGETHER BEING THERE LOCATIONS AND STATE/DISTRICT CURRICULUM STANDARDS

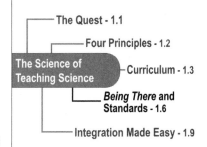

Just as a magnet attracts metal shards, a *being there* experience[12] helps attract important concepts and skills from your state standards or district-adopted curriculum and clump them into meaningful chunks. At this stage of your implementation, allow this magnetic quality of *being there* locations to do your curriculum integration and development work for you. Rather than trying to chase down various curriculum pieces, allow the intrinsically interesting aspects of the *being there* location and the most important points from your curriculum standards to simply pull together, creating a natural fit of related patterns. Make it fun. Give yourself the best chance at succeeding.

The answers to the two pivotal questions asked on the Curriculum Overview, Figure 1A, help you evaluate a potential *being there* location in relationship to your curriculum standards. Your answers also help create a basis for authentic assessment based on the real-life standards and expectations for what a capable person should understand and be able to do at this location.

Development of bodybrain-compatible curriculum requires an eye for the practical and lots of common sense; it's not a theoretical exercise.

Choosing a physical location as the anchor for curriculum is critical to creating a bodybrain-compatible learning environment for several reasons:

- The best way to ensure that students quickly grasp an accurate and comprehensive understanding of the concepts and skills of the curriculum is to allow them to experience those concepts in their real-world contexts.

- Once students understand concepts in one location, they can generalize them to other locations and use them to make predictions about events past and future. This speeds up and deepens the pace of future learning.

- Each of us must understand how our community works in order to become an informed citizen.

BRINGING TOGETHER
BEING THERE LOCATIONS
AND STATE/DISTRICT
CURRICULUM STANDARDS

Guidelines for Selecting
***Being There* Locations**

MARY FROGGINS

Many will think that basing science curriculum in being there locations and going on study trips to visit them is a foolish idea because it's too difficult, too costly, can't be done because of insurance and liability risks, and is just too foolish to contemplate. However, I believe that the ultimate foolishness is doing what we've always done and expecting a different result.

The United States will continue to lag behind industrial nations until it decides to commit itself to using science to teach science—until we commit to using what we now know from brain research about how the human brain learns.

The readers of this book stand at a crossroads. Which path will you choose?

Guidelines for Selecting Being There Locations

Selecting physical locations upon which to build your curriculum is the most critical curricular decision you will make for the year. Like any builder, choose your site with care. The more solid the foundation, the more empowering your curriculum can be.

Before selecting a physical location, do your homework. Think through the following steps.

Step 1—Analyze the Potential of a Site to Teach What Your Students Need to Learn. Let the world integrate your curriculum naturally. For example, consider the common grocery store. Been there a million times? Of course. But have you ever been behind the scenes and looked at it from a business perspective? Would you be amazed to discover that the typical profit margin for grocery stores is two to three cents on the dollar? Ever wonder how many items change price? How often? And just where does this stuff come from anyway? Grown in the United States? Imported from a country with far less stringent environmental safeguards? The possibilities for study are unlimited: profits and losses, employer-employee relationships, the demographics of the clientele and producers, legal restrictions, health inspections, competition, energy costs, OSHA (Occupational Safety and Health Administration) requirements, and so forth.

After your preliminary match of state standards to the concepts best illustrated at the *being there* site, go visit the location.

Step 2—Visit the Site. Go to the location; look with new eyes. Pretend you've never been there before. Get curious! Look everything over from a fresh perspective. Look behind the scenes. Imagine what others see. What do they need to know to competently perform their roles as seller, buyer; service provider, service recipient; guide, visitor; host, guest; and employer, employee? What do visitors need to know to get the best value for their dollar, to make the wisest decisions, to avoid being taken advantage of, or to enjoy it most fully?

Be sure you take time to interview people—those who create the environment (employees and owners) and those who come to use or enjoy (clients, customers, and sightseers). Skip past the knowledge and comprehension questions of Bloom's Taxonomy. Dive right into the levels of application, analysis, evaluation, and synthesis. That's where the fun and engagement are! Ask the interviewees why they choose to work or shop here. What about this place makes them proud to work or visit here?

Always put yourself in your students' shoes. What is gripping about this location? What would bring you back again and again?

Step 3—Expand Your Knowledge Base. Solid curriculum can't be developed from information off the top of one's head; also, our typical curriculum tools are limited. For example, state standards and district curriculum offer an outline and textbooks provide superficial information in summary form. Expect to become a learner. Open yourself up to the joy of discovery. Don't expect to have all the answers. Long gone is the era when what you knew by age 25 would carry you through a lifetime. Learning how to learn and learning to embrace the necessity for learning with enjoyment are the demands of our time. Model this and let your excitement and passion transfer to your students.

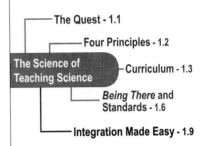

Pursue concepts that you believe will allow students to unlock meaning in other settings. Ask yourself several questions: What can be generalized and what can be used to predict events or happenings in other locations? From the students' point of view, what's useful? What are the most empowering concepts and skills you can help them understand?

To create an immersion environment in your classroom to replicate the *being there* location, expect to have at least 50 resources in your room, such as books (e.g., Eye Witness, Usbourne series), magazines, print of all kinds written at a range of reading levels (including children's books that provide clear explanations and lots of visuals), plus multimedia options which capitalize on today's technologies (Internet, DVDs, encyclopedias, and so forth). And, very importantly, real things for hands-on exploration.

Step 4—Revisit Your Curriculum. However small or large this chunk of curriculum for the *being there* experience, is it as conceptual as you can make it? Have you prioritized the content so students will have time to understand and learn to apply the most important concepts, significant knowledge, and skills? Are your curriculum choices solid and acceptable to your supervisors? Can you explain them thoroughly to the parents? If so, you are ready to begin developing key points and inquiries.

For an in-depth discussion of how to plan, conduct, and follow up on a *being there* study trip, see Appendix A.

INTEGRATION MADE EASY

Look out the window: Science is everywhere we look, the results of history and social interaction are unavoidable, the arts are everywhere we turn, and all are going on together. Basing your curriculum in *being there* locations makes integration easy and natural; simply let your curriculum match the world we see when we look out the window, walk down the street, and window-shop in the mall.

INTEGRATION MADE EASY

Integrating Subject Content
Assessment

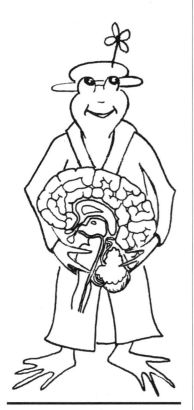

MARY FROGGINS

This is an exciting time to be in education. The same kind of scientific endeavors that put man on the moon 50 years ago, and recently focused on how the brain operates, has rewritten our assumptions, about how the human brain learns.

It is up to us to demand that our schools use that information to transform our public schools.

Integrating Subject Content

If you're still on the fence, not yet ready to base your curriculum in *being there* locations, consider this: *Being there* locations are the great mixer—blending together subject areas and skills in natural and engaging ways. Basic skills—universally essential—can be taught using any location where they are used routinely.

Almost any mixture of natural and man–made settings will demonstrate the concepts, significant knowledge, and skills from your state standards.

History/Social Studies. Just add people to your location and you will have a window through which to view human nature past, present, or future.

Mathematics. Any location drips with numbers; all you have to do is decide what math functions and concepts you want to apply to those numbers.

Start with the obvious—how far, how long, how tall, how wide, how much, how many, what volume, what angle, which direction, how many years since, how much per square foot or per square mile, and so forth. Keep a running list of numerical data inherent in each *being there* location. Have students use data from these lists instead of those from worksheets. This allows them to create their own problems, the answers to which deepen their understanding and application of the content they are learning. Get real . . . show practical applications of geometry and algebra and more.

Reading, Writing, and Language Development. *Being there* locations offer students something real to read about and a real audience to write to. Provide the opportunity for students to communicate their discoveries and thank resource people who helped them learn. Provide a means to journal what is discovered, or compose an article to submit to the school or class newsletter or, better yet, the local newspaper.

The Arts. Wherever there are people, there is art—clothing, marketing materials, interior design, architecture, paintings, cultural expressions, and more. Give students the option to sketch some of the objects they notice. Music is everywhere. Pay close attention ot rhythm and sound, both indoors and out. Analyze what is heard. What mood does it induce? Identify which instruments or objects created the sounds.

Assessment

Anchoring curriculum content in the real world also allows us to develop assessment that mirrors performance standards that students and teachers encounter in their everyday lives. For example, we write a letter with perfect grammar and spelling because we want a real person to take our opinion seriously; we want to calculate math problems accurately when the answers have an impact on our personal lives.

For a discussion about how to make assessment bodybrain-compatible for students and meaningful and useful to teachers, see Chapter 7: Assessment.

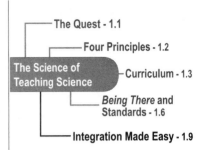

HEADS UP

This chapter, merely a heads up for the rest of this book, provides an outline for information gathering throughout your journey through these pages. Although we have placed the discussion about how the brain learns in Chapters 9-13, the science of teaching science should be at the core of every curriculum- and instruction-related question you encounter in your teaching day. *We strongly recommend you read Chapters 9 through 13 before you continue.*

END NOTES

1   For a discussion of the scientific thinking processes, see Chapter 5.

2   The brain research for these four principles emerged as early as the 1970s. Subsequent research, which has been extensive, has validated and expanded these summaries.

3   Marian Diamond, a professor of anatomy at Berkeley for over 30 years and pioneer brain researcher, conducted numerous lines of research into the effect of the environment and hormones on the forebrain. Her ground breaking work in the 1970s and 1980s studying the impact of enriched and impoverished environments culminated in her "enrichment theory." Enrichment theory should be read by all teachers, administrators, and parents. A layman's description can be found in *Magic Trees of the Mind: How to Nurture Your Child's Intelligence, Creativity, and Healthy Emotions from Birth Through Adolescence* by Marian Diamond and Janet Hopson (New York: A Dutton Book, 1998). Also see Diamond's most recent research project, Enrichment in Action in a Cambodian Orphanage.

4   Research in these areas has emerged from many different lines of research. When stitched together, it's indeed compelling. See the work of Carla Hannaford, Elkhonon Goldberg, John Ratey, and John Medina, among others. See the bibliography for a list of their books.

5   The most readable, and eye-popping, account of the power and omnipresent processing of emotion is Candace Pert's work; see her *Molecules of Emotion: Why You Feel the Way You Feel* (New York: Scribner, 1997), 139-140, 178.

6   Robert Sylwester has synthesized a good deal of research into a very useful and memorable phrase: "Emotion drives attention, attention drives learning/memory/problem-solving/just about everything else." See Sylwester's "The Role of The Arts in Brain Development and Maintenance," 6. Available at http://ode.state.or.us/teachlearn/subjects/arts/resources/ rolesbraindevelopment.pdf. Also see his lastest book, *A Child's Brain: The Need for Nurture* (Thousand Oaks, CA: Corwin, 2010).

7   The work of three easy-to-read authors provide compelling information about this concept: Elkhonon Goldberg, John Ratey, and Carla Hanaford. An especially good source is *Spark: The Revolutionary New Science of Exercise and the Brain* by John Ratey (New York: Little, Brown and Company, 2008), 53.

8   Howard Gardner's theory of intelligence is widely received and well ensconced; it's also our choice for the Highly Effective Education (*HET*) model. We use Gardner's work because it rings with our experiences with children and adults and because it so readily lends itself to practical applications when developing curriculum and selecting instructional strategies. See Gardner's *Frames of Mind: The Theory of Multiple Intelligences, Revised* (New York: Basic Books, Inc., 2004), xxiii-xxxiii.

9   Howard Gardner's definition of intelligence is an extremely useful alternative to the standard IQ number. See *Frames of Mind*, xxiv.

10   Leslie Hart was a man ahead of his time. From his impressive personal library of firsthand research studies, he was the first to understand that the brain is a pattern seeker that builds programs for using what it understands. With each succeeding book he wrote about how the brain learns, and how schools ignore this fact, Leslie Hart continued synthesizing his conceptualization of the two fundamental brain concepts: pattern detection and program building. His initial definition was simple and to the point:

The process of learning is the extraction, from confusion, of meaningful patterns

and

Learning is the acquisition of useful programs.

Since the late 1960s, this view of learning has become standard vocabulary. Patterns and programs is an accurate and useful description of learning. See Hart's *Human Brain and Human Learning*, 3rd ed. (Books for Educators, Black Diamond, WA, 2002), 117 and Chapters 7–10.

This conceptualization of learning is an extremely important contribution to the field of education because it's comprehensive enough to cover the wide range of practicalities that teachers, administrators, and parents face on a daily basis—from curriculum to instruction to assessment.

11   These recommended *being there* locations are excerpted from *Science Continuum of Concepts for Grades K-6*, 4th ed., by Karen D. Olsen (Black Diamond, WA: Books for Educators, 2010). Used with written permission of the author.

12   *Being there* experiences are not just activities, they are a key structure in the *HET* model. They are the base for localizing curriculum—bridging the gap between national and state standards and the prior experiences of your students. They're the key tool for delivering massive amounts of sensory input to spur learning.

MAKING CURRICULUM BODYBRAIN COMPATIBLE

Before we launch into another round of science improvement and reform, we should first ask ourselves why our previous efforts have failed. Certainly it wasn't due to lack of inspired rhetoric or good intentions or because the ideas of the reform movement were wrongheaded. Not at all. In fact, the vision of what constitutes good science has been remarkably consistent over the past 80 years.

This consistency of content, as we shall see, is both good and bad. Good because curriculum has changed very little and thus has given us time to figure out what's amiss. Bad because the way the content has traditionally been stated does not fit how the brain learns. This is often true of even the best state standards.

THE CHALLENGES

To create a quality science program, there are numerous major challenges to overcome—lack of time, fragmentation that frustrates the brain, traditional content that is inappropriate for the developmental level of children, and failure to make national and state standards relevant to students in their neighborhood.

Time

As discussed in Chapter 1, the chief challenge is lack of time, solvable only by integration of science with other subjects including application and practice of the basic skills.

Fragmentation

At Grades K-6, science content has changed little in the past 100 years. New discoveries in the sciences, made possible by astonishing advances in technology, apply to curriculum for high school and university levels.

Fragmentation has several causes:

- Failure to integrate the fields of science. We still teach biology separate from earth science, chemistry from physics. However, in life, such tidy divisions do not exist. Critical issues in the ballot box require integration of all areas of science in order to understand the implications of a yes/no vote. Examples abound: the cause and effects of critical environmental challenges, habitat destruction due to pollution, and the thermodynamics of global warming to name but a few. Such

THE CHALLENGES

Time

Fragmentation

Age-*In*appropriate Content

Creating Relevance

MARY FROGGINS

For many students, it's a long way from national and state standards to their neighborhood and the experiences they bring to school. Making such curriculum relevant to students is a process we call localizing curriculum, the key to which is basing curriculum in being there *locations that can be studied through frequent study trips.*

issues simply can't be grasped by an electorate raised on fragments of science taught in isolation and spread out over years. The world students experience is integrated and so should be the curriculum we teach.

- An overdose of factoids—piecees of content so small that they are meaningless and fail students' "So what?" test. Traditionally, science content has consisted of never-ending lists of definitions. Without context, these definitions lack relevance and perceivable pattern and thus lack meaning. Lacking meaning, they are all but impossible to wire into long-term memory.

- Lack of context. Because students rarely see the fragmented science they study in action, it's nearly impossible for them to grasp its meaning and understand its relevance to their lives—now or in the future.

Solution. To eliminate fragmentation, we need to base each chunk of conceptual curriculum in a *being there* location that can be easily visited by students and that integrates not only the areas of science but also all subject areas. Such firsthand experience with what concepts and skills look like in real life and how they affect students' lives spurs learning. As you will see in Chapters 2, 10, and 13, the context of real life provides the rich sensory input the brain needs and activates the amazing power of our mirror neurons—two of the most powerful tools in the teaching/learning process.

Age-Inappropriate Content

Much of our traditional science content is wildly age inappropriate. By that we mean that something is not understandable due to the developmental level of the student's brain at that grade level. As a result, students are forced into memorizing content that doesn't make sense to them. In the end, students come to hate science and believe they're poor students.

Solution. Ensure that the content we teach is age appropriate and thus understandable. (For more information about age-appropriate curriculum, see Chapter 7.)

Creating Relevance by Localizing Curriculum

For many students, it's a long way from national and state standards to their neighborhood and the experiences they bring to school. If significant learning is to occur, that gap must be bridged. Content must connect to students as they are, not as we wish them to be; it must be made relevant to the experiences they bring with them.

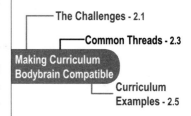

Relevance depends on two factors. The first is well illustrated by the backmapping process begun by Project 2061.[1] It does an excellent job of pointing out the concepts that students must understand in order to make sense out of subsequent concepts. Teaching into thin air is a bad place to be—for both teachers and students.

Second, context is critical. Science should be taught through the locations that students experience in their daily lives.

Solution. Localize your curriculum. Base it on locations familiar to students so that they can bring prior experiences to bear on their learning tasks. Behind-the-scene tours are fascinating because they fill in missing pieces. Likewise, applying science concepts to familiar locations speeds and deepens learning because everything isn't new all at once. (See Chapter 3.)

COMMON THREADS

Bodybrain-compatible curriculum has several common threads.

Localized in a *Being There* Location

The gap between national and state standards is bridged by basing curriculum in being there locations that students can visit frequently throughout study trips.

As Conceptual as Possible

Curriculum content is stated as conceptually as possible to enhance pattern seeking (constructing meaning) and learning how to apply what is learned. However, statement of concepts varies as appropriate to the grade level. For example, kindergarten curriculum looks like a stringless necklace, i.e., the beads, or concepts, aren't attached to teach other. The concepts are experienced one at a time, in no particular order, although they can be and should be repeated again and again at varying locations. In contrast, by fifth grade, the concept of systems is highly interconnected, like a multistrand necklace with connections among the strands. (For examples of grade-level content mindmaps, see *Science Continuum of Concepts, K-6.*)

New Brain-Based Definition of Learning

The new brain-based definition of learning described in Chapter 13—the underpinning for all decisions about curriculum, instruction, and assessment—radically changes our pictures of learning.

COMMON THREADS

Localized in a
Being There Location

As Conceptual as Possible

New Brain-Based Definition
of Learning

Age-Appropriate Content

MARY FROGGINS

As you will soon see, this instructional process fits the new brain-based definition of learning just beautifully.

See Chapter 13 for a discussion of this new definition of learning.

The diagram below contrasts the old notions about learning science that underlie traditional teaching practices (i.e., focusing on terminology and reading about science in hope that understanding and learning will occur) with how learning occurs most powerfully. The fading ink illustrates the loss of learning that occurs when science begins with vocabulary definitions instead or high sensory input.

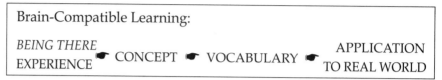

Brain-Compatible Learning:

BEING THERE
EXPERIENCE ☛ CONCEPT ☛ VOCABULARY ☛ APPLICATION TO REAL WORLD

versus

Old Notions About Learning:

VOCABULARY ☛? CONCEPT ☛? ☛? ☛ APPLICATION

Figure 2A

Conceptually, the learning process begins with *being there* input from which the mental pattern or concept is extracted, then acquiring a word or words to represent that concept, and applying what is understood to the real world until a mental program is built. Thus, students need discovery time to explore and manipulate until patterns, uniquely theirs yet accurate, are pieced together and woven into meaningful wholes. (See Chapters 12 and 13.)

For students also learning a second language, the importance of a brain-compatible approach is even more profound.

Age-Appropriate Content

Curriculum must be age appropriate. Respecting the developmental unfolding of the brain is vital. Pushing content that is not understandable by students forces them to resort to rote memory and a lifelong aversion for science. (See Chapter 7.)

For example, appropriate content for kindergarten appears less coherent from a science point of view than can be expected in later grades as concepts are less interconnected. However, by upper grades, students should learn to impose earlier understandings on a *being there* location—to hold a concept in their minds and compare what they experience against that template. This comparison expands and deepens their prior understandings and, when necessary, corrects them. A concept such as systems needs to be used as a lens through which to study what's at the site. The concept is huge, has many facets, and is a powerful way to view the world—in science, history/social studies, economics, civics, and the learner's personal life.

A useful rule of thumb for judging age inappropriateness was suggested by Dr. Larry Lowery, Lawrence Hall of Science, University of California Berkeley: If, after ample time to explore (observe, communicate, and compare), you still have to tell the student what you wanted him or her to get, the content is inappropriate at this time.[2] *We must avoid complexities and abstractions which students can memorize but not understand.*

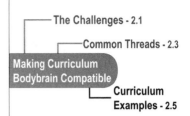

Another way to ensure that curriculum is age appropriate is to make the primary grades heavy in life sciences and light in earth and physical sciences. As students move upward in the grades, this should flipflop as shown in the following illustration:

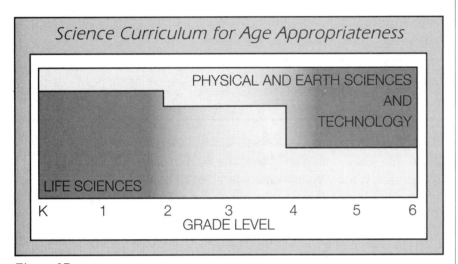

Figure 2B

Science curriculum that solves these challenges would look something like the following examples for Grades K-6. Called a continuum of concepts for Grades K-6, it also invites integration, is conceptual, is age appropriate, and can be based in *being there* locations to provide context.

CURRICULUM EXAMPLES

The organizing concepts on the next page are age appropriate, relevant, and can easily integrate the strands of science and other subjects.

Beginning on the next page, and continuing through page 2.34, are examples of K-6 curriculum based on the above continuum of concepts. Excerpted from *Science Continuum of Concepts for Grades K-6*, 4th edition, by written permission of the author, they provide a model for localizing your state standards. See *Science Continuum of Concepts for Grades K-6*, 4th edition, by Karen D. Olsen (Black Diamond, WA: Books for Educators, 2010.) This first edition was developed for the

CURRICULUM EXAMPLES

A Continuum of Concepts

MCSIP (Mid-California Science Improvement Program) science initiative funded by the David and Lucile Packard Foundation from 1987 through 1996. Our thanks to Project 2061 for providing educators a beginning place for developing curriculum. See Project 2061 and their curriculum recommendations in *Science for All Americans* and *Benchmarks for Science Literacy.*[3]

Please note that the excerpts don't include the entire curriculum for a grade level, thus the irregular numbering of the concepts and significant knowledge key points.

\	
\	

Science Continuum of Concepts – Grades K-6

GRADE LEVEL	ORGANIZING CONCEPTS
Kindergarten	**Exploration**—We can learn about things around us by carefully observing, comparing them, and interacting with them.
First Grade	**Basic Needs**—All living things, including humans, have basic needs that their habitat must provide.
Second Grade	**Form and Function**—Physical characteristics of living things vary greatly and determine what they can do and how they do it in order to meet their basic needs. Similarly, the physical characteristics of nonliving things vary greatly and determine what changes can occur and how they can be used.
Third Grade	**Change**—Things are changing around us all the time. Change can occur in a variety of ways and for different reasons. Rate and size of change may require tools to observe/measure change. Change can be helpful, harmful, or neutral.
Fourth Grade	**Interdependence**—Within a habitat, resident plants and animals interact with each other and their environment to meet their basic needs.
Fifth Grade	**Systems**—All structures and systems, living and nonliving, are made up of smaller parts and/or processes.
Sixth Grade	**Constancy and Change**—Cause is an action or event that brings an effect, which could be a single consequence or a chain of events. Every cause has an effect.

Figure 2C

KINDERGARTEN

The main goal for kindergarten is to convey to students that the world is an exciting place worthy of intense investigation. Identification of patterns through observing similarities and differences in nature is a precursor to children being able to identify, at later grades, more abstract patterns such as the unobservable happenings studied in science (particularly in earth and physical science areas) and abstract concepts in history/social studies, fine arts, and so forth. Giving students as many opportunities as possible to experience and interact with their environment and the living and nonliving things in it expands students' capacity to learn from the world they live in.

ORGANIZING CONCEPT— EXPLORATION

People can learn about things a̶ṛ̶ them by observing carefully—what things are made of, how they are put together, what they do, and how they are similar and different. Observing and comparing similarities and differences is a key way to help interpret and understand our world. Often we can learn even more about those things if we do something to them (especially if we use tools) and note what happens.

From the students' perspective, this might appear as a lot of messing around with fascinating things; from the teachers' perspective it's to ensure that students have rich, varied, and numerous daily experiences with the scientific processes of observing, communicating, and comparing those things that are the real stuff of the students' world. In doing so, teachers should avoid things that cannot be explored on a *being there* basis, such as tropical rain forests. Instead, choose local experiences that will engage all 20 senses. In the words of the theme song from the movie *The Lion King*, "There is more to see than can ever be seen . . . more to do than can ever be done." Localize your curriculum.

However, a focus on those things that are directly experienceable by kindergarteners can and should lead to in-depth and rigorous exploration of science through many, many real-world experiences with each of the concepts identified here. The young learner shows up at a new location ready to take in all that he or she sees. It's all about expectations and anticipation, an enjoyment of the surface, a what-you-see-is-what-you-get experience. An open mind meets the joy of surprise. Therefore, expect to repeat application of the concepts by allowing the nature of the *being there* location to select the concepts to be taught. Just ask yourself, "What are the obvious elements of attraction to a five-year old?"

At kindergarten level, formal science experiments utilizing two or more variables are age inappropriate. The goal is exploration and practicing the observation skills needed to do so.

Concepts and Significant Knowledge to Learn

Conceptual Key Point 1: People, and animals, use their many senses to explore and find out about their environment, each other, and themselves. Exploring and finding out about is a process called *observing,* a process that involves much more than watching or looking at. Good observation requires the use of all our senses because different senses provide different information during observation.

Significant Knowledge Key Point 1a: Tools, such as magnifiers, thermometers, and X-ray machines, often give more information about things than can be obtained by observing things with our senses without their help.

Significant Knowledge Key Point 1b: Different information can be taken in by moving closer to or farther away from the thing being observed and by comparing and contrasting them to something else.

Significant Knowledge Key Point 1c: [Select a related state standard that is prominently illustrated at the *being there* location; develop as many such related significant knowledge key points as needed for students to understand Conceptual Key Point 1.]

Conceptual Key Point 3: Some animals and plants are alike in the way they look and in the things they do; others are very different from one another.

Significant Knowledge Key Point 3a: People have different external features, such as their size, their shape, and the color of their hair, skin, and eyes, but they are more like one another than they are like other animals.

Significant Knowledge Key Point 3b: All animals have offspring, usually with two parents involved.

Significant Knowledge Key Point 3c: [Select a related state standard that is prominently illustrated at the *being there* location; develop as many such related significant knowledge key points as needed for students to understand Conceptual Key Point 3.]

Conceptual Key Point 4: Water is a home for many plants and animals. Some plants and animals can live only in salt water (oceans), others only in fresh water (rivers, lakes, marshes). Only a few are equipped to survive in both.
[Note: This is an important concept for students to ensure they do not imperil the lives of animals and plants as they study them.]

Significant Knowledge Key Point 4a: Most animals that live in water "breathe air" (absorb oxygen) directly from the water, absorbing oxygen from the water through their gills. Others, like humans, must come to the surface to breathe air, absorbing oxygen through their lungs.

Significant Knowledge Key Point 4b: [Select a related state standard that is prominently illustrated at the *being there* location; develop as many such related significant knowledge key points as needed for students to understand Conceptual Key Point 4.]

Conceptual Key Point 8: Objects can be described in terms of their physical properties (color, size, shape, weight, texture, flexibility, hardness/softness, and so forth) and the materials they are made of (such as clay, cloth, paper, wood, or metal).

Significant Knowledge Key Point 8a: Things can be done to materials (pulling, pushing, twisting, squeezing, submersing in water) to change some of their properties, but not all materials respond the same way to what is done to them.

Significant Knowledge Key Point 8b: [Select a related state standard that is prominently illustrated at the *being there* location; develop as many such related significant knowledge key points as needed for students to understand Conceptual Key Point 8.]

Conceptual Key Point 9: Most things are made of parts. Something may not work if some of its parts are missing.

Significant Knowledge Key Point 9a: Building something with parts makes it easier to build (especially large, heavy things such as a house). Building something with parts also allows the parts to move (such as a skateboard, a bicycle, or an automobile with its steering wheel and wheels).

Significant Knowledge Key Point 9b: [Select a related state standard that is prominently illustrated at the *being there* location; develop as many such related significant knowledge key points as needed for students to understand Conceptual Key Point 9.]

Possible Being There Locations

Schooyard, backyard of a nearby home (for examples of the natural world and relevant hobbies), nearby pond, creek, or man-made pond on the school grounds, nearby park or empty lot, pet store, and animals living in or visiting the classroom, and so forth.

Examples of Expected Performance Levels

- Responds with enthusiasm when faced with learning new things in science and proceeds with high confidence that he or she will be interested in and can understand what he or she will be learning.

- When comparing two animals, such as a skunk and a porcupine or a sea anemone and a shark, readily identifies at least five ways in which the two animals are similar and five ways in which they differ.

- When given five animals (that are very different from each other and live in different ecosystems), readily states at least five ways the animals use their bodies to locate food, shelter, and a mate and to avoid predators.

- Compares, with minimal prompting, any two nonliving things in terms of at least three of the following four categories: what they are made of, how they are put together, what they do, and how they are similar and different.

FIRST GRADE

The goal for first grade is an extension of that for kindergarten: To teach students how to learn from the natural world and to convey to them that the world is an exciting place worthy of intense investigation. To achieve such a goal, students must be given as many opportunities as possible to experience and interact with their environment and the living and nonliving things within it.

> ### ORGANIZING CONCEPT—
> # BASIC NEEDS
>
> All living things, including humans, have basic needs—for food, water, and oxygen, for protection from weather, disease, and predators, and to reproduce. A habitat is the place where the animal or plant lives while meeting these needs.

At first grade, larger patterns should begin to form for students. For example, all living things have the same basic needs but may go about meeting them differently. Therefore, if you know the characteristics of one mammal, you can guess many characteristics about another. For example, a means to help retain body heat is needed, such as fur, feathers, or hair. In short, the exploration begun in kindergarten that focused primarily on the process of observation and interacting with the natural world begins to spin into big ideas, information from which students can generalize to other similar situations or environments.

Identification of the patterns of similarities and differences in nature is a precursor to children being able to identify more abstract patterns such as the unobservable happenings studied in science at later grades (particularly in earth and physical science areas) and abstract concepts in history/social studies, fine arts, mathematics, and so more. Thus, students need discovery time to explore and manipulate until patterns, uniquely theirs yet accurate, are pieced together and woven into meaningful wholes.

Each *being there* experience should provide students ample opportunities to begin to generalize (extract patterns) and predict (apply previously learned patterns to new situations) about the living and nonliving things they experience using the organizing concept. Orchestrating science as a discovery of understandable patterns, especially of the organizing concept, is effective and efficient. For example, by studying a few members of a group, students can often find out a lot about the entire group or any other member of that group. This is a level of scientific "predicting" that is not only age appropriate for first graders but also very powerful for organizing and storing memories.

Study of the basic needs of all living things to survive should begin with immediately experienceable plants and animals in the schoolyard, backyards, playgrounds, gardens, and school Life Labs. A wonderful focus for first grade is "Beneath the Ground" because it opens up a world heretofore unseen by most students and thus invites conscious application of the science behavioral thinking processes. Such a focus on animals and plant parts found below ground level opens new doors to a new yet immediately experienceable world.

Once the patterns of survival of local plants and animals are constructed, students can transfer this knowledge to their learnings about other plants and animals in less frequently visited locales; for example, nearby ecosystems that are visited by students as part of family travel. Study of survival should always be related, at some point, to humans and what they would have to do to survive in a similar setting.

Concepts and Significant Knowledge to Learn

Conceptual Key Point 1: All living things have basic needs that must be met in order for them to survive. These are the needs for oxygen to breathe; water to drink; food for energy; protection from weather, disease, and predators; and the need to reproduce more of their own kind.
[Note: Study of the need to reproduce more of their own kind should not delve into the details of how reproduction occurs; such concepts are studied later in second and fourth grade. At first grade, stay with a general understanding of the need for reproduction to repopulate the species.]

Significant Knowledge Key Point 1a: Animals breathe oxygen in numerous ways. Mammals (such as humans, horses, dolphins, and whales) breathe air into their lungs; fish extract oxygen through their gills. Others, like earthworms, absorb oxygen through their skin.
[Note: Select for study animals that can be found at your *being there* locations, ones that students haven't studied before. This is true for selection of animals and plants for all conceptual and significant knowledge key points for the primary grades.]

Significant Knowledge Key Point 1b: Fresh, non-polluted water is essential for all living things. It provides an essential element that makes the bodies of animals and plants work; it also protects against diseases.

Significant Knowledge Key Point 1c: Animals eat a wide range of living things. Some eat other animals (from animals so small we can't see them with our naked eye to very large animals, such as whales and elephants. Some of these meat eaters, called carnivores, catch their prey while others are scavengers that eat what's already dead. Other animals, called herbivores, eat only plants. Others, like humans, eat both; these are called omnivores.

Significant Knowledge Key Point 1d: Many animals, including humans, have the ability to move to new places if their needs are not met. Many animals spend part of the year in one place and then migrate to another place when conditions become too harsh or when the needed food or shelter is no longer available.

Significant Knowledge Key Point 1e: Humans often rely on manufactured goods in the forms of food, clothing, and homes to help them survive.

Significant Knowledge Key Point 1f: All animals reproduce their own kind, usually with two parents involved. Many babies are unable to care for themselves; their survival depends on the care and protection received from their mother and other adults.

Significant Knowledge Key Point 1g: Animals reproduce in different ways. Some lay eggs from which the babies hatch; some produce live births.
[Note: This is an opportunity to closely examine local animals, especially those from the students' world that they may interact with but about which they may actually know little.]

Significant Knowledge Key Point 1h: The babies of mammals grow inside their mother until their birth. After birth, their mothers provide milk until the babies can eat on their own.

Significant Knowledge Key Point 1i: [Select a related state standard that is prominently illustrated at the *being there* location; develop as many such related significant knowledge key points as needed for students to understand Conceptual Key Point 1.]

Skill Key Point 1: When studying plants and animals, care must be taken to know about and provide for their needs when they are being studied. We must respect them as living things.

Conceptual Key Point 2: A habitat is a place where an animal or plant lives while meeting its basic needs.

Significant Knowledge Key Point 2a: Plants and animals have more limited capacity than humans to adapt; therefore, their environment must fit their needs. Therefore, some plants and animals can be found only in a few and relatively small areas of the world and will die if moved elsewhere, while others can live and thrive in many kinds of habitats.

Significant Knowledge Key Point 2b: Animals that live underground have very different features and behaviors from those that live aboveground.

Significant Knowledge Key Point 2c: Soil is an important habitat. How healthy it is determines what, if anything, can grow in it, such as corn, wheat, or alfalfa, and thus what animals can live in it. Soil is not just dirt, nor is it the same everywhere; it varies from place to place. Soils consist of different particles such as clay, sand, coarse gravel, small and large rocks, decaying bits of small and large animals, and so forth. Soil is a home for many living things. Different plants and animals need different kinds of soils. [Note: Don't get too technical here; work with the most important elements of soil. This is an opportunity for children to explore, share observations, and compare and report data resulting from their observations of soils from different locations. Let them explore such questions as Which kinds of soils do local plants grow best in? What should we add to our garden to grow the biggest, most healthy plants? What kind of soil do earthworms prefer? What lives in sand on beaches?]

Significant Knowledge Key Point 2d: Animals, including humans, and plants sometimes cause changes in their surroundings. Some of these changes are highly noticeable almost immediately and can be long lasting (for example, the work of beavers or the spread of water hydrangeas, which can quickly result in obstruction of water flows and clogging of waterways); others occur more slowly and may or may not be long lasting such as undergrowth reappearing in a recently flooded creek or riverbed. [Note: Select local examples of change that students have experience with. For example, ask the kindergarten teachers which physical locations they used for *being there* experiences last year and then find out what changes have occurred during the past year. The comparison of two intense observations (then and now) will provide an excellent vehicle for teaching the concept of change.]

Significant Knowledge Key Point 2e: [Select a related state standard that is prominently illustrated at the *being there* location; develop as many such related significant knowledge key points as needed for students to understand Conceptual Key Point 2.]

Conceptual Key Point 4: Everybody can "do" science, invent things, and have ideas. Doing science is a way of observing and thinking and learning about the world.

Significant Knowledge Key Point 4a: Describing things as accurately as possible is important in science because it enables people to compare their observations and understandings with those of others. Tools such as rulers, magnifiers, thermometers, balances, and scales allow us to observe and describe things more completely and accurately.

Significant Knowledge Key Point 4b: Tools are used to do things better or more easily and to do some things that could not otherwise be done at all.

Significant Knowledge Key Point 4c: When people give different descriptions of the same thing, it is usually a good idea to make some fresh observations instead of just arguing about who is right.

Significant Knowledge Key Point 4d: [Select a related state standard that is prominently illustrated at the *being there* location; develop as many such related significant knowledge key points as needed for students to understand Conceptual Key Point 4.]

Conceptual Key Point 6: Objects move in many different ways.

Significant Knowledge Key Point 6a: Common patterns of movement are straight, zigzag, round and round, back and forth, and fast and slow.

Significant Knowledge Key Point 6b: The way to change how something is moving is to give it a push or a pull. Objects do not move because they want to or because someone asks them to or because of magic or other fictional explanations presented in cartoons, movies, and books.

Significant Knowledge Key Point 6c: [Select a related state standard that is prominently illustrated at the *being there* location; develop as many such related significant knowledge key points as needed for students to understand Conceptual Key Point 6.]

Possible Being There Locations

Underground in the schoolyard or backyard of a nearby home, local habitats that are rich in animal and plant life, farm, nearby garden (school Lifelab or nearby backyard), larger bodies of water such as lakes, rivers, ocean, and a zoo, aquarium, or pet store.

Examples of Expected Performance Levels

- Responds with enthusiasm when faced with learning new things in science and proceeds with high confidence that he or she will be interested in and can understand what he or she will be learning.

- Given five animals from the local area, describes key characteristics of each animal that allow it to meet its needs and succeed in its habitat. Describes why two of the animals could not survive in the desert or tundra.

- Identifies four local, belowground animals and describes their role in helping plants grow.

- Given half a dozen local animals and plants, can describe what change in the environment would result if that plant or animal died out.

- When confronted with unfamiliar objects, readily uses common instruments and tools to observe, compare, and describe the objects. Understands the importance of remeasuring when descriptions of an object or event differs among members of their collaborative group.

- After reading a fictional story about animals and plants, can chart which characteristics are true and which are make-believe.

- Compares the animals, plants, and objects in a fictional story to the characteristics and behaviors of these animals, plants, and objects in real life. Distinguishes between make-believe and ascription of human qualities to animals from scientific fact.

SECOND GRADE

By second grade, students can begin to work with large ideas or concepts that add cohesiveness to their study of science. This Organizing Concept is powerful. It helps students understand that the characteristics of things and of animals and plants are not whimsical or random. Shape, size, and other characteristics are directly related to function—what something can do or be used for and how it does it or how it works.

> ORGANIZING CONCEPT—
> ## FORM AND FUNCTION
>
> The physical characteristics of animals and plants vary greatly and determine what they can do and how they do it in order to meet their needs (form and function). Similarly, the physical characteristics of nonliving things vary greatly and determine what changes can occur in them and how they can be used (form and function).

This is true of all things—living and nonliving. Plants and animals, including humans, have distinct external features that help them to live and thrive in different kinds of places. Thus, students should have experience with a wide range of animals and plants (beginning with local species and moving outward as is age appropriate) in order to gain an appreciation of the wide range of adaptations developed to allow each to thrive in its particular niche. In so doing, always examine such characteristics in relationship to basic needs, the Organizing Concept for first grade. For example, food (how to locate, capture, and eat it), shelter in which to raise young (for example, those born hairless, sightless, and dependent upon parents for months versus those ready to keep up with the herd in a matter of hours).

Students should also note what tools allow humans to perform similar tasks, for example, fins for our feet for swimming and guns to compensate for speeds slower than those of our prey.

Similarly with nonliving things, we should help students understand that all materials, objects, and tools have different characteristics that determine how they can be used, and how and if they can be changed. Such behaviors are observable and predictable. Emphasis must be placed on providing students with ample opportunities to mess around, to explore the materials, objects, and tools from their immediate world.

The organizing concept for second grade provides students their first experience with the basis of the biological classification system and the if-then thinking in fields such as geometry. This is a level of predicting in science that's not only age appropriate for second graders but also very powerful for organizing and storing long-term memories. It's also smart curriculum for smart use of time, the preconditions for Effective First Teaching (EFT).

Concepts and Significant Knowledge to Learn

Conceptual Key Point 1: Living things have physical characteristics that allow them to survive. They use these characteristics to meet their basic needs for food, water, air, protection, shelter, and reproducing.

Significant Knowledge Key Point 1a: Knowing what animals do to survive (such as eat meat or swim) allows one to make predictions about their physical characteristics.

Significant Knowledge Key Point 1b: Some animals and plants are alike in the way they look and in the things they do, while others are very different from one another.

Significant Knowledge Key Point 1c: [Select a related state standard that is prominently illustrated at the *being there* location; develop as many such related significant knowledge key points as needed for students to understand Conceptual Key Point 1.]

Conceptual Key Point 3: Circles, squares, triangles, spirals, and other shapes are patterns that occur in nature and in human-made things. They are the building blocks of nature and human creations.

Significant Knowledge Key Point 3a: Each shape has its advantages.

- The circle holds the most mass relative to surface area; thus, most animals with self-regulated body temperatures are roundish in shape in order to reduce surface area compared to body mass. In contrast, most reptiles have flat bodies which increase surface area to body mass, therefore allowing them to use the environment to heat and cool their body.

- The triangle is the strongest shape. It is a common shape in bridges, buildings, and structures which must bear weight.

- Squares and rectangles are a good shape for efficient stacking, such as some support structures in plants or containers for storing items in a closet or warehouse, and for measuring, such as in surveying and computing distance and volume (acreage, perimeter, and so forth).

- Hexagons, such as in bee hives, maximize the enclosed region and minimize the perimeter construction materials and allow for efficient stacking. And when stacked, they make strong structures (for example, the concept behind the method of timber shoring developed in the Comstock Mines of Virginia City, Nevada in the 1860s).

Significant Knowledge Key Point 3b: Patterns can be made by putting different shapes together or taking them apart; they can be simple or complex, symmetrical or not.

Significant Knowledge Key Point 3c: Shapes such as circles, squares, and triangles are useful in describing many things that one person can see but another cannot. They are also useful for artists as they begin to sketch their subjects.

Significant Knowledge Key Point 3d: [Select a related state standard that is prominently illustrated at the *being there* location; develop as many such related significant knowledge key points as needed for students to understand Conceptual Key Point 3.]

Conceptual Key Point 4: The function or use of something is usually related to its shape.

Significant Knowledge Key Point 4a: The design of objects and tools determines what the object or tool will be able to do and how it will get something done.

Significant Knowledge Key Point 4b: People use objects and tools to solve problems, take measurements, do observations, make work easier, and create change. Some tools have changed little in hundreds of years, such as a carpenter's hand tools; others, like computers and related tools, change rapidly, almost daily.

Significant Knowledge Key Point 4c: [Select a related state standard that is prominently illustrated at the *being there* location; develop as many such related significant knowledge key points as needed for students to understand Conceptual Key Point 4.]

Possible Being There *Locations*

Natural history museums, taxidermy shop, construction sites and repair shops where a variety of tools are used, local businesses, and city agencies and resources such as police, fire, hospitals, medical clinics, and so on.

Examples of Expected Performance Levels

- Compares the physical characteristics of four plants and four animals and explains how they are able to live where they live.

- Designs a new animal by determining how the animal would meet its survival needs given the weather (summer and winter extremes and amount and kind of precipitation), terrain of its habitat, and its food sources, and then creates the body parts accordingly. Student first draws a picture and/or makes a diorama in a shoebox showing the animal's habitat and physical characteristics needed to survive; describes or imitates how the animal would move; and depicts (oral, written, drawing) how the animal would meet each basic need. [Note: Although the animal is fictional, the characteristics must be consistent with established physiological precepts.]

- Given five tools or objects, determines what each can do or be used for based on its physical characteristics. Can demonstrate how each object is used. Can speak for two minutes each about where and how each is used locally (job sites) and about the location occupations (at least four) which use the tool on a regular basis.

THIRD GRADE

The goal of third-grade curriculum is to alert students to the dynamic nature of the world around them. Experiencing many and varied examples of change will provide opportunities to sharpen their ability (and inclination) to observe, analyze, communicate, and record typical patterns of change in daily life and the wider world. Such skills are the necessary foundations for further science study. They should, however, be taught as means to making meaning of the world, not as ends in themselves.

> ORGANIZING CONCEPT—
> ## CHANGE
>
> Things are changing around us all the time. Change can occur in a variety of ways (reversible, irreversible; controllable, not controllable; steady or repetitive and thus fairly predictable or not and thus unpredictable) and for different reasons. The rate and size of change may not be observable with human senses; tools to measure such change are needed. Change can be helpful, harmful, or neutral.

Change is not a subject to be studied separately but rather to be seen as a pattern in much that occurs around us. Use this year of study as a way of deepening students' awareness and understanding of the plants, animals, earth and physical sciences, and technology of their immediate surroundings. The pattern of change being studied can be used to compare and contrast, to connect, and to extend objects, actions, and ideas into larger understandings. A cautionary note, however, is to remember to stay within content that is appropriate for eight-year-olds (see Chapter 7).

The observation and recording of change is an excellent time to integrate mathematics and language arts. It gives purpose to learning math and improves recording thinking, writing, spelling, and more). It is also a golden opportunity to make students conscious practitioners of the scientific thinking processes appropriate to this age level: observing, communicating, comparing, and simple means of organizing, all of which leads to making predictions (based on extending the patterns they understand). Students can then prove or disprove these predictions as they go to similar but different situations and environments.

Remember that students need discovery time to explore and manipulate ideas (concepts) until they can be pieced together and woven into meaningful wholes. This means that, despite the more developed levels of basic skills and study skills, science at the third-grade level should be every bit as experiential of the real thing as one would expect for very young children. The power of the real world to propel learning never fades, even for adults.

Concepts and Significant Knowledge to Learn

Conceptual Key Point 1: All things change over time.

Significant Knowledge Key Point 1a: Some changes are so slow or so fast or on such a massive or minute scale that they are hard to detect with our senses. Instruments are needed to take measurements; information must be graphed over time.

Significant Knowledge Key Point 1b: Change occurs in different ways (such as in size, weight, color, movement, in chemical composition, and from birth to death).

Significant Knowledge Key Point 1c: Living things can be sorted into groups by the way they change, such as metamorphosis (butterflies), renewal by root rather than seed (perennial plants versus annual plants), aquatic to land (tadpoles to frogs), and so on.

Significant Knowledge Key Point 1d: [Select a related state standard that is prominently illustrated at the *being there* location; develop as many such related significant knowledge key points as needed for students to understand Conceptual Key Point 1.]

Conceptual Key Point 2: The nature of change can vary.

Conceptual Key Point 2.1: Change can be steady or repetitive and therefore fairly predictable. An example of repetitive change is a cycle.

Significant Knowledge Key Point 2.1a: Cycles are changes that occur in a pattern which repeats itself. Examples of cyclical change include night-day, seasons, life cycles (with their usual sequences of physical and mental development), water cycle, shape of the moon, tides, and more.

Significant Knowledge Key Point 2.1b: A garden is a complex microcosm of change that illustrates many cycles, such as reproduction, growth, dying, decaying, recycling, and so forth.

Significant Knowledge Key Point 2.1c: Cycles and change happen over time. Some take place over short periods, such as the life cycle of a butterfly, and others over long periods (such as the seasons of the year, generations of a family, or even millions of years, such as the change in the horse from the size of a rabbit to today's horses).

Significant Knowledge Key Point 2.1d: Some physical objects, plants, and animals change in some way when they are part of a cycle, such as the metamorphosis of a butterfly from caterpillar to butterfly. Other physical objects may also change but not be part of any cycle, such as changes in a hillside as a result of mining for gold or coal.

Conceptual Key Point 2.3: Some change can be controlled; some cannot.

Significant Knowledge Key Point 2.3a: Examples of change that can be controlled include water flow levels in a watershed downstream from a dam, temperature inside a house or space station, or production levels in a garden. Whether humans choose to control some change depends upon cost and the political will to do so.

Significant Knowledge Key Point 2.3b: Examples of change that cannot be controlled include flooding upstream from a dam, the weather, earthquakes, and volcanic eruptions. Although humans may not be able to control a change, we can plan how we will respond when such change happens, e.g., emergency evacuation plans, stockpiling food and medical supplies, and so forth.

Significant Knowledge Key Point 2.3c: [Select a related state standard that is prominently illustrated at the *being there* location; develop as many such related significant knowledge key points as needed for students to understand Conceptual Key Point 2.3.]

Conceptual Key Point 3: Change can occur as a result of a single cause or numerous causes or variables.
[Note: Select examples of change from your *being there* locations.]

Significant Knowledge Key Point 3a: Common causes or variables include being combined with other things (mixing water and flour to make paste, mixing water with Jell-O powder, and so forth); being bent, stretched, or squeezed by motion (such as a car wreck, bungee cord, and rolling the center of a fresh piece of bread into a ball); and the disappearance of an element in the system (such as a wheel falling off a skateboard or no cable between computer and printer, and so forth).

Significant Knowledge Key Point 3b: Many kinds of change occur faster under hotter conditions, such as melting copper or gold into a liquid in order to quickly reform it into something else. Change can also happen as a result of cooling, such as when molten asphalt applied on a road surface hardens, providing a surface for cars and trucks to drive on.

Significant Knowledge Key Point 3c: [Select a related state standard that is prominently illustrated at the *being there* location; develop as many such related significant knowledge key points as needed for students to understand Conceptual Key Point 3.]

Conceptual Key Point 5: Humans use machines to make change happen.

Significant Knowledge Key Point 5a: [Select a related state standard that is illustrated at the *being there* location; develop as many significant knowledge key points as needed for students to understand Conceptual Key Point 5.]
[Note: Use students' favorite toys and machines as examples of simple machines. Based on knowledge of how work is done through these toys, select examples of work being done in the immediate surroundings of the school and at *being there* locations; analyze what simple machines are being used to accomplish these tasks and how they are like the toys they studied.]

Significant Knowledge Key Point 5b: [Select a related state standard that is illustrated at the *being there* location; develop as many significant knowledge key points as needed for students to understand Conceptual Key Point 5.]
[Note: Use examples of construction equipment on projects near the school, such as excavator, backhoe, bobcat, and so on.

Conceptual Key Point 6: Change can be helpful, neutral, or harmful.

Significant Knowledge Key Point 6a: [Select a related state standard that is prominently illustrated at the *being there* location; develop as many such related significant knowledge key points as needed for students to understand Conceptual Key Point 6.]
Note: Use the *being there* locations you are studying to provide examples of changes that fit each of these three categories.]

Possible Being There Locations

The best approach to teaching these concepts about change is through in-depth study of four to six child-engaging locations. For example, diverse and rich natural settings which demonstrate a domino chain of events, and so forth. Without in-depth and varied experiences with the concept of change, content becomes a memorization chore. Remember that the purpose of starting locally is to provide real-world, *being there* experiences for students that can provide rich sensory input for pattern seeking and meaning making. This shifts the burden of teaching from talking about science to exploration and discovery that makes pattern identification, transfer of learning, and program building for long-term memory more likely. When possible, select locations for science study that can also serve as *being there* locations for studying history/social studies.

Introduce a range of observational techniques such as the 1′ x 1′ grid for 10 minutes; below, on, and above; pick a tree (and graph all observable residents), "birds of a feather flock together" (If you know three residents of a habitat, how many others can you predict?), and so on. For resources for framing observations, see the science resources at the end of this chapter. Be sure to include chemical testing of water and soil as natural investigatory tools for examining the quality of habitats.

It's important to visit and revisit selected sites to notice change occurring over time, e.g., nearby road cuts that expose changes in landscape, before and after a flood or earthquake, recycling operations from pick-up to remanufacturing to resale, and lots of neighborhood illustrations of life cycles, machines, and so forth. Also, community landmarks, businesses (grocery store, mall, mom-and-pop stores of any kind). And don't forget observation of the nighttime sky, daily weather, and the seasons.

Examples of Expected Performance Levels

- For three local habitats, identifies things that have not changed in hundreds of years, those that have changed within the past year, evidence of at least five life cycles, and things whose degree of change would require measurement by various instruments (such as a ruler, magnifier, scale, hand lens, or chemical lab). Identifies human-made changes potentially harmful to the habitat and those potentially helpful to the habitat.

- Through interviewing people from three generations (family and/or neighbors), identifies the most significant changes that have occurred in the past 100 years. Compiles such information (as a whole class or a collaborative group) and creates a bar graph of the most frequently mentioned items.

- After selecting a location, talks for two minutes about the kinds of changes that occur there. Provides examples of change, different ways things can change, whether change is controllable or reversible, cyclical, and/or predictable.

- Draws or constructs a model of a machine (which may or may not work) to do the work of a task he or she is responsible for performing at home. Predicts if and how his or her regular use of that machine would change his or her life (helpful, harmful, neutral effect).

- Identifies at least 10 examples of change based on the front page of the local newspaper, TV nightly news, or Internet sources.

- Using examples of change locally, identifies at least three examples of change in each of the following categories:
  —So slowly that we cannot detect their change without assistance of tools
  —So fast we cannot determine their change without tools
  —On a scale so large that we need tools to determine the change
  —On a scale so small that we need tools to determine the change
  —On a chemical level we cannot detect without laboratory tools.

  Can identify the most effective tools for observing each of the examples of change given above, such as measuring tape, hand lens, scale, stethoscope, stove or refrigerator (as source of heat or cooling), graphing, or calculator.

FOURTH GRADE

The goal of fourth-grade curriculum is to give students many opportunities to investigate the interaction of plants and animals and their environment so that they can construct for themselves the concepts of habitat, food web, and the impact of weather and terrain (landforms) as a

> ORGANIZING CONCEPT—
> # INTERDEPENDENCE
> Plants and animals interact with each other and their environment in ways that allow them to meet their basic needs. Keep in mind that humans are animals.

basis for understanding the many issues of ecology which they will face in the polling booth and in their personal lives. What we wish to eliminate is the teaching of ecology as preaching about or object lessons in good versus evil without a firm scientific understanding of what is actually happening.

Scientific understanding of our world is essential preparation for citizenship and the increasing complexity of science-based decision making demanded in our polling booths. Developing a deep understanding of interdependence and of cause and effect in the natural world (which students can observe and experience firsthand) is also excellent preparation for understanding systems, living, nonliving, or a combination of both (which are not directly observable but can be followed in the mind by understanding their inputs and outputs).

Remember that students need discovery time to explore and manipulate until the Organizing Concept is internalized. Thus, despite the more developed levels of basic skills and study skills, science at the fourth-grade level should be every bit as experiential of the real thing as one would expect for very young children. The power of the real world to propel learning never fades, even for adults.

Concepts and Significant Knowledge to Learn

Conceptual Key Point 1: Within a habitat, the resident plants and animals interact with other plants and animals and the environment in ways that allow each to meet its basic needs (for food, water, oxygen, sunlight, protection from predators, weather, and disease, and to reproduce). This interaction is called *interdependence.*

Conceptual Key Point 1.1: Interactions to meet the need for food within a habitat are called a food chain or, more accurately, a food web. The disappearance of even one animal or plant can have a disastrous domino effect on the food web.

Significant Knowledge Key Point 1.1a: Food webs are significantly and often disastrously disrupted by human activities, such as land use and development and pollution.

Significant Knowledge Key Point 1.1b: Food preferences can usually be predicted based upon the physical characteristics of the plant or animal (form and function as studied in second grade) and can be categorized as carnivorous, herbivorous, and omnivorous.

Significant Knowledge Key Point 1.1c: [Select a related state standard that is prominently illustrated at the *being there* location; develop as many such related significant knowledge key points as needed for students to understand Conceptual Key Point 1.1.]

Conceptual Key Point 1.2: The weather (climate—temperature ranges, amount and frequency of precipitation, and amount of sunlight) and terrain (landforms and soil) significantly shape a habitat.

Significant Knowledge Key Point 1.2a: Weather and terrain determine availability of needed shelter and food.

Significant Knowledge Key Point 1.2b: Ability to survive in a particular climate and terrain can often be predicted based on physical characteristics of the animal and plant (refer to the organizing concept for second grade, form and function).

Significant Knowledge Key Point 1.2c: [Select a related state standard that is prominently illustrated at the *being there* location; develop as many such related significant knowledge key points as needed for students to understand Conceptual Key Point 1.2.]

Conceptual Key Point 1.5: Essential factors in reproduction are extremely varied.

[Note: Use local plants and animals as examples. Variances include how the egg is fertilized, how it is carried/not carried by the female, the thickness of the egg's exterior membrane, lengthen of incubation, and so forth.]

Significant Knowledge Key Point 1.5a: The reproductive process of some plants and animals is extremely dependent upon other plants and animals. A species may completely die out without its partner, thus becoming endangered or extinct; for example, honey bees that pollinate fruit trees, the lesser long-nosed bat (the foremost pollinator of the saguaro cactus), and the cow bird that lays its eggs in other birds' nests and relies on them to raise their young.

Significant Knowledge Key Point 1.5b: Other species rely on constants to disperse their seeds or young (such as wind) with no interaction of other species and are thus considered very hardy (for example, the tumbleweeds, dandelions, and baby spiders carried by parachute-like webs).

Significant Knowledge Key Point 1.5c: Those species relying on interaction of other species are highly at risk when human intervention in the environment negatively impacts a partner species. Chemicals used by local businesses and people in their personal daily lives disrupt the food and reproductive cycle of many plants and animals in our area.
[Note: Identify the chemicals involved in the most pervasive pollution problems in your area. Where do they come from, what are their intended uses, how did they get out of hand, how are they carried into and through the environment, what's their effect on plants and animals, including humans?]

Conceptual Key Point 3: Machines make work easier. Machines and other forms of technology extend the ability of people to change the world: to cut, shape, or put together materials; to move things from one place to another; and to reach farther with their hands, voices, senses, and minds. Such changes may be for survival needs (such as food, shelter, or defense), for communication and transportation, to gain and share knowledge and express ideas, or to satisfy a market need and thus make money.

Significant Knowledge Key Point 3a: Machines allow us to apply force (push or pull) to objects to move them. Motion is the act of changing place or position, usually measured in distance and time.

Significant Knowledge Key Point 3b: Machines used during the gold rush locations (mid- and late 1800s) took many forms, e.g., the wheel on wagons, water wheels in mills and steam ships, and fly wheels in stamp mills and most manufacturing settings; levers in jacks needed to remove or install a wagon wheel or shore up timbers in mines; inclined planes for ramps, mountain roads; screws for augers, drill bits, hydraulic presses; and pulleys for lowering men and supplies into mines and loading ships.

Possible Being There *Locations*

The best approach to teaching the above issues is through in-depth study of four or five complex ecosystems such as a nearby creek, slough, marsh, tide pool, lake, forest, or biodiverse park or backyard garden. Also have **students create and maintain as many habitats in the classroom and schoolyard as possible, e.g., the Salmanoid**

project hatching salmon, a pond with all its inhabitants. What is learned in-depth there can then be extended through numerous being there experiences in varying ecosystems. Also include a state historical site or its replication that parallel your state history curriculum.

Remember that the purpose of starting locally is to provide real-world, *being there* experiences for students, thus allowing rich input for pattern seeking and meaning making. This shifts the burden of teaching from talking about to exploration and discovery, thus making pattern identification, transfer of learning, and program building for long-term memory more likely. When possible, select locations for science study that can also serve as *being there* locations for studying history/social studies.

Take advantage of a wide range of observational techniques such as the 1' x 1' grid for 10 minutes; below, on, and above; pick a tree (and graph all observable residents); "birds of a feather flock together" (If you know three residents of a habitat, how many others can you predict?), and so forth. Be sure to include water chemistry and soil testing as natural investigatory tools for examining the quality of habitats.

Examples of Expected Performance Levels

- Selecting a favorite wild animal from his or her local ecosystem, creates a diorama of this animal and its food web. Includes at least four animals and/or plants in each direction of the web from the chosen animal outward.

- Using a local ecosystem, compares and contrasts the food web needed to support the most common carnivore, herbivore, and omnivore in the area. Describes how that food web has changed in the past 20 years and why.

- When given six local plants, researches what kind of soil each plant most prefers; finds (from the local environment) or makes such soils for each plant.

- Describes how the landforms influenced the early migration of Europeans into our state—how they came, where they settled, and what they did to survive.

- Describes how machines influenced the early migration of Europeans into our state—how they came, where they settled, and what they did to survive.

- Creates an invention for an Invent America-like program that would solve a major problem in the local environment.
  [Note: Such an invention does not have to work; the focus is on design.]

FIFTH GRADE

Exploring systems parallels one of the essential components of higher-order thinking—the ability to think about a whole in terms of its parts and, alternatively, about parts in terms of how they relate to one another and to the whole.

> **ORGANIZING CONCEPT—**
> # SYSTEMS
>
> All structures and systems, living and nonliving, are made up of smaller parts and/or processes.

The main goal of the fifth-grade curriculum is to have students learn about systems, not as an exercise in talking about systems in abstract terms, but has a means to enhance students' ability (and inclination) to closely observe systems all around them—living, nonliving, and combinations of both—especially those that shape their daily lives. For example, the complexity of a global economy and today's technology and its effects on ecology and quality of life cannot be understood without a firm and very concrete grasp of the notion of systems. Nor can history and the study of societies and cultures be understood in any useful way without a sense of the interactions among ideas, events, and peoples.

The fifth grade should provide many, many investigations of experienceable, hands-on-of-the-real-thing examples of systems made up of smaller parts. Abstract concepts, topics, and systems that cannot be directly experienced and investigated by students should be left to later grade levels when they would be age appropriate. As there is no shortage of experienceable systems to study, avoid the abstract and intangible.

The key idea to be conveyed to students is that systems are everywhere and that examining things as systems will teach us more about them. We can learn more about the parts of a system when considering them as part of the whole and, conversely, more about the whole when we understand the parts. Examples include living systems (such as ecosystems and the systems of our bodies), nonliving systems (such as electrical systems in cars and houses, water systems to and from our houses, weather), and combinations of living and nonliving systems, such as watersheds, transportation and communication systems, and so forth). Be sure you choose for study those systems that students can directly experience on a daily basis.

Concepts and Significant Knowledge to Learn

Conceptual Key Point 1: A system is a collection of things and processes (and often people) that interact to perform some function.

Conceptual Key Point 1.1: Most systems, living and nonliving, are made up of smaller parts that, when put together, can do things the parts couldn't do by themselves. Examples include skateboards, clocks, flashlights, bicycles, roller blades, cars, electrical circuits, habitats, large corporations (such as agribusinesses or solid waste removal operations), economics systems (such as banks, stock market, or housing market), and political systems (such as a monarchy, democracy, or socialist system).

Significant Knowledge Key Point 1.1a: [Select a related state standard that is prominently illustrated at the *being there* location; develop as many such related significant knowledge key points as needed for students to understand Conceptual Key Point 1.1.]

Conceptual Key Point 1.2: Thinking about things as systems means looking for how every part relates to others.

Significant Knowledge Key Point 1.2a: *Living systems*—Every plant and animal is a living system; each is made up of smaller parts whose processes are essential to the survival of that plant or animal.

[Note: A simultaneous study of plants and animals, the similarities and differences of their structures will provide a useful compare and contrast, discovery-oriented context and thus minimize rote memorization; for example, microscope examination of the difference in thickness of cell walls of plants and animals, source and distribution of nutrients, and so forth.]

Significant Knowledge Key Point 1.2b: *Nonliving systems*—Nonliving systems are also made up of smaller parts, each contributing to what the system can do.

Significant Knowledge Key Point 1.2c: *Combination systems*—Some systems are a combination of living and nonliving parts or processes. For example, in a watershed, the nonliving parts of the watershed system include sunlight, soil, water, air, and gravity. The living parts are animals and plants, including algae, bacteria, and fungi.

Significant Knowledge Key Point 1.2d: In manmade systems, such as the Boeing 747, there are often redundant or backup systems that are or can be activated if the first system fails.

Significant Knowledge Key Point 1.2e: [Select a related state standard that is prominently illustrated at the *being there* location; develop as many such related significant knowledge key points as needed for students to understand Conceptual Key Point 1.2.]

Conceptual Key Point 1.3: Something may not work as well (or at all) if a part of it is missing, broken, worn out, mismatched, or misconnected.

Significant Knowledge Key Point 1.3a: [Select a related state standard that is prominently illustrated at the *being there* location; develop as many such related significant knowledge key points as needed for students to understand Conceptual Key Point 1.3.]

Conceptual Key Point 1.4: In something that consists of parts, the parts usually influence each other. When parts are put together, they can do things that they couldn't do by themselves.

Significant Knowledge Key Point 1.4a: [Select a related state standard that is prominently illustrated at the *being there* location; develop as many such related significant knowledge key points as needed for students to understand Conceptual Key Point 1.4.]

Conceptual Key Point 1.5: No matter how parts of an object are assembled, the weight of the whole object made is always the same as the sum of its parts. Likewise, when a thing is broken into parts, the parts have the same total weight as the original thing. For example, all the individual parts for a bicycle or car weigh the same as the assembled bicycle or car.

Significant Knowledge Key Point 1.5a: [Select a related state standard that is prominently illustrated at the *being there* location; develop as many such related significant knowledge key points as needed for students to understand Conceptual Key Point 1.5.]

Conceptual Key Point 2: Systems are everywhere.

Conceptual Key Point 2.1: To study a system, one must define its boundaries. [Note: Examples of boundary definition occurred in fourth grade when looking at habitats within habitats, such as the habitat of an individual animal (one mountain lion) or of a specific species (grizzly bears remaining). Also, in the study of machines, boundary definition can be limited to the gears of a bicycle or established to include the entire bicycle. This basic notion about defining the boundaries of systems in order to study them should be examined using systems in students' everyday world and your *being there* location(s) before moving to less familiar or more abstract systems. Allow plenty of lead-up time during which students can explore and analyze the nature of systems they already know but have not viewed as systems before.]

Significant Knowledge Key Point 2.1a: A watershed is a system whose boundaries are the region from which a river, stream, creek, pond, or lake receives its water supply. A watershed is an area of land that drains its rain water to a river, a creek, a wetland, a lake, or an ocean. It can be huge, covering many states, such as that for the Mississippi River whose boundary includes all the land area from which water trickles and flows to get to the creeks and rivers that feed the Mississippi River. Watersheds can also be much smaller, such as our local _____ Creek. Its watershed covers _____ square miles. [Note: Whatever your *being there* location(s), there are literally dozens of systems that could be defined and studied there.]

Significant Knowledge Key Point 2b: An organic garden is a system that includes the garden plus its key components which include the composting area and processes and the natural methods of protecting the garden from pests (for example, a fenced area encircling the garden into which the gardener puts chickens who eat the pests before they can crawl into the garden).

Significant Knowledge Key Point 2c: Simple electrical circuits are made of smaller parts, and each part plays a different role in the circuit. Combining such circuits can create a large electrical system for houses, buildings, automobiles, and so on. To analyze electrical circuits to troubleshoot or determine if amperage is sufficient, you must first define the system to be analyzed.

Conceptual Key Point 3: A system is usually connected to other systems, both internally and externally. Thus a system may be thought of as containing subsystems and as being a subsystem of a larger system.
[Note: An example is all the systems within a city or town that are essential to the existence of the city, such as transportation, water, garbage, sewer, hospital, police, and fire. Other examples include the human body, ecosystems, human-made habitats such as a shopping mall, school and regional transportation systems, and the International Space Station and similar attempts at creating self-sustaining environments.]

Significant Knowledge Key Point 3a: Gardens are a system connected to other systems, both internally and externally. A garden contains many subsystems, such as soil, composting, pests, pest controls, and water systems. A garden is part of larger systems of product preparation, sales, distribution, and consumption.

Significant Knowledge Key Point 3b: [Select a related state standard that is prominently illustrated at the *being there* location; develop as many such related significant knowledge key points as needed for students to understand Conceptual Key Point 3.]

Conceptual Key Point 3.1: A change in one system may disrupt all the other interrelated systems.

Significant Knowledge Key Point 3.1a: Water flow and soil type are interrelated parts of the watershed. The interaction between water and soil affect the quality of life within the watershed. Increases in the amount of soil runoff (erosion) will increase the turbidity (amount of particulate matter) of the water. This can have negative effects on the animals living in the water, e.g., interfering with oxygen absorption or disrupting food sources.

Significant Knowledge Key Point 3.1b: [Select a related state standard that is prominently illustrated at the *being there* location; develop as many such related significant knowledge key points as needed for students to understand Conceptual Key Point 3.1.]

Conceptual Key Point 3.2: The output of one system becomes the input for another. For example, water flows out of a watershed (output) to the ocean and, in doing so, provides nutrients to animals and plants (input) along the way. Likewise, the energy output of an automobile engine, a complex system consisting of thousands of parts, provides input to the transmission, air-conditioning and heating system and to the electrical system needed to operate gauges, radio, moving seats, windshield wipers, and so on.

Significant Knowledge Key Point 3.2a: [Select a related state standard that is prominently illustrated at the *being there* location; develop as many such related significant knowledge key points as needed for students to understand Conceptual Key Point 3.2.]

Conceptual Key Point 3.3: The solution to one problem may create other problems. For example, a town's new subdivision provides new housing for humans, but the construction destroys the habitat for resident animals which must leave or die.

Significant Knowledge Key Point 3.3a: [Select a related state standard that is prominently illustrated at the *being there* location; develop as many such related significant knowledge key points as needed for students to understand Conceptual Key Point 3.3.]

Possible Being There Locations

Fortunately, systems are everywhere, so start with those right under your students' noses: school transportation systems, school food system (including where food comes from and where the leftovers go), schoolyard, local gardens and parks, the telephone company, television and radio stations, a nearby creek or river, water treatment plants, car repair shops, malls, city and county bus systems, and theme parks such as Sea World, Great America, Boardwalk, Disneyworld, and Epcot.

Examples of Expected Performance Levels

- After selecting three out of four kinds of systems (mechanical, electrical, transportation, business), can speak knowledgeably for two minutes on each, describing the boundaries of the system (how and why he or she chose such boundaries in order to study and describe the system), the major inputs and outputs of the system, how the major parts of the system influence each other, and what part of the system is most vulnerable to breakage or overloading.

- Using a broken item made up of parts (student brings item of choice to class), uses knowledge of systems to identify why the item (as a system) doesn't work—which parts are missing, broken, worn out, mismatched, or misconnected. Can describe what is needed to repair the item and which parts must be put together to create or bring in the input to the system and which to utilize or take out the output of the system.

- Identifies five systems in his or her classroom, school, or home life that he or she finds most interesting. Defines their boundaries, their parts, and how they work, including their inputs and outputs.

- Identifies at least a dozen systems in the city or town he or she lives in (or, if in a rural area, a nearby town). Defines their boundaries, their parts, and describes inputs and outputs as a way of identifying and describing at least three systems within a system. Identifies how the elimination or failure of each of the systems would disrupt another. Describes ways in which city life would be significantly disrupted if each of these systems were eliminated.

SIXTH GRADE

Understanding the reasons underlying change and constancy in systems is critical to being able to predict such situations and events that affect our daily lives and about which citizens must cast an informed vote. This is especially vital for the citizenry of a democratic society in the 21st century, with its challenges of global warming and resource consumption, to name but a pressing few.

> ORGANIZING CONCEPT—
> # CHANGE AND CONSTANCY
> Both living and nonliving systems have situations in which they change in some way and other situations in which they remain essentially unchanged or constant. Why situations in such systems change and why they remain constant can be explained in terms of particular variables. Much change in our world is human-made; some is intended and some inadvertent.

Study of constancy and change in systems requires that students develop the capacity to mentally coordinate two or more properties or concepts at a time, a capacity that may occur as early as age 8 or as late as age 10.

Critical conceptual building blocks for this sixth-grade curriculum include concepts from both third and fifth grade. If your students have not mastered these concepts, you must begin your year with them. They are necessary prerequisites.

- From the third-grade curriculum, students must understand and be able to use conceptual key points 1 through 3. Use the significant knowledge key points to ensure students' understanding is comprehensive and accurate.

- From the fifth-grade curriculum, understanding and predicating one's life on these building blocks is crucial. While they should have been acquired in early experiences with science, it would be a mistake to assume they are in place.

For example, the recent economic turmoil has amply illustrated that all things change. One of the major goals of teaching about change is to help students truly internalize this notion and change their behavior accordingly. Economic housing bubbles burst, family members and friends die, life continues to surprise us, and so on. That is the norm. What's artificial is believing that the value of things always goes upward, that our personal lives (be they, at the moment, happy or miserable) will always be so.

Also, students must internalize that change can be, and usually is, complex. That is, some features or aspects of things may stay the same while others change and the nature of change can vary: steady, repetitive, or irregular and in more than one way at the same time.

The goal for sixth grade is to study constancy and change in a wide variety of situations so that students can develop the ability to use the language of constancy and change and an ability to discuss and apply, in their daily lives, the ideas that lead systems to be stable or to change. This conceptual framework of change forms an ideal foundation or lens through which to study government and history as well as science.

Please note that the notion that all systems have situations in which they change and others in which they remain essentially unchanged, and why and how they change, is an enormously powerful idea for students when understood at the application levels. Although the concepts here are organized under living things, landforms, mechanical systems, chemical interactions, and technology, do *not* develop your curriculum in such clumps. Instead, let your *being there* locations drive the integration of your study. For example, if a dam is chosen as one of your locations, you could study elements of mechanical systems relative to changing water levels, chemistry (water purity), landforms (erosion downstream due to varying release rates such as Glen Canyon Dam on the Colorado River), and living things (changes in up- and downstream habitats due to varying release rates). Let the real world integrate your curriculum naturally.

Concepts and Significant Knowledge to Learn

All things change over time — living things

Conceptual Key Point 1: All living things, animals and plants, have changed over time.

Significant Knowledge Key Point 1a: This change over time shows that the genetic information passed along over the generations changes slowly. As a result, significant change can come about over long periods.

Significant Knowledge Key Point 1b: [Select a related state standard that is prominently illustrated at the *being there* location; develop as many such related significant knowledge key points as needed for students to understand Conceptual Key Point 1.]

Conceptual Key Point 4: Biological systems tend to change until they become stable and then remain that way unless their surroundings change.

Significant Knowledge Key Point 4a: Old-growth forests are an example of an eco-system that has become stable and can remain so for hundreds of years.

Significant Knowledge Key Point 4b: The human body is another biological system that tends to change until it becomes stable. For example, the body changes from conception to birth, birth to adolescence, during adolescence, and adolescence to adulthood, at which time it becomes stable until old age, injury, and/or disease occurs.

Significant Knowledge Key Point 4c: Many changes occur in our bodies during puberty.

Significant Knowledge Key Point 4d: [Select a related state standard that is prominently illustrated at the *being there* location; develop as many such related significant knowledge key points as needed for students to understand Conceptual Key Point 4.]

Conceptual Key Point 5: The human body can be viewed as a system which remains stable when healthy, during which times there are normal ranges for temperature, heart rate, and the content of blood and urine. When sick, these ranges change.

All things change over time—landforms

Conceptual Key Point 2: Landforms will be stable unless some force acts on them to change them. For instance, a piece of ground might have supported a redwood tree for 1,000 years, while another piece of ground very nearby might have been radically changed by the erosion of a stream.

Significant Knowledge Key Point 2a: Lack of forces, such as erosion and human activity, leads to stability.
[Note: This concept should first be applied to the schoolyard or the yard of neighbors and in miniature scale model before attempting to study large-scale changes.]

Significant Knowledge Key Point 2b: [Select a related state standard that is prominently illustrated at the *being there* location; develop as many such related significant knowledge key points as needed for students to understand Conceptual Key Point 2.]

All things change over time—mechanical systems

Conceptual Key Point 1: Constancy and change are states that are determined by some variable(s) that acts upon a situation, keeping things stable or changing them. These variables are often referred to as change agents; in mechanical systems, they are also known as physical agents.

Significant Knowledge Key Point 1a: Physical agents include heat, light, sound waves, water, physical forces (gravity, pushes and pulls). All of these factors can play an important role in determining whether a system is stable or unstable. For instance, an ice cube is stable until heat is added to it; cloth maintains its color unless light is shined

on it for a long time; water waves can cause a beach to be unstable; a bike will roll along at a constant speed unless some force(s) act on it to slow it down (such as wind resistance, gravity, or friction); a teeter-totter can be balanced (stable, constant), or it can be unbalanced and will begin to move until one end comes to the ground or counterbalancing weight is applied at the ends and constancy is reestablished.
[Note: The important idea here would be for students to understand what causes differentiate the stable (constant) situation from the unstable (changing) situation.]

Conceptual Key Point 2: Sometimes physical agents are part of a system of forces that act upon an object or situation to keep it stable or to make it change. Sometimes a single physical agent keeps things stable or changes them.

Significant Knowledge Key Point 2a: Examples of physical agents that are part of a system of forces that act upon an object or situation to keep it stable or make it change include the weather. The world's oceans drive our weather. Changes in one part of the world, such as the warming called El Niño, can significantly change weather patterns in other parts of the world.

Significant Knowledge Key Point 2b: An example of a common single physical agent at work is heat.

All things change over time—chemical interactions

Conceptual Key Point 1: When a new material is made by combining two or more materials, it has properties that are different from the original materials. For that reason, a lot of different materials can be made from a smaller number of basic kinds of materials.

Significant Knowledge Key Point 1c: Although most of us learn to cook and clean our houses by imitation as a child, most simple, day-to-day tasks are the result of a huge array of chemical interactions. Most are harmless, e.g., the multiple ingredients of cooking. Some could be deadly if mishandled (such as the mistaken mixing of cleaner and bleach).
[Note: An excellent resource for exploring everyday examples of chemical stability and change is *Kitchen Chemistry, Science Projects About* by Robert Gardner. For the true chemistry devotee, try *Kitchen Science: A Compendium of Essential Information for Every Cook* by Lisa Howard Loring Hillman, which offers "practical scientific principles, plainly stated, which take the mystery out of cooking and free you to adapt or improvise successfully."]

Change through technology

Conceptual Key Point 4: Any invention is likely to lead to other inventions resulting in unanticipated events of constancy and change, usually change.

Significant Knowledge Key Point 4a: Once an invention exists, people are likely to think up ways of using it that were never imagined at first.

Significant Knowledge Key Point 4b: Technologies often have drawbacks as well as benefits. A technology that helps some people or organisms may hurt others—either deliberately (as weapons can) or inadvertently (as pesticides can). When harm occurs or seems likely, choices have to be made or new solutions found.

Possible Being There Locations

Yards in the neighborhood whose growth is old and diverse, biodiverse city and state parks, waste and water treatment plants, health clinics, locations of airplane and satellite photos that illustrate change and constancy, recent cuts in hillsides due to highway building or major real estate development, agricultural fields, local manufacturing plants, local engineering firms and biotech labs, human-made systems such as a school campus or a mall with its heating/air-conditioning system, water and electrical systems, plus family homes or condos (examples of energy efficient and inefficient).

Examples of Expected Performance Levels

- Traces the lineage of a pet—parentage and offspring. Identifies the features that prove the statement that there is stability in genetic information from generation to generation. Using photographs of student's own family over several generations, traces his or her characteristics back through family members. [Note: If many students do not have pets, start a mini-breeding program in class with mice or rats or find a community person who can bring multiple generations of cats or dogs.]

- After graphing illnesses in the classroom or in his or her extended family for two months, develops a class handbook describing the means of transmission of the three most frequently occurring diseases, the effect on various body systems, and the methods of prevention and cure of the 10 most common illnesses.

- Selecting a land use issue from local news, analyzes pro and con arguments in terms of kind and degree of change that would occur as a result of implementing the proposal. Develops recommendation on the issue to share with the principal people involved.

- Charts and identifies constancy and change of own body systems by charting the ranges of body function in terms of temperature, heart and breathing rates, urine color, bowel movement (time frames, color, and consistency) from the middle of an illness to return to health.

- Using a T-chart (fast changes, slow changes), identifies at least ten local locations which have been shaped by natural forces. Indicates the change force that shaped each location.

- Collects newspaper stories over a one-week period describing an aspect of an engineering problem(s). Selects one for in-depth study (e.g., visitation, interviews, library and internet searches, and more). Prepares and presents a five–minute report to class regarding the main problem to be solved, major trade-offs involved, political and/or economic forces involved, and his or her recommended solution.

SCIENCE RESOURCES

Examples of resources for framing observations include:

- *Creepy Crawlies and the Scientific Method: Over 100 Hands-On Science Experiments for Children* by Sally Stenhouse Keidel (Golden, CO: Fulcrum Publishing, 1993).

- *Kitchen Science: A Compendium of Essential Information for Every Cook* by Howard Hillman and Lisa Loring (Yonkers, NY: Consumer's Union, 1989).

- *One Small Square: Backyard* by Donald Silver (New York: W. H. Freeman and Company, 1993).

- *Science Is . . . : A Source Book of Fascinating Facts, Projects, and Activities* by Susan Bosak (Richmond Hill, Ontario, Canada: Scholastic Canada, 1991).

- *Science Project Ideas About Kitchen Chemistry* by Robert Gardner (Berkeley Heights, NJ: Enslow Publishing, Inc., 1999).

END NOTES

1 Project 2061, a project of the National Science Foundation, began in the 1980s. As its name suggests, it was believed that substantive change in science education would take time, perhaps until the return of Haley's Comet in the year 2061. The staff, headed by the first director James Rutherford, built well and carefully. Their curriculum outline provided an invaluable base for the curriculum developed for the MCSIP program, excerpts from which appear here. See *Benchmarks for Science Literacy* (Oxford, UK: Oxford Press, 1993); also available online at www.project2061 .org/publications/bsl/default.htm.

2 Larry Lowery, science inservice training for the Mid-California Science Improvement Program (MCSIP), 1988.

3 The curriculum work done by Project 2061 is thorough and thoughtfully done, a foundational work against which to check your state and district standards. We particularly like their "backmapping" process which helps in thinking through what prior knowledge students need to be successful. We wouldn't, however, assign so much of the content to earlier grades but rather make it a conscious part of current study. See Project 2061's *Atlas of Science Literacy* (Washington, DC: American Association for the Advancement of Science and National Science Teachers Association, co-publishers, 2001).

MARY FROGGINS

Fortunately, there are many, and I do mean many, science content books for children that also meet the requirements for good literature. When you next visit your neighborhood book store or library, ask for an experienced children's literature person. Ask him/ her to point out science as literature books. Be especially alert for titles written at your students' readability level. Select other books for your daily read-aloud topics.

CHAPTER 3

LOCALIZING CURRICULUM

Bridging the gap between national and state standards and the prior experiences of students is a process we call localizing curriculum. There are five aspects to the process:

- Basing curriculum from state standards in *being there* locations, discussed in Chapters 1 and 9

- Using an **organizing concept** to organize and integrate content for *being there* curriculum, discussed in this chapter

- Stating what you want students to know as **key points**, also discussed in this chapter

- Developing **inquiries** that state what you want students to do with what they understand, discussed in the next chapter

- **Social/political action** projects—actions that apply what students understand in ways that improve their world

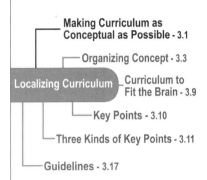

MAKING CURRICULUM AS CONCEPTUAL AS POSSIBLE

The organizing concept is but one among many concepts used as building blocks for your curriculum. It just happens to be the most powerful, capable of organizing all the needed elements of your curriculum.

While there are many brain-research based reasons for making curriculum as conceptual as possible (see the discussion of Two-Step Learning Process in Chapter 9), the practical reason is efficiency. Just as a picture is worth a thousand words, understanding a concept makes absorbing details and related information quick and easy for students. For the teacher, conceptual curriculum is far easier to organize and integrate, a means of buying time for science and making curriculum look to students like what they experience in real life.

What Is a Concept?[1]

Concept = 1. A general notion or idea

2. An idea of something formed by mentally combining all its characteristics or particulars; a construct

In the world of our biological brain, patterns are neural food. They are what our brain seeks and from which it makes meaning. Concepts are rich, powerful patterns for the brain, useful in unlocking meaning around us and much easier to store in long-term memory

MAKING CURRICULUM AS
CONCEPTUAL AS POSSIBLE

What Is a Concept?

Many Reasons for Concepts

Concepts: Curriculum Structures Without Borders

than curriculum fragments and factoids. To learn fragments and factoids, students mostly resort to memorization; in contrast, concepts allow students to leapfrog from today's lesson to yesterday's personal experience to tomorrow's situations in life. Concepts are powerful curriculum builders.

Many Reasons for Concepts[2]

1. Concepts provide structure for a discipline.

2. Concepts provide a framework within which details can be more readily understood and remembered.

3. Concepts are the primary bridges which make transfer of learning possible.

4. Concepts provide the framework for lifelong learning.

5. Concepts provide the cognitive framework that makes it possible for us to construct our own understandings of the world in which we live.[3]

Concepts: Curriculum Structures Without Borders

Concepts travel. They don't stay where we last put them, such as in science or art. They know no curriculum borders. They aren't stopped by time or space—which is precisely why they are so good for integrating curriculum.

Example 1: Consider this statement: *"A system is a collection of processes and often people that interact to perform some function."* Clearly this invites an exploration of science—ecosystems, mechanical engineering, and so forth. But it's also a powerful lens through which to view civics. For example, our democratic government is a collection of laws, government bodies, and citizens and processes (those described in or allowed by laws). Our federal constitution, including its Bill of Rights, describes the systems of our government. Democratic governments are rule-based systems of government rather than power- or people-based forms, such as dictatorships, oligarchies, monarchies, and theocracies.

Economics? Yes. Supply and demand are two interacting components of the capitalist system. Art? Of course. The Munsell Color Wheel is a system of analyzing color combinations and intensity of hue. The potential for integration goes on and on.

Example 2: Consider the rich exploration that could come from study through a related concept: *"To study a system one must define*

MARY FROGGINS

When searching for an organizing concept, choose one whose pattern is intuitively understood by students.

its boundaries." For example, in science, a watershed can't be studied if its boundaries aren't established.

History/social studies: Our federal constitution, including its Bill of Rights, sets the boundaries of our government. Laws considered outside this boundary are considered unconstitutional and are set aside or repealed. (Without such boundaries, there would be chaos.)

Boundary lines could also be drawn to include philosophical precursors to our constitution such as the Declaration of Independence, the writings of Thomas Paine, and the 500-year-old, unwritten constitution of the Iroquois Confederation, many ideas of which found their way into our constitution.

Example 3: Consider the further depth and power from studying another related concept: *"Thinking about things as systems means looking for how every part relates to others. Most systems, living and nonliving, are made up of smaller parts that, when put together, can do things the parts couldn't do by themselves."*

In science, this is a powerful lens through which to study the danger of extinction of animals and plants: Together plants and animals create a self-sustaining ecosystem; however, if missing a partner, many or all may die out.

In history/social studies, an equivalent idea is: Our constitution establishes a system with three parts or subsystems: executive, legislative, and judicial. They are designed to provide checks and balances to preserve a balance of power. If one branch dies back, democracy is imperiled.

Concepts are like computer worms. Once they infect your hard drive, they never stop moving; once they lodge in your brain, your brain keeps extending the patterns, using them to make sense of more and more of the external world.

CHOOSING AND USING AN ORGANIZING CONCEPT

Twenty years ago, themes were used to integrate content. However, without knowledge from brain research about the power — the innate drive — of the brain to seek pattern, we often ended up with some pretty powerless themes, such as the color red, apples, spiders, clever catch phrases, or titles of songs, movies, and TV shows.

Today, armed with brain research, we now know that we should be looking for an organizing concept inherent in the content to be taught, one that should, by itself, be powerful enough to quick start

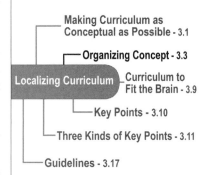

CHOOSING AND USING AN ORGANIZING CONCEPT

Getting Started

What Makes a Concept Powerful?

Basing Curriculum in Sensory-Rich *Being There* Locations

us into learning that can be generalized and transferred so as to help us learn more, faster, and more comprehensively. It should connect both our state standards and our *being there* location (see page 3.9).

Getting Started

Start small; build carefully. Begin organizing your curriculum around a powerful concept. Invest small amounts of time frequently. This will provide opportunities to learn from your experiences.

Starting Small . . . One Step at a Time. A topic is the smallest piece of an integrated curriculum. Starting small means starting with one *being there* location and selecting a conceptual key point that is well illustrated by that location, engaging to your students, and an important aspect of your state standards.

MARY FROGGINS

Although your goal may be integrated curriculum for a year, remember to start with small chunks.

Implementing small chunks frequently is a superior strategy because it gives you time to learn from your successes and mistakes while the investment of time and energy is still small. This approach eliminates backtracking and all the lost time and energy that goes with it.

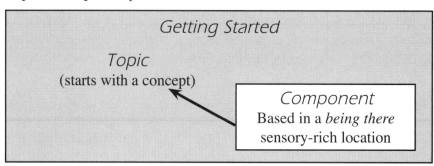

Getting Started

Topic
(starts with a concept)

Component
Based in a *being there*
sensory-rich location

Figure 3A

Around this nucleus, determine what you want students to understand (key points, Chapter 4) and be able to do (inquiries, Chapter 5). This first topic, a part of a component, is often designed for one to three half-days. It is big enough to take you through the tools for building an integrated curriculum but small enough that you can get started with relatively short lead-up time. How long a topic lasts depends on your purpose and planning.

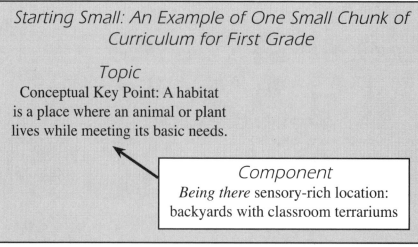

Starting Small: An Example of One Small Chunk of Curriculum for First Grade

Topic
Conceptual Key Point: A habitat
is a place where an animal or plant
lives while meeting its basic needs.

Component
Being there sensory-rich location:
backyards with classroom terrariums

Figure 3B

You choose the time frames; the curriculum structure will work with time spans long or short, full days or partial. However, be aware that curriculum often takes on a life of its own; be prepared to follow the teachable moments. Feel free to extend or shorten any topic as best serves students and your responsibilities for curriculum content.

Focusing on a single component or topic at a time is a good beginning point for teachers working alone or those who find it easier to work from details to big picture rather than from big picture to details. It allows you to master the three critical integrated curriculum strategies—basing curriculum in *being there* locations, starting with concepts, and integrating content and skills. As you master these strategies, you will be ready to delve into the power of concepts to create memorable patterns for the brain.

Stepping Out. You will need to take the next step in curriculum development by adding more than one topic to your component. For example, if the *being there* location is a local watershed, the topics might be "Watersheds: An Irreversible System" and "We All Live Downstream."

[Note: Each topic has at least one conceptual (transferable/generalizable) key point plus related significant knowledge and skill key points as well as their inquiries. In this example, the concept could be systems, habitats, interdependence, change, or cause and effect. Choose the one that would provide the best umbrella for your state standards.]

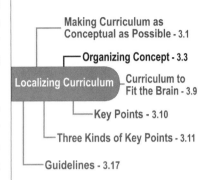

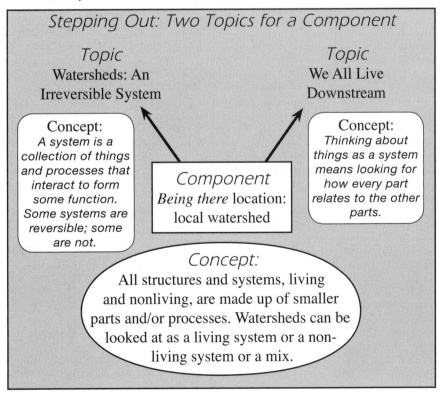

Figure 3C

Starting With the End in Mind. Starting with the end in mind means beginning with four *being there* locations (and thus four components). Then, you can increase the number of topics for each component as your curriculum development expertise increases through the year.

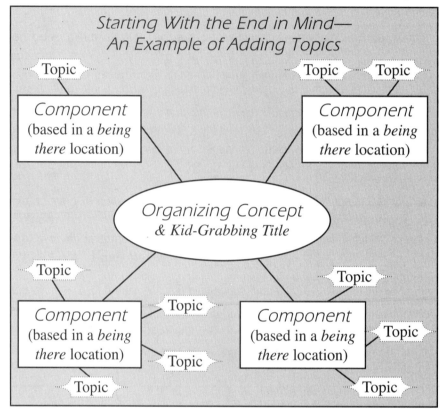

Figure 3D

MARY FROGGINS

The immersion board is part of the curriculum wall. It's a 3-D representation of the being there location. Go for classy; avoid clutter.

In constructing it, hands-on-of-the-real-thing items are preferable to secondhand and symbolic.

Involve students in its design and construction.

Starting with a skeletal mindmap for integrated curriculum allows you to start small but use the tools for building integrated science curriculum: Find an organizing concept that webs together all the content and skills for the year and a kid-grabbing title for it that stirs up enthusiasm, conveys the essence of the concept, and is memorable.

For example, if habitat is the organizing concept for your integrated curriculum, then the *being there* location for the components can be various kinds of habitats such as underground, airborne, or water-related (pond, lake, tidepools, creek, river, or watershed.) Choose those that can be easily visited by your students and readily turned into an immersion board in the classroom or on the school grounds. For an underground habitat, for example, study animals in the food web of a particular animal or ways they locate and get food.

What's important is ensuring that the pattern or conceptual relationship between the organizing concept and each component and between each component and its topics is obvious to students. The greater the conceptual webbing of the organizing concept, the more connections students can make. This quickens and deepens learning and makes efficient use of instructional time. It also makes the content easier for the students to understand. It integrates your content and skills in a natural way that students can recognize as they look out the window, walk down the street, visit a mall, or relax with Mother Nature.

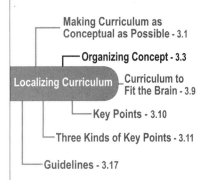

What Makes a Concept Powerful?

What makes a concept powerful? It's universal, meaning that it explains a great deal about many things and examples of it can be directly experienced (seen and touched). Consider the following examples of organizing concepts:[4]

Kindergarten: EXPLORATION — People can learn about things around them by observing them carefully—what they are made of, how they are put together, what they do, and how they are similar and different. Observing and comparing similarities and differences is a key way to help interpret and understand our world. Often, we can learn even more about these things if we do something to them and note what happens.

First Grade: BASIC NEEDS—All living things, including humans, have basic needs—for food, water, and oxygen, for protection from weather, disease, and predators, and to reproduce. A habitat is the place where the animal or plant lives while meeting these needs.

Second Grade: FORM AND FUNCTION—The physical characteristics of animals and plants vary greatly and determine what they can do and how they do it to meet their needs. Similarly, the physical characteristics of nonliving things vary greatly and determine what changes can occur in them and how they can be used.

Third Grade: CHANGE— Things are changing around us all the time. Change can occur in a variety of ways (reversible, irreversible; controllable, not controllable; steady or repetitive and thus fairly predictable or not steady or repetitive and thus unpredictable) and for different reasons. The rate and size of change may not be observable with human senses; we need tools to measure such change. Change can be helpful, harmful, or neutral.

Fourth Grade: INTERDEPENDENCE—Plants and animals interact with each other and their environment in ways that allow them to meet their basic needs. Keep in mind that humans are animals.

Fifth Grade: SYSTEMS— All structures and systems, living and nonliving, are made up of smaller parts and/or processes.

Sixth Grade: CONSTANCY AND CHANGE—Both living and nonliving systems have situations in which they change in some way and

CHOOSING AND USING
AN ORGANIZING CONCEPT

Getting Started

What Makes a Concept Powerful?

Basing Curriculum in Sensory-
Rich *Being There* Locations

MARY FROGGINS

"Why," you may ask, "am I designing curriculum when I'm supposed to teach my state standards?"

Answer: Because it's a long way from national and state standards to the experiences of your students.

The purpose of designing classroom curriculum is to localize your content—to bridge the gap between the standards you're expected to teach and the prior experiences and knowledge of your students.

If you don't bridge that gap, your students will fail. Basing your standards in being there *experiences is hands down the most effective and efficient way to bridge that yawning gap.*

other situations in which they remain essentially unchanged or constant. Why situations in such systems change and why they remain constant can be explained in terms of particular variables. Much change in our world is human-made; some is intended and some is inadvertent.

Just as students have to learn and practice how to write in different genres, such as essay, short story, journaling, technical writing, or poetry, so must teachers. Writing key points is definitely a different genre—part essay, part technical writing, part sales pitch, and part revelation of one's soul (or at least your prior life experiences and knowledge base).

Tips for Getting Started. If looking for an organizing concept trips you up and nothing comes to mind, or the options are overwhelming, go back through your standards. Are there some big ideas that catch your interest?

If not, use the list below to jog your thinking. Compare your top three candidates to your standards. Is there any overlap? If yes, work with that content to distill out a sentence that captures the essence of a chunk of standards.

adaptations	*balance*	*cause/effect*	*conflict/resolution*
change	*cycles*	*dependence*	*diversity*
ecology	*form/function*	*habitat*	*interdependence*
independence	*matter*	*nature*	*power*
relationships	*stewardship*	*survival*	*symbolism*
systems	*time*	*wisdom*	

If still at a loss, review the discussion of selecting a *being there* location in which to base your curriculum in Chapter 1, pages 1.3–1.4.

A Reminder. Choose an organizing concept that you know interests you, engages your students, will integrate all subjects, and is well illustrated by a *being there* location that your students can readily visit.

Basing Curriculum in Sensory-Rich Being There Locations

The power in curriculum comes not from educators who toiled over the writing of state standards but from the connections it helps make in a learner's head. For example, how an idea in this setting can help explain things in a similar but different setting and connections to prior experiences, the lives of past and current role models, and the power and efficiency of our mirror neuron to mimic and simulate the actions of others, essentially learning by doing.

Thus, although curriculum planning begins with state and district standards, the content must then be sliced and recombined as needed so that the curriculum as stated fits together in the same integrated way that students will experience it at the *being there* location.

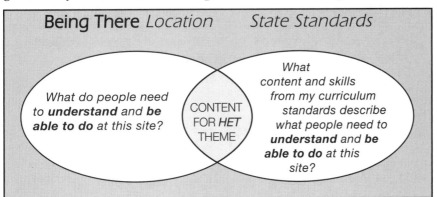

Figure 3E

Effective First Teaching (EFT) demands that we enhance student abilities to make and utilize such connections as quickly, accurately, and comprehensively as possible. Basing curriculum in *being there* locations gives us our best shot at doing so.

See the discussion of learning as a function of intelligence; see Chapter 10.

DESIGNING CLASSROOM CURRICULUM TO FIT HOW THE BRAIN LEARNS

As early as 1969, brain research into how the human brain learns has described learning as a two-step process. Curriculum should be designed to fit this process.

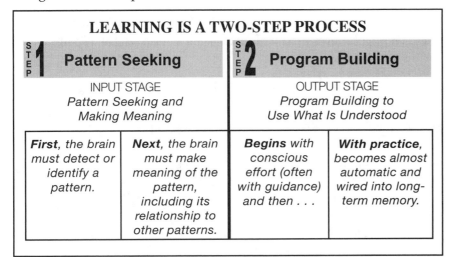

Figure 3F

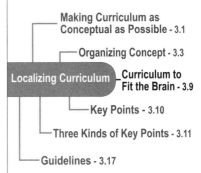

MARY FROGGINS

Remember to state your key points EXACTLY the way you want your students to remember.

Through the subsequent 40 years, this perspective has become widely accepted as both accurate and useful. It has been used in the ITI/*HET* model with great successful for 30 years.

- Curriculum for Step One of the learning process consists of the content that you want students to understand. This is described in key points.

- Curriculum for Step Two of the learning process consists of inquiries—activities that ask students to apply what they understand to real-world situations and practice those applications until they are wired into long-term memory. This is described in inquiries (see Chapter 4).

KEY POINTS: WHAT YOU WANT STUDENTS TO UNDERSTAND

Identifying what you want students to understand—and stating it exactly the way you want them to remember it—is the most the most critical step in curriculum development. Everything flows from this decision—lesson planning, selection of instructional strategies, student exploration and application, and assessment.

The goal of this aspect of curriculum development is to enhance student's ability to detect patterns, i.e., to readily identify the collection of attributes that is essential for recognizing and understanding the concept, the significant knowledge needed to understand the that concept, and the aspect of a skill needed to apply it.

Concepts Versus Factoids

Because every concept is a pattern and factoids are devoid of pattern, it's critical that you make you key points as conceptual as you can. Factoids are good for playing Jeopardy but aren't useful in real life.

Traditions to Avoid

Avoid curriculum that begins with "The student will understand" and ends with a generality. For example, "The student will understand photosynthesis," or "The student will understand the important role a food web plays in an ecosystem." Such statements leave teachers clueless about what to teach about the topic and students clueless about what they are expected to learn.

Remember, key points should be written exactly the way you want students to remember them.

THREE KINDS OF KEY POINTS

To help you stay focused on stating curriculum as conceptually as possible, you'll find it easier to use three kinds of key points:

- Conceptual key points—the pattern, the big idea

- Significant knowledge key points—content needed to understand the concept, and

- Skills—basic skills and those specific to the content area that are necessary to allow students to apply the concept they're learning

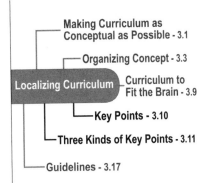

Conceptual Key Points

 Conceptual key points are big ideas, the gist of something that, once understood, explains a great deal about similar situations and thus eliminates the need for memorization.

 Conceptual key points are rich in patterns and allow students to create meaning. Such patterns, encoded with the massive sensory input from *being there* experiences, help establish a post office box in the brain, a location where patterns from prior and current experiences can be pieced together into meaningful wholes and where long-term memories can be stored.

Some conceptual key points are sufficiently global that they can organize study across subject areas, such as the organizing concept for each grade level in the continuum of science concepts in Chapter 2. For example, the study of constancy and change in systems (sixth grade) could lead to a concept in science such as, "Prevention is the best cure," which can be applied in many ways:

- **History**—The importance of resolving conflicts before they escalate into wars

- **Economics**—The failure to regulate institutions considered too big to fail (Wall Street brokerage firms, AIG, banks, and other financial institutions); the value of taking necessary steps to avoid catastrophic floods as occurred in New Orleans when inadequate levies failed during Hurricane Katrina; spending on new prisons rather rather than improving educational outcomes in schools

- **Civics**—The failure to maintain checks and balances in government and between citizens and the powerful corporations

The size of the umbrella of a concept for your conceptual key point is not the issue here; what's important is that it is freighted with patterns for the brain to munch.

THREE KINDS OF KEY POINTS

Conceptual Key Points

Significant Knowledge Key Points

Skill Key Points

Why Three Kinds of Key Points?

For examples of conceptual key points specific to your grade level, see Chapter 2.

Guidelines for Improving Conceptual Key Points. As you develop your conceptual key points, keep the following guidelines in mind. Pardon the pun but concepts—patterns—are the GUTS of your curriculum.

MARY FROGGINS

As you can see, these significant knowledge key points are DIRECTLY related to the concept. Their purpose is to provide the patterns needed to understand the conceptual key point.

Significant knowledge key points are essential building blocks to make meaning of the concept and prepare for applying it to real-world situations.

> ## Guidelines for Improving Conceptual Key Points
>
> G = **G**eneralizable—a principle or conclusion that can be used to explain specifics; pulls idea into general use
>
> U = **U**nderstandable by students this age
>
> T = **T**ransferable to new locations and/or situations
>
> S = **S**uccinct and clear

Figure 3G

Significant Knowledge Key Points

 Significant knowledge key points state the knowledge that is needed to understand a concept as stated in the key point. Nothing more, nothing less.

Significant knowledge key points provide examples of the concept that students can experience at the *being there* location. Because they are not stand-alone statements, but are innately connected to the conceptual key point, they are easier to remember as they are part of a larger pattern. Relationship, as illustrated in the song "Dem Bones," is powerful neural food. Instead of isolated curriculum statements that must be memorized one by one, relationships allow the brain to weave ideas together into a comprehensive, understandable whole. This also greatly enhances recall: The learner need only recall one aspect of the web in order to bring to mind the entire pattern.

Significant knowledge key points provide information (patterns) necessary to arrive at an understanding of the concept. They are not random, unrelated statements. Nor are they factoids. Significant knowledge key points illustrate important attributes of an example of a concept that add a piece to the puzzle of the concept. Preferably, these illustration can be found locally. For example:

Significant Knowledge Key Point: Animals breathe air (oxygen) in different ways. Many, like humans and dolphins, breathe air into their lungs. Others, like fish, have gills that extract oxygen from water. Some, like earthworms, absorb oxygen through their skin.

The value of a *being there* location rich in animal life is that students can observe numerous animals that breathe using each of the above methods. They can also relate what they observe to previous experience. Then, understanding takes care of learning; this significant knowledge key point and the aspect of the conceptual key point about air being a basic need is quickly wired into long-term memory.

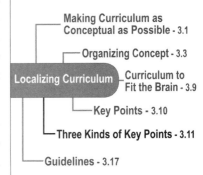

Writing a key point so that it enhances students' ability to perceive and understand a pattern is just smart use of teacher (and student) time. When such a pattern will continue to unlock meaning in future interactions with the world, curriculum becomes the powerful tool it could and should be, a prerequisite for effective first teaching. The following key point is an example.

Significant Knowledge Key Point. To find and catch their prey, predators have forward-looking eyes so they can track their prey during the chase. In contrast, prey have eyes on the sides of their heads so they have a full field of view (forward, to the side, and behind) to help them detect and flee danger.

Contrast—Conceptual to Factoids

CONCEPTUAL KEY POINTS	SIGNIFICANT KNOWLEDGE KEY POINTS	FACTOIDS
All living things have basic needs—for air, food, and water, for protection from predators, weather, and disease, and to reproduce.	Animals breathe air (oxygen) in different ways. Many, like humans and dolphins, breathe air into our lungs. Others, like fish, have gills that extract oxygen from water. Some also absorb oxygen through their skin.	Fish breathe air through their gills.
Function follows form: The body of each animal (form) matches what tasks it needs to perform to survive (function).	To find and catch their prey, predators have forward-looking eyes so they can track their prey during the chase. In contrast, prey have eyes on the sides of their heads so they have a full field of view (forward, to the side, and behind) to help them detect and flee danger.	Owls have eyes in the front of their head.

Figure 3H

In contrast, factoids are statements of curriculum so fragmented or piecemeal that they contain no patterns for the brain to seek. Like the examples in the chart above, they elicit an "And? So what?" response or restrict the learner to but one mode of learning, rote memory. Factoids are interest killers and should be avoided at all costs. If you find them in your state standards, find a way to relate them to a larger story (significant knowledge key point) that can be related to a concept (conceptual key point). If that is not possible, apply the principle of selective abandonment; move the item to the end of the year. In all reality, the year will end before you get that far through your curriculum.

THREE KINDS OF KEY POINTS

Conceptual Key Points

Significant Knowledge Key Points

Skill Key Points

Why Three Kinds of Key Points?

As you look through the side-by-side comparison of conceptual and significant knowledge key points versus factoids on the next page, it's clear that the more conceptual your statements, the richer the pattern-seeking potential and the more useful the information. By useful we mean that it can be generalized to other situations/things and transferred to other settings, all of which greatly speeds up and deepens learning.

Skill Key Points

Skill key points are those skills needed to apply the the concept or significant knowledge stated in a key point. This includes the basic skills of reading, writing, oral language, and mathematics as well as skills specific to a content area such as how to use a magnifying lens or telescope or lay out a transet and record observations.

Consider the following examples.

Science: There are several steps to follow when you measure liquids with a graduated cylinder. These steps must be followed so that accurate measurements are obtained each time and the risk of experimental error is minimized. The steps are:

1. Fill the cylinder to approximately the correct level.

2. Leave the cylinder on the flat surface. Move your head so that you are at eye level with the gradations on the cylinder while it sits flat on the table.

3. Read the bottom of the meniscus (the curve that forms at the top edge of the water).

4. Read the measurement to the nearest tenth.

MARY FROGGINS

Be alert to skills that students will need to successfully complete an inquiry.

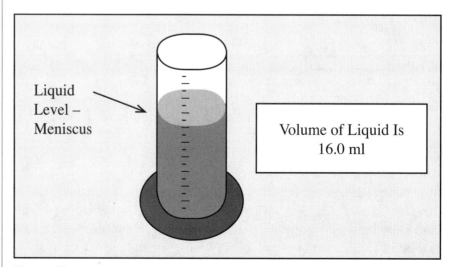

Liquid Level – Meniscus

Volume of Liquid Is 16.0 ml

Figure 3I

Science: SCAMPER:[5] S (substitute), C (combine), A (add), M (modify), P (put to other use), E (eliminate), and R (reduce, re-use, recycle) is an acronym for a procedure used by inventors and design experts wanting to modify a basic design. Following this acronym can help one "think outside of the box."

Math: A bar graph is used to display information in a way that makes quantities easy to see and comparisons easy to grasp. A bar graph must include a title, a scale of quantity (such as amount of money, number of cars, or percentage of items), and labels for each part of the graph. Bar graphs may include a key or legend to identify information.

Math: Drawing to scale is used on maps so that large areas can be fit onto a small piece of paper. In scaling, the concept of ratios is used. A ratio is a relationship of one numerical item to another. For example, on a map, two miles might equal one inch. Therefore, if we measure the distance between two places and find it to be two inches, then we know the number of miles we will have to travel is four miles. This is a two-to-one (2:1) ratio.

Math: Mode, median, and mean are three statistical terms that are useful for analyzing data. Mode is the number in a set of data that occurs most frequently. Median is the number that is in the middle when they are organized from smallest to biggest. Mean, sometimes called average, is really no more than finding the middle point between the extremes (least and greatest). There are two steps to finding an average:

1. Add the numbers,

2. Divide the sum by the number of data items in the set.

Reading: To aid comprehension and memory of what you read, make pictures in your mind as you read, like making a motion picture frame by frame. For example, picture in your mind Charlotte talking with Wilbur and weaving her web message. At the end of each page or chapter, review these images; make them stick in your mind before continuing on with your reading.

Language: An interview is a strategy to obtain information from another person or persons. The interviewer prepares for the interview by researching the person or the topic the person will discuss in order to learn as much as possible. The interviewer then formulates questions about the person or topic that the interviewer thinks will prompt the information he or she wants to learn. During the interview, the interviewer speaks in a pleasant, polite voice that can be easily heard. The interviewer uses body motions such as nodding, smiling, and making eye contact to show that he or she is interested in the information and to encourage the interviewee to continue.

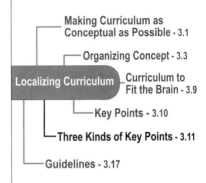

THREE KINDS OF KEY POINTS

Conceptual Key Points

Significant Knowledge Key Points

Skill Key Points

Why Three Kinds of Key Points?

MARY FROGGINS

Remember, curriculum development is a pattern-enhancing activity.

Social Studies: Time lines are linear representations of the chronology of events. They are graphic organizers that can help us understand the temporal relationship among events.

Study Skill: Because they provide a visual way of recording information and showing how ideas are related, mindmaps are useful analytical and study tools. Single words or short phrases, color images, and symbols help give a visual picture of information. The most common mindmap, the web, places the main idea in a circle in the center of the page and links related ideas on branches off the center idea.

Why Three Kinds of Key Points?

Early in the development of the *HET* model, there was just one kind of key point. We learned two lessons. First, when content is truly integrated, students didn't recognize they were learning math or how to write a paragraph. Designating skill key points as such helps teachers communicate to students, parents, peers, and supervisors that skills are being taught and learned, which ones, and when. Second, we learned that key points tended to mirror the district's curriculum which, until the recent state standards movement, consisted heavily of factoids. Focusing on conceptual key points pushes us to make curriculum as conceptual as possible. By requiring that significant knowledge key points directly relate to those concepts helps prevent drift, fluff, and loss of focus when writing curriculum.

When we think back over the enormous volume of information we ourselves covered during high school and college and the almost equally enormous volume of information we no longer remember, we should be more humble and honest about curriculum planning for today's students. If covering volumes of details—dates, definitions, names of famous people, and other fill-in-the-blank items—didn't stick with us, why do we pass it on? Especially when brain research clearly tells us why such an approach doesn't work.

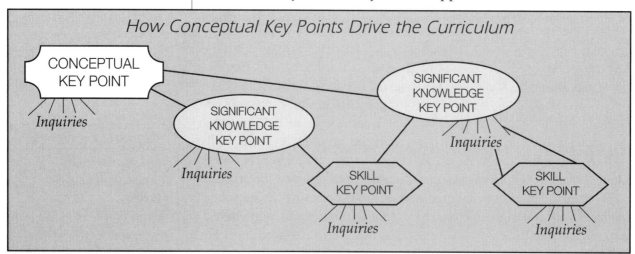

Figure 3J

Carefully pick through your standards to identify concepts and to "chunk up" ideas to make them more conceptual. This chunking up process is vital, the only way to eliminate factoids which are largely devoid of patterns and thus appear meaningless to the students.

Look with new eyes at everyday locations; select those concepts that will best serve responsible citizenship. Stretch yourself to find a few powerful concepts that will explain a lot of things instead of collecting a lot of content under many organizers.

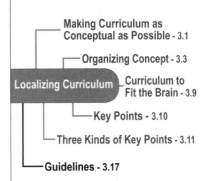

GUIDELINES FOR IMPROVING KEY POINTS

To guide you in improving the quality of your key points, keep the following guidelines in mind:

Guidelines for Writing Key Points – S.T.U.D.E.N.T.S.

S = **S**uccinct and clear, **s**imple but not simplistic

T = **T**ied to real-world situations

U = **U**niversal concepts that naturally organize and integrate subjects and skills at a being there *location*

D = **D**esigned for students

E = Understandable by **e**very student (age-appropriate)

N = **N**ot lesson planning

T = Worthy of the **t**ime of teacher and students

S = **S**ignificant knowledge key points tightly connected to the conceptual key points they help explain

---

Figure 3K

S = **S**uccinct and clear, **s**imple but not simplistic

Learn to cut to the chase and say exactly what you wanted to say, no more and no less. Keep a copy of Strunk and White's little book, *The Elements of Style*, for a clear and simple writer's guide.

THREE KINDS OF KEY POINTS

Conceptual Key Points

Significant Knowledge Key Points

Skill Key Points

Why Three Kinds of Key Points?

MARY FROGGINS

Don't lose heart. In the beginning, the time it takes to localize curriculum may seem like a waste of time—time you don't have to spare. However, every minute you invest up front increases the likelihood that your students will master a concept and wire it into long-term memory and greatly speeds up the time needed to do so.

So, take the gamble. Find a colleague to team with so you can half your time and double your results.

T = **T**ied to real-world situations

Select concepts and skills from your state and district standards that students see illustrated at their *being there* locations. Context is very important to the brain when seeking patterns. Context enables students to see what something is and what it's not plus how and when it is used and why. The understandings reached are always deeper and broader than when the concept or skill is taught in the classroom isolated from its real-world context.

U = **U**niversal concepts that will naturally organize and integrate subjects and skills at a being there *location*

Concepts are memorable. Factoids are statements of fact that offer little potential for detecting patterns because they represent such a small dot of life and thus offer few attributes for students to grab on to. Factoids rarely make it past short-term memory. A week after the test, all is forgotten. Unfortunately, most textbooks consist primarily of factoids and thus are difficult to learn from. Their content is watered down; written in short, simple sentences for low readability; and summarized so briefly as to be cryptic and seemingly unrelated to real life or student experiences. Most curriculum—state standards as well as district level—has traditionally been overweighted with factoids. Examples include weekly vocabulary-building lists in English classes that do not relate to concurrent areas of study, definitions in science with which students have no prior or current experience, and strings of historical dates for which students have little context.

D = **D**esigned for students

State exactly what you want your students to understand so they can use that concept or skill. State it just as you want it remembered, just as they will retrieve it to use in the real world. Avoid starting with "The student will. . . ." For example, don't say, "The student will understand why civilizations fail." Instead, state that "Civilizations fail for five main reasons, which are. . . ."

E = Understandable by **e**very student (age appropriate)

While much content in today's curriculum standards may impress the public, much of it is not age appropriate. For example, compare the table of contents of your science textbook with the concepts in the Science Continuum of Concepts. You'll find many concepts should be moved upward to later grades when students' brains are organized to process the content, not just memorize it. See discussion of age appropriateness in Chapter 7.

N = **N**ot lesson planning

Always complete writing key points and inquiries *before* you begin to lesson plan.

For example, a skill key point about journal writing might look like this: "Journal writing helps us clarify our thoughts, make connections, summarize things to help us remember them, and/or sort through our emotions."

However, mixed in with lesson planning or advice to yourself, it could well end up like: "Journal writing is a learning tool based on the ideas that students write to learn. Students are actively engaged in using the journals to write about topics of personal interest, to note their observations, to imagine, to wonder and to connect new information with things they already know."

The above key point fails on several key criteria: First, it doesn't state clearly what students are to understand and apply nor is it concise. It also treats students as third persons not present for part of the conversation. Writing key points and lesson planning at the same time ALWAYS distorts the key points.

T = Worthy of the **t**ime spent on it—yours and your students

For all the criticism of textbooks and related worksheets, homespun curriculum is no better if it's more of the same and doesn't fit how the brain learns. As you gather information about your components and topics, you'll become more knowledgeable about the world around you and thus better able to craft your key points. Spend your time well.

S = **S**ignificant knowledge key points tightly connected to the conceptual key point they are supposed to help explain

Make sure the significant knowledge key points are what students need to know to understand how the conceptual key point applies locally at their *being there* location and elsewhere in their area. Resist the temptation to toss in tidbits that, although interesting in themselves, don't actively contribute to understanding the conceptual key point.

EXAMPLES OF KEY POINTS

For examples of good key points for your grade level, see Chapter 2: Making Curriculum BodyBrain Compatible.

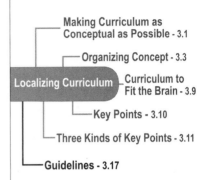

Making Curriculum as Conceptual as Possible - 3.1

Organizing Concept - 3.3

Localizing Curriculum

Curriculum to Fit the Brain - 3.9

Key Points - 3.10

Three Kinds of Key Points - 3.11

Guidelines - 3.17

MARY FROGGINS

Taking time to localize your curriculum by basing it in being there locations creates huge gains in science achievement and in other subjects and social and personal growth.

According to Lieberman and Hoody,[6] general gains include:

- *Better performance on standardized measures of academic achievement in reading, writing, math, science, and social studies*

- *Reduced discipline and classroom management problems*

- *Increased engagement and enthusiasm for learning*

- *Greater pride and ownership in accomplishments (for students and staff)*

For more information, see pages 10.11–10.12.

END NOTES

1 *Webster's New Universal Unabridged Dictionary* (New York: Barnes & Noble Books, 1996).

2 Adapted in 1989 from Benjamin Bruner's work by Jeanne Herrick, Assistant Superintendent, Monterey County Schools Office, California.

3 Conceptual curriculum is the best material for a constructivist approach.

4. *Science Continuum of Concepts for Grades K-6,* 4th ed., by Karen D. Olsen (Black Diamond, WA: Books for Educators, 2010).

5 Developed by Bob Eberle. See *SCAMPER: Creative Games and Activities for Imagination Development* (Austin, TX: Prufrock Press, 1997) and www.mindtools.com/pages/article/new CT—02.htm.

6 Gerald A. Lieberman and Linda I. Hoody, *Closing the Achievement Gap: Using the Environment As an Integrating Context for Learning,* Executive Summary (Poway, CA: Science Wizards, 1998), 1.

CHAPTER 4

MAKING LEARNING MEMORABLE

Brain research over the past 40 years makes it painfully clear that until—and unless—learning becomes wired into long-term memory, all teaching and learning efforts are wasted. Short-term memory is just that, short term.

What students deserve, and taxpayers have every right to expect, is that schools send students out the door with concepts and skills stored in their long-term memory, not left in the pages of textbooks or on worksheets long ago thrown in the trash.

USING INQUIRIES TO ADD ACTION

The new, two-step definition of learning from brain research clearly explains how the brain learns. And curriculum development must follow. Key points provide the content for pattern seeking and making meaning, as seen in Chapter 3. Inquiries provide opportunities to apply the concepts and skills of a key point in real-world situations and the necessary practice to wire it into long-term memories.

Inquiries Defined

Inquiries are carefully crafted activities that enable students to understand and apply the concept, skill, or significant knowledge of a key point. The primary purpose of inquiries is to enable students to develop mental programs for applying each key point in real–world situations and wire those programs into long-term memory. They make learning active and memorable fully engaging a learner's sensory system, mirror neurons, and bodybrain learning partnership (see Chapters 10 and 11). They answer the question, "What do we want students to do with what they understand?"

How to Write Inquiries

Once you have stated what you want your students to understand as conceptually as possible and included significant knowledge and skills, think through ways students can apply these understandings in real-world ways. Go back to your *being there* location and watch how these concepts and skills are applied by the people who work and visit there. Then, keeping in mind the age of your students and what is appropriate for their stage of mental development, start writing these applications down on paper. Jot down as many as you see and others that come to mind. You are now ready to write inquiries.

GUIDELINES FOR WRITING INQUIRIES

As you write inquiries, keep the following rules in mind.

The ABC + D² Rules for Writing Inquiries

- **A**lways start with the action in mind. What are students to do? How can they practice applying what they understand to real-world situations? (For a wealth of action words, see the next page.)

- **B**e specific with your directions so that students can see the outcome or finished product in their minds' eye. What is the inquiry asking them to do?

- **C**onnect to the key point. Will doing this inquiry help students both understand and be able to apply the concept, significant knowledge, or skill described in the key point? Never select an activity just because it's fun or clever or cute. If it doesn't help students understand and practice the key point, throw it out. Learning is serious business; stay focused on what you want students to understand and what you want them to do with what they understand.

- Requires **d**eep thinking.

- **D**on't stop writing until you have enough inquiries for each key point to address all the multiple intelligences and to take students through mastery to long-term memory.

Figure 4A

MARY FROGGINS

Think of inquiries as a bridge between a key point and long-term memory of how to apply the content of that key point.

Unfortunately, state standards do not provide such a curriculum bridge. This leaves a serious hole in the tools available to classroom teachers.

So, may I venture to say that, no matter how good the statements of what students are to learn, without how they are to use it in the real world, there will be no change in student achievement.

The good news, however, is that inquiries are not difficult to write and students, third grade and up, can help write them.

Providing Choice Through Inquiries

One of the biggest benefits of developing your own curriculum at the classroom level is the opportunity to build in choices for students. Choices allow them to learn through the intelligences in which they are strong and then, while completing the last phase of the Two-Step Learning process, strengthen those less-developed intelligences. Choices also allow students to expand interests and deepen motivation to learn. Inquiries are your major means of providing meaningful choice; fortunately, it's easy to do. Simply refer to the Inquiry Builder Chart on the next page. Select action words from each segment of the chart and you will be able to write inquiries that meet the multiple intelligences.

Inquiry Builder Chart

Adapted from Bloom's Taxonomy[1]

Starting Point with being there experience →

Ending Point for test preparation →

MULTIPLE INTELLIGENCES		APPLICATION	ANALYSIS	EVALUATION	SYNTHESIS	COMPREHENSION	KNOWLEDGE
	LOGICAL / MATHEMATICAL	• apply • convert • expand • organize • schedule • sequence • solve	• compare • differentiate • distinguish • inventory • question • solve	• assess • choose • estimate • judge • measure • predict • rate • review • select • value	• classify • design • formulate • hypothesize • infer • prepare • propose	• calculate • describe • explain • identify • organize • recognize • retell • sequence	• compute • label • name
	LINGUISTIC	• apply • communicate • interview • teach • translate	• analyze • criticize • debate • discuss • interpret • investigate • question	• critique • discuss • interpret • judge • justify • probe • rate • relate	• adapt • compose • debate • infer • impersonate • produce • propose • rewrite	• describe • discuss • explain • express • report • restate • review	• define • label • list • name • tell • memorize • narrate • recall • record
	SPATIAL	• apply • chart • diagram • exhibit • graph • illustrate • make • summarize • teach • translate	• diagram • differentiate • disassemble • distinguish	• decipher • estimate • judge • measure • predict	• arrange • design • formulate • organize • plan • propose • restructure • visualize	• compare • describe • identify • illustrate • locate • recognize • relate parts • sort	• adapt • draw • interpret • match • sketch
	BODILY KINESTHETIC	• apply • demonstrate • dramatize • mime • operate • practice • rhythm • teach	• diagram • disassemble • experiment • interpret • inventory	• debate • measure • rehearse	• arrange • assemble • classify • construct • convey emotion • design • invent • prepare • tell a story	• locate • perform • role-play	• imitate • play • role-play
	MUSICAL	• characterize • express • harmonize • perform (solo or group) • rhythm • synchronize	• analyze • compare • interpret	• characterize • critique • interpret	• compose • convey emotion • create a variation • express • improvise • symbolize • tell a story • transpose	• imitate • rehearse	• create • recite

Figure 4B

$(C_2H_5)_2O$ $6H_2O$
Na_2CO_3 $10H_2O$
-120 CH_3 $+120$
$COOH$

MARY FROGGINS

Well-written inquiries
• *Infuse action into the day, the best antidote to poor learning.*
• *Make every day memorable and help students answer the familiar parent question, "What did you do today, son?"*

The inquiries below are examples of how a teacher can use inquiries to build in choices for students. The initials after each inquiry indicate which of the multiple intelligences is needed to carry out the task. Also, some inquiries require collaboration, while others require individual work.

Another important way to build in choices is to invite students, third grade and up, to develop inquiries for your key points. A good starter question is, "What examples of this concept (skill) have you seen today?" Collect these inquiries, and then determine which you would like to use. Designate some for the class, Learning Club,[2] or individuals to choose to do.

EXAMPLES OF INQUIRIES

 Conceptual Key Point 1: Most systems are made up of smaller parts that, when put together, can do things the parts could not do by themselves.

Inquiries:

1. With your Learning Club, investigate the bicycle that is in the classroom. Draw a picture of the bicycle in your Science Journal. Label all the smaller parts that create the bicycle. Explain how each helps the bicycle do what it does. Share your list with another Learning Club. Discuss any items about which your two Learning Clubs do not agree. Add to your own list any new ideas gained from this sharing. (BK, LM, L)
[Note: These initials identify the multiple intelligence(s) called upon by this and subsequent inquires. BK = bodily-kinesthetic, LM = logical-mathematical, L = linguistic, S = spatial, M = musical.]

2. Examine the three photos of old-fashioned cycles (unicycle, chainless bicycle, early motorcycle). Choose two to analyze using the Venn circles. Create two sets of Venn circles; compare and contrast the parts of each of the bicycles in the photos to the bicycle in the classroom. Be sure you address the following parts of the system: source of power, method of translating the power into action, steering, and braking. Work as a Learning Club. Share your findings with the class as a whole. (S, M, L)

3. With a partner, generate questions to ask the guest expert about how bicycles work. Write the questions in your Science Journal. Share your questions with your Learning Club. As a group, decide what two questions you want to ask; decide who will ask the questions. (L, LM)

4. Write a thank-you note to the guest expert. Include at least two things that you were most excited about learning. Include at least two ways you will use this information in the near future. (L)

5. Listen to the song "Bike" by Pink Floyd. Make up movements to accompany the song that demonstrate how the system and subsystems of a bike work. Perform it for the class. (M, LM, BK)

6. With a partner, discuss how our class is part of a larger system. Create a flow chart that shows all of the other parts of this larger system. Post your flow chart on the class bulletin board. Be prepared to explain it to the class. (S, LM, L)

7. Go on a 10-minute walkabout at your school. Identify an item that is part of a system yet is small enough to fit in your pocket. In your Science Journal sketch a picture of this object. Write a paragraph telling how it's part of a system. (BK, S, LM, L)

Homework Extension Inquiry: Repeat the assignment described in Inquiry 1 with a parent, sibling, or friend. Add to your list any new ideas you discover about what the parts do and how they help the bicycle do what it does. The next day, share your experience with others in your Learning Club. Compare their discoveries with your own. Add any new ideas you learn to your list. (BK, LM, S, L)

Homework Extension Inquiry: List in your Science Journal five examples of systems in your home or neighborhood that are good examples of Concept Key Point 1. Choose two of those systems; label the parts of each. Add two observations about systems that you have made as a result of studying these systems. Share your findings with your Learning Club when you return to school.

Assessment Inquiry: Working on your own, list five examples of systems you see at your school that are good examples of Conceptual Key Point 1.

Choose two of those systems to analyze. On two 8.5" x 11" pieces of paper, draw and label the parts of each system; briefly describe what each part does. In one or two sentences, tell what the system does that the parts by themselves cannot do. (Use the backside of the paper if necessary.)

Next, describe two observations about systems that you have made as a result of studying the systems you analyzed. Record these observations on the backside of one of the Venn circles.

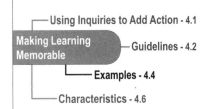

Using Inquiries to Add Action - 4.1
Making Learning Memorable
Guidelines - 4.2
Examples - 4.4
Characteristics - 4.6

CHARACTERISTICS OF GOOD INQUIRIES

Good inquiries

- Follow the ABC + D^2 rules of writing inquiries.

- Ask for action that the people who work and visit the *being there* location need to know and be able to do.

- Ask for action that supports the bodybrain partnership by adding movement and evoking emotion and that engages the mirror neurons and the 20 senses.

- Allow students to see and practice applying concepts and skills in real-world contexts so that critical details are available for ready reference.

- Connect to prior experience, knowledge, and skills.

- Address, as a set of inquiries for each key point, all the multiple intelligences.

- Nurture a sense of community that supports learning and nurtures reflective learning.

- Provide the tools for assessment—both formative and summative (see discussion of authentic assessment in Chapter 8).

- Provide interaction with the people working at and visiting the *being there* location which helps activate the mimicry neurons; engagement of these neurons can speed and make more precise students' ability to use learning.

END NOTES

1   Bloom's Taxonomy is perhaps the most widely used—and misused—attempt to categorize cognitive learning. Benjamin Bloom originally produced the taxonomy to assist fellow college professors to expand the range of questions developed for tests; he never intended it to be interpreted has a hierarchy of difficulty, which has been mistakenly the case. However, once rearranged as shown, it does parallel the learning process as it is now understood. See Benjamin Bloom, *Taxonomy of Educational Objectives: The Classification of Educational Goals, Handbook #1: Cognitive Domain* (New York: Longman, Green Publishers, 1956).

2   Learning Club is a term for a collaborative group used by Frank Smith. The word club captures the important essence of a group that has become a close-knit group whose members become valued learning friends, every bit as much as if they had chosen each other in the beginning. See Smith's *Insult to Intelligence: The Bureaucratic Invasion of Our Classrooms* (New York: Arbor House Publishing Company, 1986), 18–31.

MARY FROGGINS

Involving students, third grade and up, in writing inquiries is a win-win enterprise. It's a real time saver for teacher. For students, it's another way of practicing how to apply the concepts or skills of a key point.

Like playing Jeopardy, *if you know the answer, you can ask the question. In other words, if you know how to apply something, you know what that something is.*

THE SCIENTIFIC THINKING PROCESSES

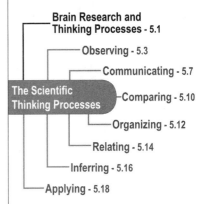

The scientific thinking processes[1] described for decades in every science textbook and teacher's manual are neither the product of a science laboratory nor mysterious. They are the natural processes of the human brain as it attempts to understand and act upon its environment, a feat it's been perfecting over millions of years. Part of our struggle with teaching science stems in large part from the mistaken belief that when we teach science we are supposed to teach kids something that they can't already do, something foreign to them, something quite difficult, something that only the very bright and able can master. Nothing could be further from the truth! Children do not have to be taught how to think scientifically because their brain already function that way naturally.

This is a critical notion for teachers of science. What the modern-day, TV-reared, urbanized child lacks is not instruction in how to think but rather daily doses of real-world input to think about. *Immersion* in *experiences* with natural phenomena of the physical, earth, and biological world provide opportunities to practice thinking scientifically, thinking processes innate to the human organism. Talking about science, reading about science. or seeing videos about science are not a substitute for a *being there* or immersion experiences which intensely activate the 20 senses in an exploratory, active process deserving of thinking time and effort.

RELATING BRAIN RESEARCH WITH THE SCIENTIFIC THINKING PROCESSES

Science is the most brain compatible of all subjects because it asks the brain for observation and thinking processes which the brain is born to do and which a child has applied with great power since infancy.

The purpose of this chapter is to discuss the scientific thinking processes in light of the brain research outlined in Chapters 1 and 10 through 13. These findings about how the human brain learns provide a conceptual framework needed for making significant and long-term improvement in science education.

THE SCIENTIFIC THINKING PROCESSES[2]—

Observing

Communicating

Comparing

Organizing

Ordering

Categorizing

Relating

Inferring

Applying

K–6

7–12

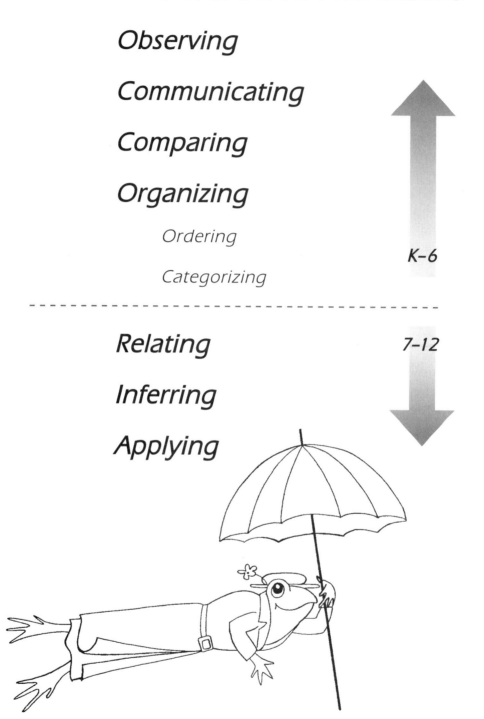

OBSERVING—
Scientific Thinking Process #1

Observing is the scientific thinking process from which fundamental patterns of the world are constructed. The main route to knowledge is through observing, using all the senses, a process through which people come to know about the characteristics of objects and their interactions.

Figure 5A

Most Fundamental

The process of observing is "the most fundamental of the scientific thinking processes . . . only through this process can we acquire information from our environment."[3] Observing requires using all 20 senses to assess everything in our environment. Observing in the real world is not a passive activity; it's all engaging of the brain and body. These are the ways by which we have made sense of the world since infancy. When you watch young children who have not yet developed language capabilities, you see the "natural way" in which they assess the world around them. In fact, young children, because they gather information so continuously and vigorously, can wear out a string of adults by noon and often have to be restrained for their own safety.

Through the Senses. The young child observes by sifting through information gleaned directly from his or her senses (see Chapter 10 for a discussion of our 20 senses). We adults also use inventive extensions of these senses such as a camera, microscopes, telescopes, gas detectors and analyzers, space probes, and so on. In either case, the desired result is the same: Observation enables the learner to construct a view of the world and how it works as a prerequisite for acting upon the environment. Of course, prior knowledge enables the observer to extract more useful information from each new observation or situation, clearly explaining why some of us can look without seeing while another person sees an entire landscape of connected events. Not knowing how to look or what to look for restricts what one sees. For example, if someone has never seen a praying mantis before, it's doubly hard to recognize one when the insect is motionless in a tree.

Science Must Be Experienced. The most powerful premise of this book is that science must be experienced in the context of real life—through *being there* experiences—because conceptual development is constructed primarily through sensory input. *Being there* experiences help overcome inequities in student experience, provide a base for second-language acquisition, deepen the learning for all students, and ensure learning becomes wired into long-term memory.

The process of learning then looks like this:[4]

Brain-Compatible Learning:
BEING THERE   APPLICATION EXPERIENCE ☞ CONCEPT ☞ VOCABULARY ☞ TO REAL WORLD

MARY FROGGINS

The "scientific thinking processes" are natural processes of the mind, what Smith terms as "commonplace thinking." Commonplace because such thinking:

- Goes on all the time; everyone does it, and it's not unusual or special in any way;

- Is widely shared, developing largely as a result of association with other people; and

- Reflects an accumulation of personal experiences.[5]

High levels of sensory input from *being there* experiences are processed by the pattern-seeking brain to identify and construct meaning—the concept, thing, or event is understood. Language (the attachment of a word to this new understanding) then makes possible further exploration and application through comparing understandings with others. The brain readily learns (makes meaning) and applies (builds a program for using) information learned in this sequence.

In contrast, conventional schooling starts with language and definitions about things and attempts to move to concept development. Typically, ability to apply to the real world isn't part of the expectation.

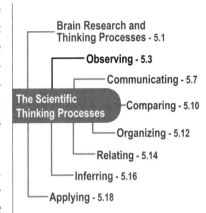

Brain Research and Thinking Processes - 5.1

Observing - 5.3

Communicating - 5.7

The Scientific Thinking Processes

Comparing - 5.10

Organizing - 5.12

Relating - 5.14

Inferring - 5.16

Applying - 5.18

Old Notions About Learning:
VOCABULARY ☞ ? CONCEPT ☞ ? ☞ ? ☞ APPLICATION

"Talking about" science works only with those students who have had prior experience with what is being talked about. The fading ink on the arrows and dots above is not a printing error. It is intended to represent the fading ability to achieve accurate and full meaning during the learning process when instruction begins with and focuses on vocabulary rather than on high sensory input. Basing instruction on the textbook when there is no prior experience makes it difficult or impossible for the brain to fully understand and learn.

Every Brain Is Unique

Every child's brain is unique; a portion of this uniqueness comes from genetic wiring which is then shaped by environment. According to Jane Healy, in her book *Endangered Minds: Why Our Children Don't Think,* "Experience—what children do every day, the ways in which they think and respond to the world, what they learn, and the stimuli to which they decide to pay attention—shapes their brains. Not only does it change the ways in which the brain is used (functional change), but it also causes physical alterations (structural change) in neural wiring systems."[6] What is taken in by the senses makes for profound differences in the structure of the brain. In short, the brain of Video Kid is quite different in structure from that of the Child of Print (the child whose parents have immersed him or her in books, stories, and conversation), both of which are very different from the Child of Nature (a child who spends a great deal of time living with nature).

It is not our purpose here to catalog the impact of TV and other visual, noninteractive technologies on the modern brain. Our purpose is only to make the point that today's students come with very little

OBSERVING

Most Fundamental

Every Brain Is Unique

experience of the real world and thus with minimal conceptual understanding of what makes the world work. Accompanying this deficit is minimal language development; without well-developed receptive and expressive language capability, the seven scientific thinking processes are simply not possible. Thinking demands language; according to Healy, "language is the scaffolding for thought."[7]

"I would contend that much of today's school failure results from academic expectations for which students' brains were not prepared—but which were bulldozed into them anyway. Deficits in everything from grammar to geography may be caused by teaching that bypasses the kind of instruction that could help children conceptually come to grips with the subject at hand."[8]

As Lowery points out, "We are not born with our thinking capabilities completely in place; they develop sequentially over time. There is a biological foundation for all human learning."[9] And the degree to which these capabilities develop depends heavily upon the nature of the input provided the growing mind—the amount and kinds of input received, the amount of practice in extracting meaning from such input, and the richness of opportunities to apply what is learned to new situations.

The old adage is so true: "There is no substitute for experience." Yet *Newsweek* magazine reports that time spent online has increased from 2.7 hours per week in 2000 to 18 hours per week in 2010.[10] This, coupled with concerns for children's safety, translates into fewer hours for experiencing the real world through self-organized play, hobbies, family and community-sponsored outings, such as Boy Scouts or Campfire Girls, and more.

Such a drastic shift in our culture requires an equally drastic counterbalancing change in schools. Schools simply must change their modus operandi and become experience- rather than textbook-based in order to provide the sensory input that drives learning.

MARY FROGGINS

Idea Alert: The classic scientific "experiment" with variables to control and manipulate should be used sparingly from the K-5 curriculum. Students' brain have not developed sufficiently to handle multiple variables. K-5 science curriculum should focus on the first four scientific thinking processes: observing, communicating, comparing, and organizing.[15] It should also dwell more heavily in life sciences as shown below.[16]

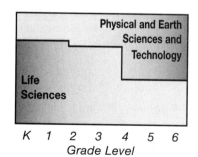

Figure 5B

COMMUNICATING—
Scientific Thinking Process #2

Communicating is the scientific thinking process that allows one to share interpretations; to clarify, correct, and expand one's understandings; to explore applications to the real world; and to determine relevance to one's own life.

Figure 5C

MARY FROGGINS

Action-oriented, study trip-driven curriculum isn't a luxury; it's imperative.

Communicating Activates the Brain

Communicating is a fundamental human process that enables one to refine what we understand by refining the patterns we perceive and to learn more about a greater range of information than could be learned otherwise. When communicating, objects are named and events are described so that we can talk to ourselves and others about what we experience. Communication is the foundation for wondering and reflecting, for manipulating data in ways which allow us to compare, organize, relate, infer, and apply what we know.

The act of communicating activates the brain and enhances dendrite growth. Tools for communicating include mathematical means (such as graphs, charts, equations); language arts skills of listening, speaking, reading, and writing (journals, diaries, essays, poetry); and the fine arts (drawing, painting, sculpture, drama, dance, music). Clearly, "the communication skills of one content area enhance the skills of the other,"[11] because, as noted in the discussion of multiple intelligences, each skill originates from a different part of the brain. Thus, the science content gets processed and stored in multiple places, thereby making later retrieval more likely and richer in detail.

Frank Smith, in his book *Insult to Intelligence: The Bureaucratic Invasion of the Classroom,* considers "much opportunity to manipulate information" a key component of a brain-compatible learning environment. By this he is not referring to physical manipulatives through which to teach students math, but rather the students' manipulation of information in their heads as they test for accuracy and application of their understandings and for possible relevance in their lives now and in the future.[12] Undoubtedly, the greatest opportunity for manipulation comes through communicating with fellow students and, on a much more limited basis, with the teacher. The lecture format of teacher "talking about" science must give way to students "doing and sharing about" science.

Communication in Community and Social Status

The neurocognitive, psychological, and sociological research grounding for "groupwork"[13] is extensive and spans many decades. Several areas are worth mentioning here.

First, building community—a sense of belonging, creating common ground, and taking action[14] to strengthen the group and eliminate passivity—is essential to establish an environment that is safe and nurtures trust. This trust between teacher and students and among students is essential to keep the brain upshifted into the cerebral cortex.

Second, social status in the classroom should neither inhibit nor distort learning. In her book, *Designing Groupwork: Strategies for the Heterogeneous Classroom,* Elizabeth Cohen makes the point that "small groups are not a panacea for all instructional problems. They are only one tool, useful for specific kinds of teaching goals and especially relevant for the classroom with a wide mix of student academic and linguistic skills. . . . If a teacher wants to produce active learning, then groupwork, properly designed, is a powerful tool for providing simultaneous opportunities for all class members."[17]

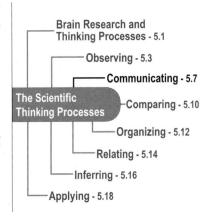

Brain Research and Thinking Processes - 5.1

Observing - 5.3

Communicating - 5.7

The Scientific Thinking Processes

Comparing - 5.10

Organizing - 5.12

Relating - 5.14

Inferring - 5.16

Applying - 5.18

COMMUNICATING

Communicating Activates the Brain

Communication in Community and Social Status

COMPARING—
Scientific Thinking Process #3

Comparing is the scientific thinking process that deals with the concepts of similarities and differences; comparing builds upon the process of observing and invites pattern detection and making meaning.

Figure 5D

Comparing . . . Not a Simple Task

Comparing is not the simple task it often appears. It's an extremely complex, simultaneous, high-speed process. To begin with, it is an enormous pattern-seeking task that draws from all the senses and the multiple intelligences. The process of comparing depends heavily upon the patterns inherent in prior knowledge and upon a wide range of experiences practicing the skills of observing. This allows the student to identify key attributes of things, events, and actions and thus begin to place information in specific relationships, the basis for comparing.

By systemically examining objects and events in terms of similarities and differences and by comparing the unknown to something known, the learner practices making predictions based on prior knowledge and current sensory input and thus sharpens his or her ability to make meaning and extract knowledge. Comparing is also the earliest stage in using what we understand.

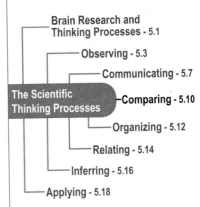

Additional Notes From Brain Research

The brain is a multifaceted operator:[18]

- The brain is a parallel processor which assimilates different kinds of information simultaneously, e.g., emotional, tactile, mental, physical. The greater the number of sensory links, the better the comprehension.

- Learning is organismic, i.e. information is absorbed and stored in the body as well as the brain. Therefore, behavior and thinking draw on information from throughout the body and brain. Learning is greatly enhanced when the entire organism is engaged.

- Each brain is unique (due to genetics and personal experience). Although the "hardware," or neural wiring, is similar, it is not identical. The "software" it generates is also unique. Each brain is a different kind of learner, thinker, and conceptualizer. Some brains even savor one type of sensory information more than other types; not surprisingly, what is attended to and the input would therefore vary.

- The brain is a self-congratulator that uses neurotransmitters to reward itself and the entire organism with feelings of well-being when new meaning and comprehension are achieved.

- The brain draws heavily from and helps develop logical-mathematical and spatial intelligences as well as linguistic intelligence.

COMPARING

Comparing . . . Not a Simple Task

Additional Notes From Brain Research

ORGANIZING—
Scientific Thinking Process #4

Organizing is the scientific thinking process that generates knowledge of principles and laws through the systematic compiling, ordering, and classifying of observed and compared data. Bodies of knowledge grow from long-term organizing processes.

Figure 5E

Organizing is often divided into two parts: ordering and categorizing.[19]

Organizing by Ordering

Ordering is the process of putting objects or events into a linear or cyclical format.

Seriating, a way of ordering, is the placing of objects in order along a continuum, e.g., from large to small, loud to quiet, bright to dim, roughest to smoothest, dullest to sharpest, softest to hardest, coolest to warmest, and so on. This establishes the extremes and ranges which often then reveal patterns that could otherwise not have been seen. Seriating objects can involve an almost limitless number of properties.[20] Examples of properties by which to seriate include the various scales for measurement such as length in centimeters or yards, wind speed scales (Beaufort's), temperature scales (Celsius, Fahrenheit, Kelvin), elevation scales (below or above sea level in feet or meters), brightness scales (star magnitudes), tensile strength scales, decibel scales, and so forth.

Sequencing, linear or cyclical, is ordering according to time. Linear stories tell us about how our favorite valley came to be, the motion of an object, the cause and effect of an event. Cyclical stories tell us about recurring events such as the water cycle, the seasons, animal seasonal migrations, or the life cycle of the butterfly.

Organizing by Categorizing

Categorizing is the process of putting objects or events together using a logical rationale. Useful categories are those that increase understanding of individual items by recognizing a common characteristic among different items. There are two kinds of categorizing: grouping and classifying.

Grouping is the process of putting items together based on a similar property or properties. Young children, ages 3 to 6, group objects using a single characteristic. Beginning at age 7, children can group multiple items using a single characteristic and, at age 9, more than two simultaneously. (See Chapter 8, age-appropriate curriculum.)

Classifying things, events, or actions, is grouping at a more complex level than that used for comparing. It involves assigning a rationale(s) to the relationship(s) that exist among groups of things. *Being there* interactions with real things in their natural context is the best environment for organizing because the attributes of the patterns involved are more apparent than when representational things are handled or when secondhand input is used.

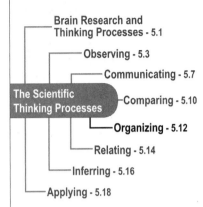

The Scientific Thinking Processes
- Brain Research and Thinking Processes - 5.1
- Observing - 5.3
- Communicating - 5.7
- Comparing - 5.10
- Organizing - 5.12
- Relating - 5.14
- Inferring - 5.16
- Applying - 5.18

ORGANIZING

Organizing by Ordering
- Seriating
- Sequencing

Organizing by Categorizing
- Grouping
- Classifying

RELATING—
Scientific Thinking Process #5

Relating is the scientific thinking process that deals with principles concerning relationships—interactions, dependencies, and cause-and-effect events.

Figure 5F

Relating is not the same as comparing or organizing objects based on their characteristics. Relating is a process by which concrete and abstract ideas are woven together to test or explain phenomena through understanding relationships such as cause and effect, dependencies, and interactions. Success in relating requires a very firm foundation—ample and successful experiences in observing, communicating, comparing and organizing. Otherwise, studies of relationship are word studies and vocabulary drill, not conceptual science.

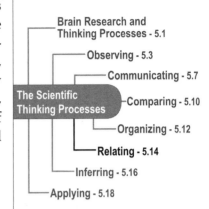

The Scientific Thinking Processes
- Brain Research and Thinking Processes - 5.1
- Observing - 5.3
- Communicating - 5.7
- Comparing - 5.10
- Organizing - 5.12
- **Relating - 5.14**
- Inferring - 5.16
- Applying - 5.18

Beyond K-6

The traditional science "experiment" is a mentally sophisticated affair. It requires that the scientist or student use the scientific thinking process of relating through hypothesizing and by controlling and manipulating variables.

For example, what factors influence the rate of swing of a pendulum? This can be investigated by isolating possible factors and testing them one at a time while holding all others constant. For example, the weight attached to the pendulum (heavy or light) or the length of the pendulum (long or short). The scientist might then set out the four combinations of possible variables:

1. Heavy and long

2. Light and long

3. Heavy and short

4. Light and short[21]

However, do note that although relating is included here in the discussion of science for Grades K-6, most K-6 students' brains have not developed sufficiently to handle relating until students are nearing their twelfth birthday. Thus, experiences that require relating can be a powerful culmination of the year's study during the last quarter of the sixth-grade year, but not before then.

A reminder: The more abstract and complex the thinking required, the more important it is to ground your curriculum in *being there* experiences.

RELATING

Beyond K-6

INFERRING—
Scientific Thinking Process #6

Inferring is the scientific thinking process that deals with ideas that are remote in time and space.

Figure 5G

Because the scientific thinking process of inferring deals with matters that are often beyond the here and now, and thus one cannot experience them directly, inferring should be relegated to high school and college. Concepts necessitating inference such as photosynthesis and other such abstractions can wait.

Remember, there is no shortage of phenomena to explore in the real world using the scientific thinking process of observing through organizing levels. There is no reason to attempt to include inferring in the K-6 curriculum.

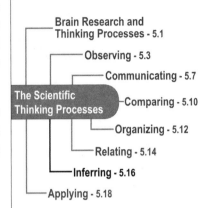

APPLYING—
Scientific Thinking Process #7

Applying is the scientific process by which we use scientific knowledge to solve new problems or problems in new circumstances. It's "a process that puts extensive scientific knowledge to use. Sometimes that knowledge is used in a practical sense as in the building of a bridge. Sometimes it's used to tie together very complex data into a comprehensive framework or theory. And sometimes, the goal is to elaborate and extend the theory."[22]

Figure 5H

Applying Versus Applying

The word *applying* has both a strict scientific meaning and an everyday, commonsense meaning. The scientific definition of applying appears on the previous page. The everyday, commonsense definition is used throughout this book to mean using knowledge and skills from all subject areas in real-world ways—in students' personal lives and in the voting booth. This sense of usefulness is a key element in a learner's decision that something is meaningful and should therefore be transferred from short- to long-term memory.

As Smith points out in his book *to think,* "The brain is always thinking." Further, he says, "It is remarkable that the idea ever got abroad that children cannot think, or that they can lack 'essential thinking skills'."[23] By way of example, he provides a scenario of the brain applying what it understands to making endless decisions: "We decide to get up at a particular time, we decide to dress, and how to dress, and what to have for breakfast (if we decide to have breakfast), and where to go first, and how to get there, and what to do when we arrive. Every step along the way during the day, with scarcely any call on our conscious attention, the brain plans, organizes, anticipates, categorizes, chooses, infers, solves problems, determines relationships, and makes decisions. Life would be a shambles without constant thought of the most complex kind even among children."[24] In short, the scientific thinking processes are innate operations of the brain that unfold automatically over time.

However, when it comes to the scientific thinking process of applying—as defined on the previous page—know that your K-6 students are not yet equipped for the job. Such mental processing requires mental operations not available until much later.

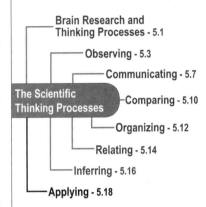

Brain Research and Thinking Processes - 5.1
Observing - 5.3
Communicating - 5.7
The Scientific Thinking Processes
Comparing - 5.10
Organizing - 5.12
Relating - 5.14
Inferring - 5.16
Applying - 5.18

APPLYING

Applying Versus Applying

END NOTES

1   Of all the descriptors of the scientific thinking processes we've seen over the years, we like best those that appeared in the California State Department of Education's *Science Framework for the California Public Schools, 1990.*

2   Every field has a ways of thinking unique to that field. In the field of science, the scientific thinking processes—whether applied consciously or unconsciously—are powerful means to deepen understanding. They are a way of thinking that is important for students to recognize and emulate. As such, they need to be consciously taught and continually reinforced.

   However, in Grades K-6, it's essential to recognize that the developing brain of 5- to 11-year-olds isn't capable of operating in the last three modes—relating, inferring, and applying. See Lawrence F. Lowery, *Thinking and Learning: Matching Developmental Stages with Curriculum and Instruction* (Black Diamond, WA: Books for Educators, 1995), 2.

3   California Department of Education, 145-146.

4   This view of the process of learning was first developed during the Mid-California Science Improvement Program (MCSIP), a 10-year, $3 million project funded by the David and Lucile Packard Foundation, 1987 to 1996. Basing the science program in *being there* experiences proved especially effective for bilingual instruction and outcomes.

5   Frank Smith, *to think.* (New York: Teachers College Press, 1990), 11.

6   Jane M. Healy, *Endangered Minds: Why Our Children Don't Think* (Simon & Schuster, New York, 1990), 23 (A study of "typical" fifth graders by Dr. Bernice Cullinan, New York University. Ninety percent read four minutes or less per day. Cullinan concludes that "our society is becoming increasingly alliterate." She defines alliterate as a person who knows how to read but chooses not to. Such an alliterate says Healy "is not much better off than an illiterate, a person who cannot read at all.")

7   Healy, 86–104.

8   Healy, 69.

9   The idea of matching curriculum to the developmental stages of a child's brain is long overdue. See Chapter 7 for an introduction to Larry Lowery's translation of this body of research into understandable applications to curriculum.

10 "Exactly How Much Are The Times A-Changin'" (*Newsweek*, July 26, 2010), 56.

11 California Department of Education, 147.

12 Frank Smith, *Insult to Intelligence: The Bureaucratic Invasion of Our Classrooms* (Heinemann, NH, 1986), 32–34.

13 See Elizabeth Cohen, *Designing Groupwork: Strategies for the Heterogeneous* Classroom (Teachers College Press, New York, 1994).

14 Susan J. Kovalik and Karen D. Olsen, *Exceeding Expectations: A User's Guide to Implementing Brain Research in the Classroom,* 5th ed., (Federal Way, WA: The Center for Effective Learning, 2010), 9.2–9.6.

15 Larry Lowery, *Thinking and Learning: Matching Developmental Stages With Curriculum and Instruction.* (Federal Way, WA: The Center for Effective Learning, 1989 and 1996), 81–86, 97.

16 The MCSIP program, see End Note 4, taught us many things about making science curriculum understandable to students. The idea of focusing on life science that is far more readily experienceable through the 20 senses than many areas of physical and earth science concepts, and technology, was a hard-learned lesson. Equal time for the three areas of science at K–3 is a groundless idea, slavish adherence to politics rather than to the brain.

17 Cohen, 1.

18 This summary of brain research findings is based in research that is more than 20 years old, yet continually validated by ongoing research. See Paul Messier, "The Brain: Research Findings Undergirding Innovative Brain-Based Learning Models" *Summer Institutes: Dedicated to the Decade of the Brain* (Village of Oak Creek, AZ: Susan Kovalik & Associates, 1990), 1–2.

19 California Department of Education, 147–148, 150–151.

20 When having student organize using seriating, use caution. Do not expect them to seriate using more properties simultaneously than is appropriate to their developmental age.

21 California Department of Education, 147–148, 150–151.

22 California Department of Education, 147–148, 150–151.

23 Smith, *to think,* 13, 16.

24 Smith, 13, 16.

CHAPTER 6

INSTRUCTIONAL LEADERSHIP

For the most part, decisions about instruction should flow from brain research, from the *being there* locations in which you will base your curriculum, and from determining what you want your students to understand (key points) and be able to do (inquiries). This chapter discusses several key areas of instructional leadership in the classroom which will help you best implement those three decisions:

- Setting the groundwork

- Preparation

- Mindful selection of strategies

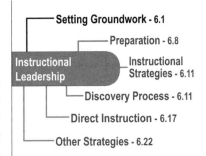

SETTING THE GROUNDWORK

Your leadership in the classroom is at the heart of a bodybrain-compatible classroom. Who you are, how you behave, and your emotional consistency are all critical factors in modeling for students what you expect.

Three important leadership tasks are:

- Replacing the rules of traditional discipline programs with agreed-upon behaviors for all[1]

- Creating and maintaining a safe and predicatable classroom environment supported by consistency and continuity

- Establishing and maintaining the behaviors of civil discourse

Agreed-Upon Behaviors

The difference between agreed-upon behaviors and rules is not subtle; it's the difference between behavior that is internally motivated and monitored versus behavior that is externally imposed and controlled — and therefore typically resisted.

Brain research and sociological and psychological studies provide overwhelming evidence that punishment-reward systems fail to create young adults who have internalized a code of behavior and ethics with which they monitor their own behavior versus those who still depend on external controls by parents, teachers, police, or boss.

The Lifelong Guidelines and LIFESKILLS help students internalize the values and habits of behavior that allow one to succeed in life.

SETTING THE GROUNDWORK

Agreed-Upon Behaviors

How to Teach the Lifelong Guidelines and LIFESKILLS

Creating a Safe and Predictable Environment

Civility

The Lifelong Guidelines were developed by Susan Kovalik and her associates in response to the question, "What qualities do you want in a lifelong partner?" Conversely, these Lifelong Guidelines also ask you to consider what qualities you should possess to make someone want to spend a lifetime with you. Also, what qualities would you hope a stranger on the street would have? A neighbor? However you ask the question, under whatever circumstances or length of time of interaction, these five qualities come out high on the list. They form the foundation for positive, valued relationships and make learning joyous and powerful. They are also the keystone to good classroom leadership as you shape the culture of your classroom.

Lifelong Guidelines

TRUSTWORTHINESS—*To act in a manner that makes one worthy of trust and confidence*

TRUTHFULNESS—*To act with personal responsibility and mental accountability*

ACTIVE LISTENING—*To listen attentively and with the intention of understanding*

NO PUT-DOWNS—*To never use words, actions, and/or body language that degrade, humiliate, or dishonor others*

PERSONAL BEST—*To do one's best given the circumstances and available resources*

Figure 6A

Trustworthiness – To act in a manner that makes one worthy of trust and confidence

Do you remember that adult who was worthy of your confidence? The day in, day out sense of fairness, no surprises, no tantrums, no misplaced anger, the unflagging joy of learning—a person you could rely on. If a teacher models this behavior, he or she can engender a sense of trust in the class which will enable students to seek help, ask questions, deal with difficult situations, and generally look forward to being at school.

Trustworthiness is fostered by consistent modeling of dependability.

Truthfulness – To act with personal responsibility and mental accountability

Truthfulness is an important motivator behind rigorous intellectual pursuit—to get it right to fully understand. And, in terms of relationship in the classroom, it's a fundamental cornerstone.

MARY FROGGINS

I'll be blunt here: Most "discipline" programs are brain antagonistic and DO NOT work in the long run because the locus of control remains external rather than internal.

Rather than investing in management and discipline programs after the fact, invest in leadership. Lead in such a way that misbehavior is drastically reduced.

This is not to say that one should always blurt out what one thinks; tact is an important social skill to learn. Absence of threat rests heavily upon knowing that people around us are truthful with us—we know where we stand with them and we know what to expect.

Active Listening – To listen attentively and with the intention of understanding what the speaker intended to communicate

Active Listening is the greatest gift we can give another. Think for a moment, who listens to you, really listens? Who hears you—what you are saying and feeling?

Some years ago during a cooperative learning training, we were introduced to the Chinese symbol tang (Figure 6B).[2] The symbol means to listen with your eyes, ears, and heart—with undivided attention—a perfect description of active listening. It's useful in the classroom because it identifies for children what the skills of listening are.

Television programming that makes no mental demands on children and commercials that assail their senses in order to gain their loyalty do not ask for active listening or considered responses. We shouldn't be surprised then that so many students come to us without listening skills, yet such skills are critical to success in school. Teaching students to listen, understand, and ask thoughtful questions is critical to the study of science.

No Put-Downs – To never use words, actions, and/or body language that degrade, humiliate, or dishonor others

Put-downs are a way of saying, "I am better than you, smarter than you, verbally quicker than you, and have more options than you." The goal is to elevate the speaker to a position of being noticed, controlling the behavior of those around them, undermining the relationship between people, sidetracking the real issues, promoting self by creating a laugh at someone else's expense. Teachers and students need to learn how to handle put-downs and how to prevent them from controlling their lives.

Put-downs are everywhere—pandemic on TV, radio, and the Internet; they're also prevalent in many faculty rooms, homes, and in the public in general. The classroom must become an oasis, a place where students can sort out what's true about themselves and what's not.

Personal Best – Doing one's best at all times

To do one's personal best does not mean becoming a perfectionist. It means doing our best under the circumstances and, if the circumstances continually produce unsatisfactory results, taking responsibility for changing those circumstances in ways that allow us to meet expected standards.

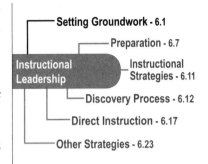

YOU
EARS
EYES
UNDIVIDED ATTENTION
HEART

Figure 6B

SETTING THE GROUNDWORK

Agreed-Upon Behaviors

How to Teach the Lifelong Guidelines and LIFESKILLS

Creating a Safe and Predictable Environment

Civility

MARY FROGGINS

The Lifelong Guidelines were created by the associates of Susan Kovalik & Associates 20 years ago in response to the question "What qualities do you want in a spouse?"

In the discussion that followed, the group observed that there's a common pattern of disintegration of these guidelines. The first to go is Active Listening, then No Put-Downs. The other three guidelines collapse quickly thereafter.

Stay alert to this cascading effect in your classroom. It's a potent indication that you have failed to adequately teach the Lifelong Guidelines and LIFESKILLS and/or to reinforce them on an ongoing basis. Never let up. Even we adults need reminders when interacting with our colleagues and family.

Remember, the LIFESKILLS don't stand alone. They define Personal Best.

Personal Best is a habit of mind defined by nineteen LIFESKILLS.

LIFESKILLS

CARING—*To feel and show concern for others*

COMMON SENSE—*To use good judgment*

COOPERATION—*To work together toward a common goal or purpose*

COURAGE—*To act according to one's beliefs despite fear of adverse consequences*

CREATIVITY—*To imagine ways to solve a problem or produce a product; to invent something original or redesign something to use for a different purpose*

CURIOSITY—*A desire to investigate and seek understanding of one's world*

EFFORT—*To do your best*

FLEXIBILITY—*To be willing to alter plans when necessary*

FRIENDSHIP—*To make and keep a friend through mutual trust and caring*

INITIATIVE—*To do something, of one's own free will, because it needs to be done*

INTEGRITY—*To act according to a sense of what's right and wrong*

ORGANIZATION—*To plan, arrange, and implement in an orderly way; to keep things orderly and ready to use*

PATIENCE—*To wait calmly for someone or something*

PERSEVERANCE—*To keep at it*

PRIDE—*Satisfaction from doing one's personal best*

PROBLEM SOLVING—*To create solutions in difficult situations and everyday problems*

RESOURCEFULNESS—*To respond to challenges and opportunities in innovative and creative ways*

RESPONSIBILITY—*To respond when appropriate; to be accountable for one's actions*

SENSE OF HUMOR—*To laugh and be playful without harming others*

Figure 6C

How to Teach the Lifelong Guidelines and LIFESKILLS

Creating acceptance for and support of agreed upon behaviors is possible only when we make the most of our mirror neurons.

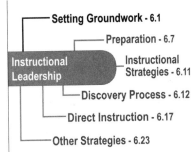

Setting Expectations. Don't just post the Lifelong Guidelines and LIFESKILLS. Teach them. Define them; provide examples. Have students analyze a recent problem on campus in terms of which Lifelong Guideline or LIFESKILL wasn't used and how that Lifelong Guideline or LIFESKILL would have enabled the student to avoid the problem before it began. Have students do the same for the main character in a book—how use resulted in success and failure to do so resulted in turmoil and possibly failure to attain goals.

Modeling.[3] The single most powerful instructional strategy— no matter what you are teaching—is modeling. As you already know, "Do what I do" is always more powerful than "Do what I say."

However, consistent modeling of the values and beliefs of a lifelong learner and a contributing citizen—core goals of a bodybrain-compatible learning environment—are more easily said than done. Also, be prepared for some self-evaluation.

Focusing on Desired Behaviors. Spotlighting desired behaviors is crucial. Many students misbehave simply because they have too many inappropriate behaviors stored in their behavior bank and not enough appropriate ones. Also, varying circumstances call for many nuances and subtleties. For example, when does trying to be caring and tactful become not truthful?

To help students succeed in a wide range of situations, it's important that desired behaviors be identified in as many settings as possible. To identify behaviors consistent with a Lifelong Guideline or LIFESKILL and gives it a label, we use Life Lingo. Because it gives feedback in the moment, teaches by modeling, and provides a dialogue frame for giving acknowledgments (sometimes called compliments, although they are not the same thing), Life Lingo is for everyone—an important social skill to be used by both teacher and students.

The three steps of Life Lingo[4] are short and to the point. For example:

- First, use the student's name. "Mike, . . ."

- Second, label the Lifelong Guideline/LIFESKILL that the student is using. "Mike, you were using the Lifelong Guideline of Active Listening when you. . . ."

SETTING THE GROUNDWORK

Agreed-Upon Behaviors

How to Teach the Lifelong Guidelines and LIFESKILLS

Creating a Safe and Predictable Environment

Civility

MARY FROGGINS

If teachers saw themselves more like leaders than managers, our classrooms would instantly become more participatory, more a learning cocoon for citizens of a democratic society.

Figure 6D

- Third, identify the action. "Mike, you were using the Lifelong Guideline of Active Listening when you faced the speaker, maintained eye contact, and were able to tell in your own words what he meant."

Using these three steps to pinpoint behaviors that work is quick and easy. The same steps should be used for short, written acknowledgments—from the teacher and from other students. Such written acknowledgments provide a long-lasting communication, a treasured note that can be referred to again and again.

Avoid Value Judgments. It's important to note that Life Lingo is decidedly not the same as praise, nor is it part of a "I like the way Johnny is doing _____" kind of dialogue. Life Lingo is neutral, just the facts, describing the key elements of an action or interaction that works.

Life Lingo acknowledges who, what Lifelong Guideline or LIFESKILL was used, and how it was demonstrated. Such clear statements provide immediate feedback. Classmates see the Lifelong Guidelines and LIFESKILLS in action and make their own judgments about how useful they are. This independent analysis is critical to building character traits, values, and attitudes—and their related behaviors—that will last a lifetime.

The "I" statement that many of us were taught to use—such as "I like the way so and so is doing such and such" or "I feel. . ." or "I notice tha . . . ," should be left behind. They can easily become bondage statements. They send the message that pleasing the teacher is the primary goal; behavior control then becomes external. Children need to become responsible for themselves and know what that looks, sounds, and feels like and does not look, sound, or feel like.

Two excellent resources for implementing the Lifelong Guidelines and LIFESKILLS in your classroom are *Exceeding Expectations: A User's Guide to Implementing Brain Research in the Classroom* by Susan J. Kovalik and Karen D. Olsen and *Tools for Citizenship and Life* by Sue Pearson.

Creating a Safe and Predictable Environment

Creating a safe and predictable environment requires investing heavily in leadership rather than control. In this leadership role, the teacher consistently leads, from the opening of the day with a written Daily Agenda to providing clear procedures plus well-planned curriculum and instructional strategies.

Daily Agenda.[5] Posted for all to see throughout the day, it continues to put forth your intentions for the day — what students will do and the key pieces that you will do. It's also an important means of teaching time management skills to students. As each task is completed, check it off your classroom agenda and have each student learn to check it off the agenda they copy down each morning upon entering the classroom.

Keep in mind that the agenda is not a time schedule. The only times written on it are for special events for which students can't be late, such as a study trip, class photo appointment, and so forth. The agenda is a mindmap of the important tasks of the day from the students' point of view. It is not the same outline as for lesson planning.

Written Procedures.[6] Procedures are not "rules" nor are they the directions for completing an assignment. Written procedures are a multipurpose instructional strategy — a systematic and unambiguous way to describe for students the personal and social skills needed to be successful as a learner and team player during specific activities. They are also a primary tool for extending your classroom leadership during times when students are working independently or in groups.

Use written procedures for all frequently occurring events and activities to provide consistency, continuity, and emotional security for students. Include graphics as well as words; visuals help students, especially younger students and English learners, learn and remember the steps to follow.

Before the first day of school, have the following written procedures ready to go. These can be revised and others for infrequent events can be developed later with the participation of students:

- Entering the classroom in the morning

- Leaving at the end of the day

- Leaving and re-entering during the day for regular events, such as recess and special subjects

- Lunchroom procedures

- Learning Club procedures for planning and debriefing

- Town Hall meetings

- Quiet time

Posting these procedures on a flipchart eliminates at least 70 percent of the "Teacher, what do I . . . ? How do I . . . ?" questions. Written procedures are an important way to create a sense of consistency, allowing everyone to feel safe in knowing what is expected. Consider

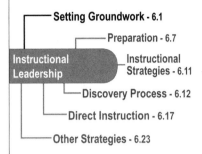

SETTING THE GROUNDWORK

Agreed-Upon Behaviors

How to Teach the Lifelong Guidelines and LIFESKILLS

Creating a Safe and Predictable Environment

Civility

MARY FROGGINS

Written procedures are a key leadership tool. Clarifying expectations before problems can occur prevents having to "manage" or discipline students after the fact.

Figure 6E

also including written procedures in Learning Club binders or in individual student binders where they can be readily accessed.

Think your procedures through carefully; involve students in developing them. Most importantly, be 100 percent consistent in having students adhere to them. These are guides for success—now and in the future—and they become useful habits of mind.

Directions. When directions—the work steps for completing an assignment—are needed, make them clear. Then, follow up with a group check for accuracy. Student failure should never occur due to poor directions or the communication of those directions.

Civility

Civility is the foundation of citizenship and close personal relationships that work over time. It is also a prerequisite to high levels of academic achievement.

Develop and use a Town Hall meeting[7] process in your classroom. The citizenry of a democracy should and must become passionate about how their government works. However, inflammatory language only serves to narrow the possible options for solving a problem.

PREPARATION

A military adage says it well: A battle well planned is a battle half won. In like vein, preparation has several critical elements:[8]

1. Powerful curriculum is all planned and ready to go.

2. Leadership requisites are in place.

3. Lesson planning is thorough and completed *after* the curriculum is developed.

4. Resources have been gathered and organized.

Powerful Curriculum

Curriculum and instructional strategies are like a good marriage; you can't have one without the other. Without good instructional strategies, good curriculum comes to naught. Conversely, superb instructional strategies cannot overcome poor curriculum. Fortunately, current brain research can help us with both.

Chapter 13 provides a summary of the brain research behind the new brain-based definition of learning, a two-step process which curriculum should parallel. Chapters 2-4 describe how to develop curriculum for Two-Step Learning.

Leadership Requisites

Leaders orchestrate their environment and set the tone and processes within which all interact. Before school even starts, there's much to do to make the physical environment of the classroom body-brain compatible.

Remove the institutional look by ensuring that the classroom is clean, healthful, aesthetically pleasing and uncluttered. Also ensure that seating is arranged in clusters with easy access to work tools.[9]

Also, carefully plan how to teach and reinforce the Lifelong Guidelines and LIFESKILLS before they are introduced. If the current discipline plan is brain antagonistic, think through ways to transition to the Lifelong Guidelines and LIFESKILLS beginning the first day of school.

The Art and Science of Lesson Design

Although there are many ways to approach lesson planning, brain research would say that there are several givens that must be built into the process:

- Do NOT begin lesson planning until you have completed writing your key points and inquiries. Mixing how you will teach something significantly distracts from the process to determining what's important and how to state it clearly and succinctly. The only way to avoid falling prey to alluring activities that become a goal in themselves is to first state what you want students to understand and be able to do. Then, and only then, look for ways to best teach that.

- Your primary goal is planning ways to activate all the senses.

- Include teaching about the Lifelong Guidelines and LIFE-SKILLS into your daily activities.

See Appendix B for the lesson design format used by the *HET* teachers of students during Model Teaching Week.

As you approach the task of lesson design, there are some common elements that must be taken into consideration. Among them are:

- Exhaust all potential sources of being there and immersion resources before moving to other hands-on activities.

- Determine which instructional approach would be most effective, i.e., discovery approach, direct instruction, or a blend of the two.

- Determine the number of inquiries.

Setting Groundwork - 6.1
Preparation - 6.7
Instructional Leadership
Instructional Strategies - 6.11
Discovery Process - 6.12
Direct Instruction - 6.17
Other Strategies - 6.23

PREPARATION

Powerful Curriculum

Leadership Requisites

The Art and Science of Lesson Design

Using Resource People

- Select inquiries most appropriate as a whole class activity, for a group project, and for individual choice.

- Set standards, criteria, and/or rubics for grading of group projects and individual work. Be sure your students understand the criteria. When possible, involve students in developing them.

- Allow adequate time for students to research, communicate, and demonstrate knowledge and skills.

Using Resource People

Finding ways to multiply your time is one of the best uses of your prep time. Resource people save you time while adding additional expertise. Parent and community resource are a gateway to a surprising array of firsthand science resources that can significantly enhance student learning. Invest the time to capture their time and expertise.

The parents of your students are a good place to begin. At your parent orientation night, held during the first week of school, share your curriculum journey and *being there* opportunities. Ask parents to indicate the area they would feel most comfortable sharing. Have them write it on their name tag and leave it with you at the door. Then be sure to contact them well in advance; provide an overview of your curriculum and agree upon the topics they will present.

Another valuable resource is a senior citizen complex. Approach the board of a local senior citizen center and ask to post requests for speakers in any area relating to your integrated curriculum. Just think of the hundreds of elderly individuals waiting to share their expertise and to once again become useful members of the community. All it takes is the asking.

To bring the added dimension of the real world to the classroom, invite a resource person at least once a month. With a little time, creativity, and a great deal of persuasion, visiting experts can be located. Most people have a difficult time saying no to a letter written by students or to an invitation asking them to share their expertise with future citizens. To ensure their success, share the following with them: The key points you want them to reinforce, the K and W columns of the class KWU chart (**k**now before study, **w**ant to know, and **u**nderstand after study), and provide ground rules, e.g., a maximum of 20 minutes for presenting, 10-15 for questions, and bringing a key hands-on-of-the-real-thing item. Then, get clear agreement upon the topics they will present.

Possible resources include the school district accountant, a civil engineer, a bridge builder, a carpenter, a beautician, a high school

MARY FROGGINS

Perhaps the biggest mistake new teachers make is thinking they should be the expert in the classroom. And it's a mistake that experienced teachers too often perpetuate.

Lighten up, teachers! The world is moving too fast and knowledge is expanding too quickly. It is no longer possible to be an expert on every subject.

Your job is to model what it means to be a lifelong learner.

chemistry teacher, a pharmacist, a state representative, a local geologist, a paleontologist, a member of a local lapidary society, a health department officer, a conservation officer, a policeman, an engineer from a utility company, a foreign exchange student, a high school principal, and many others.

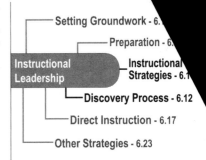

MINDFUL SELECTION OF INSTRUCTIONAL STRATEGIES

While there are dozens of useful instructional strategies, the three heavy weights are the discovery process, direct instruction, and collaboration.

THE HET DISCOVERY PROCESS

The *HET* (Highly Effective Teaching) Discovery Process is designed to encourage curiosity and initiative—key LIFESKILLS for becoming a lifelong learner and a contributing citizen. It's an opportunity to present students with an object, specimen, or problem and let them discover answers and ask new questions. This process is exciting and allows Learning Clubs to orchestrate much of their own learning. It's used most effectively when the Lifelong Guidelines and the LIFESKILLS are in place.

The steps in the Discovery Process are

1. Stimulating curiosity

2. Setting standards and expectations

3. Providing lead-up time

4. Orchestrating the exploration

5. Providing small-group follow-up time

6. Capturing the teachable moment

7. Assessing student learning

8. Creating long-term memories through outreach

When to use the Discovery Process? Whenever you introduce a firsthand item—a specimen, something unusual, something about which you want to pique student interest.

The Discovery Process takes full advantage of a child's natural curiosity. It's an opportunity to explore both questions and answers and to explore connections between prior experiences and the current challenge. Above all, it's an opportunity to lead one's own learning.

THE DISCOVERY PROCESS

Step 1—Stimulating Curiosity

Step 2—Setting Standards

Step 3—Providing Lead-Up Time

Step 4—The Exploration

Step 5—Providing Follow-Up

Step 6—Capturing the Teachable Moment

Step 7—Assessing Learning

Step 8—Creating Long-Term Memories

In the *HET* model, the Discovery Process is usually a Learning Club activity. In the spirit of two heads are better than one, working together usually uncovers the most patterns and the richest, most complex connections.

Step 1 – Stimulating Curiosity

This is your chance to open the doors to wonder and awe for your students and a chance for them to experience being active, self-directed learners. This isn't direct instruction time, it's a time to pose what-if's, anticipate problems to be solve, and drop amazing facts. Have fun! Get excited yourself! Tell your students that they are going to have a most amazing time.

Step 2 – Setting Standards and Expectations

Setting standards and expectations for behavior and performance is critical. In addition to the everyday expectations to use the Lifelong Guidelines and LIFESKILLS, clearly establish standards and expectations specific to the nature of the event.

In ten minutes or less,

- Identify the necessary procedures for working with a specimen (live or otherwise).

- Discuss use of exploratory tools, procedures, or other special equipment they will use.

- Review what teamwork looks, sounds like, and feels like.

- Identify which Lifelong Guidelines and/or LIFESKILLS will be most needed to carry out the discovery process.

It's critical that the teacher is an enthusiastic leader. Yes, handle the snake, touch the shark, open the owl pellet, reach for the worms, and watch the live owl with fascination.

A KWU T-chart is an effective tool to help students focus their thoughts. Complete the K column now, the U column during Step 3, and the U column as part of Step 7.

Step 3 – Providing Lead-Up Time

Before beginning the Discovery Process, students need time to assimilate what they have heard, seen, and experienced during Steps 1 and 2. This should be done both individually and as a group. Provide time for students to discuss their KU mindmaps, share something from their personal experience, ask themselves, "Where does

---

Sidebar:

...ed ...s must ...gn pointless ...ests.

... *oes not require coercion* ... *evant reward.* We fail to learn ...ly if we are bored, or confused, or if we have been persuaded that learning will be difficult. Schools must be places where learning can take place naturally [by desire, not force].

3. *Learning must be meaningful.* Schools must change themselves, not try to change us, to ensure we understand what we are expected to learn.

4. *Learning is incidental.* We learn while doing things that we find useful and interesting. Schools must stop creating environments where we cannot engage in sensible activities.

5. *Learning is collaborative.* We learn by apprenticing ourselves to people who practice what they teach [who don't just teach. If the child didn't learn, the teacher didn't teach]

6. *The consequences of worthwhile learning are obvious* [We use what we learn]. Schools, teachers and parents should not have to rely on marks, scores or tests to discover if we have learned.

7. *Learning always involves feelings.* We remember how we feel when we learn or fail to learn. Schools must not treat learners like machines.

8. *Learning must be free of risk.* If we are threatened by learning, then the learning will always threaten. Schools must recognize that continual testing [and many other of their practices] are intellectual harassment.

Insult to Intelligence: The Bureaucratic Invasion of our Classrooms - Frank Smith[10] Used by written permission of the author.

this fit into my knowledge and experience base?" and how they plan to go about their learning. This is the time to communicate, a time during which students must actively and purposefully manipulate information to extract as much meaning from it as possible so that information is accurately stored in the brain.

The internal dialogue that occurs in answer to the question "How does this affect me?" is critical to activating the brain's attention mechanisms and decision to store something in long-term memory.

During this period of settling in and getting comfortable, students might be sketching a specimen, comparing pictures with the real thing, predicting what they're going to discover, or sharing their experiences related to the lesson. This is their motivational lead-up for what they are about to do. For many students, this is the time to overcome fears and apprehensions about the unknown, e.g. a scary-looking owl. Not everyone is ready to jump in when the teacher says, "Go." Lead-up time, even if for only ten minutes, is invaluable.

During lead-up time, decisions must be made about who's responsible for each group task. For example, "I'll be the recorder." "John draws well; he can sketch the parts." "Who wants to label?"

Sometimes, it's appropriate for the teacher to select who will do specific jobs. This guarantees that students have an opportunity to practice various roles, especially leadership for the group. An efficient way to identify who does what is to assign every student in the group a number. All the teacher then has to do is say, "For today, number 1 is the recorder, number 3 is the organizer, and number 5 is the facilitator," and so on. Another way is to post job assignments identifying specific jobs (one for each member of the group) that can be rotated. Possible roles are

1. Facilitator — sees that each group member has the opportunity to share ideas; reviews ground rules (if any) and initiates the discussion; helps restart discussion when things bog down

2. Inquisitor — asks at least two questions about the subject or topic to reveal the big idea

3. Connector — looks for and shares connections between the topic and personal experiences of Learning Club members

4. Illustrator — draws a picture of the most important elements of the topic

5. Summarizer/recorder — summarizes discussions to clarify content or how to proceed; records events, procedures, and conclusions for the group

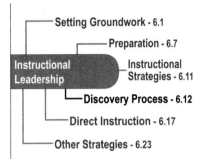

Setting Groundwork - 6.1
Preparation - 6.7
Instructional Leadership
Instructional Strategies - 6.11
Discovery Process - 6.12
Direct Instruction - 6.17
Other Strategies - 6.23

THE DISCOVERY PROCESS

Step 1—Stimulating Curiosity

Step 2—Setting Standards

Step 3—Providing Lead-Up Time

Step 4—The Exploration

Step 5—Providing Follow-Up

Step 6—Capturing the Teachable Moment

Step 7—Assessing Learning

Step 8—Creating Long-Term Memories

6. Reporter—reads the instructions or information aloud and reports the outcomes

7. Organizer—makes sure the work area is organized and clean

8. Quieter—notices when the teacher signals for active listening

Assignment of job responsibilities does not mean that such tasks interfere with the primary responsibility of full participation, in "doing" the activity, working with firsthand materials, and so on. Everyone is a learner, all must participate in the activity. Such jobs assigned on behalf of the group are in addition to the job of learning as individuals. Equal opportunity to experience responsibility and leadership is a cornerstone commitment in an *HET* classroom.

Step 4 – The Exploration

The students are mentally ready to proceed. Let them explore, help them interpret what they find, and guide only when it is necessary. Shift your role from sage on the stage to guide on the side.

Step 5 – Providing Small-Group Follow-Up

Can you remember how important it seemed to you when a teacher gave you positive, instructive feedback? Remember how good it felt and how pleased you were that he or she noticed you personally? Such feedback is critical, yet finding time to interact with students more frequently is difficult. Usually students who receive most of our time are those with behavioral problems or special needs. To solve this dilemma, limit the time allotted for direct instruction, suggest students ask each other for help ("Ask Three Before Me"), and then take this purloined time to purposefully circulate during the groupwork activity.

Purposefully circulate means interacting with each group with the intent of energizing, affirming, refocusing, using the teachable moment to provide key information, clarifying goals for the assignment, and so on. This is the teacher's time to observe, listen, and analyze student responses and to give immediate feedback. It's also a perfect opportunity to use Life Lingo to acknowledge the use of the Lifelong Guidelines, especially Personal Best as defined by the LIFESKILLS.

Step 6 – Capturing the Teachable Moment

The teachable moment is when the student's curiosity is sparked and the teacher can enhance learning by drawing on his or her own knowledge base. It's an opportunity for the teacher to model being an active and competent learner. Taking advantage of teachable moments

MARY FROGGINS

*What makes discovery so memorable is that **we** did it! We figured out what to do and how to go about. We sat in the driver's seat of our own learning.*

requires a broad knowledge base and willingness to extend learning on the spur of the moment or even to digress when appropriate.

In this information age, we're both frustrated and excited by the bombardment of knowledge all around us. To find time to increase your knowledge base, take 20 minutes a day (10 in the morning and 10 in the afternoon or evening) to read about the concepts, significant knowledge, and skills of your theme. Go online; read books, magazines, newsletters, and professional journals; listen to CDs; watch DVDs; and examine other materials and resources that relate. When you are an *HET* teacher, your conceptual curriculum will help you assimilate information, organize it, and hold it in your mind. Teachers must be active learners committed to mastering how to use information and skills, not just to talking about them.

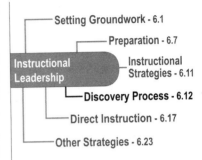

Step 7 – Assessing Learning

Because the Discovery Process is so multidimensional, assessment should be likewise.

Assessing Emotional Impact. Assessing the emotional impact of a lesson is just as important as assessing content. The feelings we experience while learning something new become the attitudes we hold for the rest of our lives. How often have we heard, "I wasn't good in that when I went to school, so I'm not surprised my child isn't doing well either," or "I've never liked science."

A daily journal is one way students can express their emotional responses to what they're learning. After a vigorous lesson such as dissecting owl pellets, it's imperative to allow students to ponder how they feel about what they learned and how this experience will affect their learning in the future. Never discount your students' feelings; acknowledge that feelings are a part of being alive and, more importantly, they are gatekeepers to the cognitive domain. Everyone has emotions; unguided or ignored emotions usually hinder learning rather than assist it.

If an activity has generated feelings of indignation, outrage, or heightened personal interest, it's time for political action—a time to write letters to the editor, school board, planning commission, Save-the-Whales committee, a chemical company, the president of the United States, local businesses, Sierra Club, and the like. Learning and internalizing information are not enough in today's society. Students must realize they have a right and a responsibility to become involved, educate themselves on the issues, and take action.

Taking action on social issues imparts a sense of importance to lessons learned at school. It provides a real-world context in which to

---

THE DISCOVERY PROCESS

Step 1—Stimulating Curiosity

Step 2—Setting Standards

Step 3—Providing Lead-Up Time

Step 4—The Exploration

Step 5—Providing Follow-Up

Step 6—Capturing the Teachable Moment

Step 7—Assessing Learning

Step 8—Creating Long-Term Memories

fully explore concepts and skills and gives an audience (and a reason) for exercising a wide range of communication skills.

Assessing Academic Learning. The authentic assessment movement is a pleasant breath of spring across the educational landscape. Brushing aside contrived, trivial standardized assessments, Grant Wiggins, Fred Newmann, and other leaders of authentic assessment admonish us to measure ability to use knowledge—producing knowledge rather than merely repeating it; thus the phrase "authentic expressions of knowledge."

In the *HET* model, we speak of mastery and competence in terms of performance. There's a large gap between selecting choice A, B, C, or D and being able to apply information to real-life situations. Measuring the ability to use what we know is what authentic assessment is all about. Mastery that matters is competence applied in real life.

The exploration phase of the Discovery Process is just the beginning and should lead onward to specific demonstrations of what is learned during the Discovery Process. See Chapter 8 for a discussion of assessment in the *HET* model.

Step 8 – Creating Long-Term Memories Through Outreach

Outreach is the purposeful connection of classroom activity to someone or something outside the classroom—a way of applying lessons to reality. Outreach can be planned by contacting a resource person or it can be spontaneous such as when students suggest a course of action. Outreach asks the question, "Knowing this information leads me where or to whom?" To have knowledge and skills is to be responsible. Does it demand we take action? In a democracy, if we don't take action to correct problems or social ills, who will? Perhaps the students want to share with other classes or schools, produce a videotape, invite someone in to answer questions, start an information center, or set up a display at the local library or school district office.

Educating fellow citizens is a major responsibility of us all. Outreach demands application of what is studied. It may have long-range effects or short-term impact, but it's an important classroom activity, one which gently prods both the students and the teacher into looking at content in an active, meaningful way.

When looking at outreach, called "political or social action" in the *HET* model, we should use the language arts skills of reading, writing, listening, and speaking. Outreach activities provide real audiences and a clear sense of purpose. What better environment in

MARY FROGGINS

For each learning experience, assessing the emotional impact of a lesson is just as important as content assessment. Too many students/adults have very negative memories of their science experiences. The feelings we develop when learning something new may become the attitudes we hold for the rest of our lives.

which to master these skills? In students' minds, it becomes clear that these skills are a means to an important end—the ability to cope and thrive in the real world.

Enjoy the moment. Your students certainly will!

DIRECT INSTRUCTION

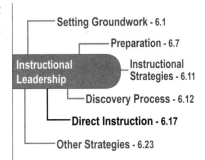

Many people define direct instruction as lecture. Lecture has its place, but it's a limited one. It's the driest version of direct instruction which typically provides little sensory input beyond hearing and seeing the speaker. Lecture is but a small part of good direct instruction.

There are many models for direct instruction. Perhaps the most widely known is the ITIP model (Instructional Theory into Practice) created by Dr. Madeline Hunter of UCLA (University of California, Los Angeles). The *HET* adaptation described on pages 6.18-6.22 is an example of deliberate, intentional steps to foster learning. Although any solid model of direct instruction will serve the purpose for *HET*, we prefer the Hunter model because it has an extensive track record and is powerful when well implemented.

The steps proposed by Madeline Hunter were a result of her research into what effective teachers do. However, she always cautioned people not to make it a static formula and not to believe that every step must be used every time the teacher selects direct instruction as the most appropriate strategy. She acknowledged that teaching is heavily contextual and that only the teacher, with full knowledge of the subject matter and his or her students, can know what is best done at any one moment.

What Is Direct Instruction?

Direct doesn't mean boring. It does mean focused, clear, interactive, well paced, and readily understandable by students. According to Linda Jordan, *HET* Associate and Associate Professor at Hope College, School of Education, in Holland, Michigan, direct instruction is

- A teaching method through which the teacher maintains a highly structured environment for teaching specific concepts and skills

- A process that enables the teacher to maximize student engagement and time spent on task

- Is characterized by teacher direction on an academic focus followed up with student practice and application

MARY FROGGINS

Direct doesn't have to be boring. It means the instructor must be focused, clear, interactive, well paced, and readily understandable by students.

Direct instruction should be a process that enables the teacher to maximize student engagement and time spent on task.

The steps of direction instruction are
- *Anticipatory set*
- *Learning objective*
- *Purpose or rationale*
- *Input*
- *Modeling*
- *Check for understanding*
- *Guided practice*
- *Independent practice*
- *Closure*

When Is Direct Instruction Effective?

Direct instruction is effective when other means to discover and explore are insufficient or frustratingly inefficient.

Direct Instruction in the HET Model. In the *HET* model, the input stage of direct instruction should be limited to 11 to 16 minutes per hour and be accompanied by full sensory input to as many of the 20 senses as possible in an immersion environment.

Direct instruction should be looked at not as an end in itself—the way to teach—but rather as one catalyst for student work on inquiries. Direct instruction can lead the way or follow the Discovery Process.

Planning and Conducting Direct Instruction

The steps in planning and conducting direct instruction are simple and straight forward. Each has a basis in brain research.

Anticipatory Set. The anticipatory set works at two levels:

- It creates an emotional hook or bridge to the new learning. In the words of Dr. Robert Sylwester, "Emotion drives attention which drives learning, memory, problem solving, and just about everything else."[11]

- It accesses prior experiences by illustrating how, where, and why this concept or skill is used in real life and how students might use it. This starts the pattern-seeking, meaning-making operation of the brain—searching for related patterns in its memory banks, a beginning place for processing incoming data.

The anticipatory sets common in the *HET* model include:

- *A being there* experience

- The *HET* Discovery Process

- Visit by an expert

- A hands-on-of-the-real-thing activity

- An inclusion activity which asks students to recall an experience common to all classmates

The goal of an anticipatory set is to get students motivated, curious, excited about the concept or skill, and aware of how the concept or skill is used in real life.

Learning Objective. The learning objective in an *HET* classroom is the key point to be learned. For Grades 2 and up, the key point should be written and posted—on the wall or in students' notebooks. For K-1, the key point is usually represented by a pictorial mindmap that students who cannot yet read can still understand.

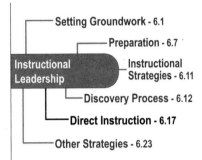

Purpose or Rationale. Purpose or rationale is always answered by how, where, and why this concept or skill is important to know and be able to do in real life. No students should be told by a teacher, as one of the authors was in her high school algebra and trig classes, "I don't know when and where you would use this. Just learn it." In the *HET* classroom, purpose or rationale should be part of the anticipatory set. Apply it to your students' lives and the *being there* experiences you've selected.

Input. This is the teacher's opportunity to give his or her best shot at making the patterns in the concept or skill meaningful, useful, and memorable. This is the "teaching" part. Will you provide a *being there* experience, immersion experience, demonstration using hands-on-of-the-real thing, a structured discovery process? Will you engage students in a set of questions for discussion by Learning Clubs or partners?

Remember, just as curriculum development is a pattern-enhancing activity, so too is the input part of your lesson. Your input should be planned to make pattern seeking by students inescapable. Think about what you are teaching from the students' point of view:

- What information do they need (don't bury them)?

- What are the patterns/programs or chunks of the task (analyze the tasks but don't splinter it into a zillion meaningless pieces)?

- In what order should I teach these patterns (concepts and skills)? Which will be picked up effortlessly through the *being there* experience?

- What teaching strategies should I use?

Modeling. The best models are the real people that work and visit your *being there* location. Choose an inquiry that best illustrates how a worker or visitor would use the concept or skill from your key point. Use it as a demonstration for the class. Then, select another such inquiry appropriate for use by the whole class.

Follow up with inquiries to be carried out by Learning Clubs as a group (peer modeling). Again, make sure that the inquiry requires application to real life; include as many of the multiple intelligences as possible (see Chapter 12).

DIRECT INSTRUCTION

What Is Direct Instruction?

When Is It Effective?

Planning and Conducting
Direct Instruction

MARY FROGGINS

Although the ITIP model of direct instruction predates brain research on this subject, Madeline Hunter's instincts were right on target.

Hunter's version of direct instruction was widely used in the United States in the 1970s and 80s. Tens of thousands of teachers and administrators passed through its training. Some states adopted it as their recommended training and provided substantial funding.

ITIP remains the preeminent model for direct instruction.

Check for Understanding. Begin checking for understanding early in the modeling process starting with modeling for the whole class, then Learning Club work, and on to partner and individual work.

Common strategies include asking questions to plumb student understanding, listening to student discussion in the Learning Club, and using collaborative structures (such as check with a partner or think-pair-share). Allow plenty of think time. Check to see who agrees or disagrees, and why. Most importantly, urge students to talk about what they think they understand and how they would apply it.

Be alert for misconceptions and the depth of understanding.

Checking for understanding is to ensure that the end of Step One of the learning process—understanding the pattern(s) of the key point—is completed (see Chapters 8 and 13).

Guided Practice. Guided practice helps students complete the final phase of Step One of the learning process and marks the beginning of Step Two—applying what is understood in real-world ways.

After modeling and checking for understanding, select another inquiry for students to complete collaboratively in either whole Learning Club or pairs. As they work, circulate among the groups, checking for accuracy and completeness of understanding. The key to providing guided practice is immediate feedback.

If misconceptions appear or if students aren't getting it, don't move on to independent practice until understanding is accurate and sufficient to complete other related inquiries, first in collaborative settings and, eventually, alone.

Independent Practice. Select an inquiry for individual or partner work. Again, make sure that the inquiry reflects real-life use of the concept or skill.

Independent practice ensures that each student can apply the concept or skill to real life and that he or she is wiring this learning into long-term memory.

Students should be given several inquiries at this stage. Hard wiring comes from applying knowledge and skills over time. The teacher must use his or her best judgment about whether students have developed a program for using the knowledge and skills and if it will be retained into the future.

Working independently gives students time to reflect on the depth and breadth of their understanding (or lack of) and their ability to apply their knowledge. With this information, they can begin to direct their own learning.

Closure. Closure to a lesson does not equal completion of wiring into long-term memory. However, the strength of the closure will likely determine whether students will persevere through sufficient practice to commit a concept or skill to long-term memory.

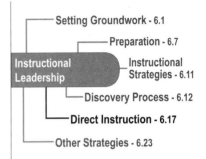

One of the most powerful elements of closure is time for reflective thinking. Ways to nurture reflective thinking include journal writing, personal think time (in writing) before sharing with a partner, writing a thank-you note to the visiting expert listing the things learned/ appreciated, writing a paragraph to parents describing what the student has learned and how it can be applied immediately in their life, creating a graphic organizer that represents what they learned, writing additional inquiries that the student thinks would help create long-term memory of the key point, and so forth.

Teachers also need closure and time for reflective thinking. For the teacher's sake, there must be reflection time to recap the key point and to clarify and check again that students learned the key point as intended. Do you move on to another key point or do you plan additional inquiries for the students to practice until the information and/or skill gets wired into long-term memory?

An Analogy. A useful analogy for direct instruction is teaching someone to bake bread. Linda Jordan describes this as follows:

Baking Bread Analogy

Steps in Direction Instruction	Baking Bread Analogy
Anticipatory set	The aroma brings you in
Stating the key point (objective)	The recipe
Stating the rationale/purpose	What are we cooking? For whom?
Input	Choosing the ingredients
Modeling	Showing how bread is baked
Checking for understanding	Tasting the bread
Guided practice	Giving them the recipe and helping as needed
Independent practice	New baker takes over kitchen
Closure	Reflect on what was learned and how to improve the product and/or process next time

DIRECT INSTRUCTION

What Is Direct Instruction?

Planning and Conducting Direct Instruction

MARY FROGGINS

In a bodybrain-compatible environment, your leadership is at the heart of everything. Who you are, what your behaviors portray, and your emotional consistency are all very important factors when modeling what you expect from your students.

Although Hunter's instructional model predates brain research on this subject, her instincts were right on target. The following chart illustrates how the ITIP elements mesh with the Two-Step Learning Process.

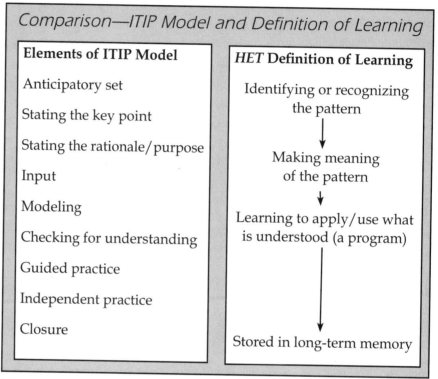

Figure 6F

OTHER STRATEGIES

For an overview of other instructional strategies especially valuable for creating a bodybrain-compatible learning environment, see *Exceeding Expectations: A User's Guide to Implementing Brain Research in the Classroom*, Chapters 7.4–7.16, 10.7–10.19, 11.1–11.6 dealing with problem behaviors. Among those referred, two bear mentioning here.

Teaching Through the Lives of Those at the Being There Location

Children are extremely adept at learning by imitation. While on site, assign students to shadow a particular employee for five to 10 minutes. Have the students use the interview/observation card they helped develop in preparation for the study trip. Have them complete the card during and immediately after shadowing.

Although not all students will identify with the employee to a degree sufficient to trigger their mirror neurons, the interview/

observation card will help them focus on the knowledge and skills needed by the employee to be successful.

Follow up discussion back at the classroom can broaden application to people students already know and identify with.

Role-Playing

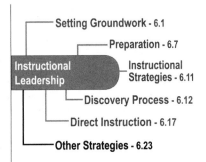

Upon returning from the study trip, develop inquiries that require students to become someone at the *being there* location—a business owner, clerk, customer, customer service rep, biologist, water treatment engineer, college student.

Schedule such role-playing sessions frequently. Each time a student plays the role of a person at the *being there* location, it broadens his or her horizons. If you can imagine it, you can do it. If students can imagine themselves doing many different roles, they can also imagine more career possibilities.

Role-playing is highly appealing to those in an audience; there is action to watch, dialogue to hear, and a story line to follow. The emotional impact makes it easier for students to see and understand connections to real life, and to remember them.

When students have difficulty learning concepts because they are new and somewhat abstract or because students hold misconceptions, role-playing can be especially powerful.

Role-playing can be formal—with time allowed to prepare and rehearse an assigned scenario—or spontaneous. Both are powerful. Role-playing is especially effective for teaching students alternative responses.

Remember, be playful. And be rigorous. Know that for many students, hearing about something is seldom as powerful as seeing it. And, because education is about giving students options in life, what better way than to have them experience those options now through role-playing in the safe environment of your classroom.

Collaboration

Collaboration in the classroom is an absolute must. Its benefits—academic as well as social and personal growth—are well researched and conclusive. However, because the practice is so widespread and how-to books so numerous, we will not address how to implement collaboration in this book. For more information, see Kovalik and Olsen's *Exceeding Expectations: A User's Guide to Implementing Brain Research in the Classroom*, pages 1.16–1.18, 2.16–2.17, 3.15–3.16, 4.22–4.23, and 5.14.

OTHER STRATEGIES

Teaching Through the Lives of Those at the *Being There* Experience

Role-Playing

Collaboration

END NOTES

1   Perhaps one of the most disconcerting implications of brain research is that conventional "discipline" programs—those that depend upon externally imposed rewards and punishments—are brain antagonistic. They are inconsistent with both brain research, as discussed and illustrated in Alfie Kohn's book, *Punished by Rewards: The Trouble With Gold Stars, Incentive Plans, A's, Praise, and Other Bribes.*

   Such discipline programs are also inconsistent with the central goal of a democratic society—the development of a citizenry willing to commit to nurturing a society that works for all.

2   We were first introduced to the tang symbol 25 years ago by Jeanne Gibbs, creator of the TRIBES program. It's a powerful way to teach the elements of active listening.

3   The discovery of mirror neurons comes as no surprise to parents. "Do what I say, not what I do" simply doesn't work. Further research can expand understanding of the power of mirror neurons.

4   By far the most impressive approach to dealing with challenging behaviors that we have seen is the work of Dr. Sigurd Zielke; see Chapter 11, Dealing with Challenging Behaviors, in *Exceeding Expectations: A User's Guide to Implementing Brain Research in the Classroom*, 5th ed., by Susan J. Kovalik and Karen D. Olsen (Federal Way, WA: The Center for Effective Learning, 2010). Neutral language to teach about behavior is essential.

5   For more information about using a daily agenda, see *Exceeding Expectations: A User's Guide to Implementing Brain Research in the Classroom*, 5th ed., 7.10.

6   For more about written procedures, see *Exceeding Expectations*, 7.10-7.11.

7   Town Hall meetings are important on many levels—as classroom forum to address issues, provide formal acknowledgments/compliments, celebrate achievements, and learn the gears of democratic processes. For more information, see *Exceeding Expectations*, 9.2-9.9.

8   For a discussion of these preparation areas, see *Exceeding Expectations*. For powerful curriculum, Chapters 12-14 and 17-19; for leadership, Chapters 6-11 and 15; for lesson planning, Chapters 7, 10, and 15; and for resources, Chapters 6 and 7; and Appendices C and D.

9   See *Exceeding Expectations*, Chapter 6.

10   Like Leslie Hart, Frank Smith was an early student of brain research which he distilled into the Learner's Manifesto. Used here with written permission of the author.

11   Robert Sylwester, "The Role of the Arts in Brain Development and Maintenance," 6. Available at http"//ode.state.or.us/teachlearn/subjects/arts/resources/rolesbraindevelopment.pdf. Also see Sylwester *A Biological Brain in a Cultural Classroom* (Thousand Oaks, CA: Corwin, 2003), 126 and *A Child's Brain: The Need for Nurture* (Thousand Oaks, CA: Corwin, 2010).

CHAPTER 7

AGE-APPROPRIATE CURRICULUM

A young child's brain is not simply a junior version of an adult brain with less information in it. It processes differently. The human brain unfolds in predictable developmental stages. Each stage is like an ever more complex template laid over the top of the previous one. At each of these stages, the brain is capable of more complex thinking, comparing, and analyzing.

Following is a brief overview of developmental stages based on Dr. Lawrence Lowery's application of Piaget's work[1] to science education. It's based on Dr. Lowery's presentations to administrators and teachers of the Mid-California Science Improvement Program (MCSIP) and his book *Thinking and Learning: Matching Developmental Stages With Curriculum and Instruction*.[2]

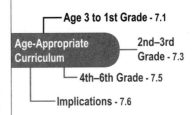

AGE THREE TO FIRST GRADE— COMPARING THE KNOWN TO THE UNKNOWN

During this stage of life, children learn to understand more words (and the concepts behind them) than they will for the rest of their lives. The child does this by putting real, concrete objects through what is called one-to-one correspondences—putting two objects together on the basis of a single property and learning from these comparisons more than was known before. According to Lowery, the child constructs fundamental concepts about the physical world and its properties (similarity and difference comparisons by size, shape, color, texture, and so forth), about ordinal and cardinal numbers (one-to-one correspondence of varying degrees), about all measures (comparison of known to unknown), and about the use of symbols to stand for meaning (word recognitions).[3]

Trial and Error

The major mode of operation at this stage is trial and error. Often, adults mistakenly try to help the child, in an attempt to reduce or eliminate error, or they reprimand the child for making an error. This is unfortunate because children, like scientists, learn as much (sometimes more) from errors as from expected, correct results. Whether putting puzzle shapes into the wrong space, putting shoes on the wrong feet while learning to dress, or falling off a tricycle, for the child, an error spurs the learning process along.

AGE THREE TO FIRST GRADE

Trial and Error

One Property at a Time

Age-Appropriate Scientific Thinking Process

Age-Appropriate Curriculum

One Property at a Time

An important characteristic of this stage is that the child does not yet have the ability to group objects using more than one property simultaneously.[4] Pairings are based on size, color, shape, texture, *or* speed—but using only one property or characteristic at a time. The three- to six-year-old may also arrange objects by chaining; i.e., the third object in the chain shares an important characteristic with the second object (which was initially chosen to pair with the first object) based on a different characteristic:

This stage is variously described as the ability to put two objects together on the basis of a single property[5] or learning by one-to-one correspondence. Piaget calls it the *pre-operational stage.*

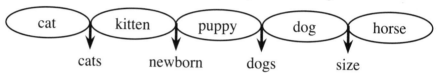

Figure 7A

MARY FROGGINS

Don't make the mistake of underestimating the power of observation. It's not a low-level kid thing. Many areas of science depend wholly on observation either because setting up experiments just aren't possible (such as the Big Bang theory of the origins of the universe or the ultimate effect of global warming) or because, at the time, the available technology couldn't accommodate it (such as nuclear fusion in the 1930s or brain scans in the 1970s).

Done well, observation is an extremely powerful thinking process.

According to Lowery, educators "have seldom provided experiences that allow the potential of this stage to develop" because they have not considered the relationships between knowledge of the learner, instruction, and subject matter.[6] As a result, "curriculum materials water down advanced concepts. The cognitive demands of these tasks are often beyond the youngster's level."[7] In contrast, "when teachers challenge children to use this stage of thinking ability, the challenge usually takes the form of a rote-memory/recall routine, something the youngsters can do—but they can do so much more! Unfortunately, teachers predominantly teach the rote-memory/recall routine throughout all the school years."[8]

Age-Appropriate Scientific Thinking Processes

The scientific thinking processes appropriate for this developmental level are observing, communicating, and comparing two items using just one property at a time.[9] At this developmental level, the emphasize should be on exploration, wide-ranging experiences with the real world, sometimes referred to as "messing around" with real things in the real world. Context is important.

Age-Appropriate Curriculum

Organizing concepts recommended for Grades K-1 are these:[10]

For Kindergarten—People can learn about things around them by observing carefully—what things are made of, how they are put together, what they do, and how they are similar and different. Observing and comparing similarities and differences is a key way to help interpret and understand our world. Often we can learn even more about those things if we do something to them and note what happens.

For First Grade—All living things, including humans, have basic needs—for food, water, and oxygen, for protection from weather, disease, and predators, and to reproduce. A habitat is the place where the animal or plant lives while meeting these needs.

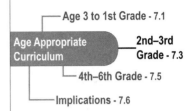

SECOND TO THIRD GRADE—PUTTING THINGS TOGETHER, TAKING THINGS APART

At this stage, a child develops the capability to group all objects in a set on the basis of one common attribute (as compared to putting only two objects together on the basis of a single property). This capacity begins at about age six (late) and is established for most youngsters by age eight.

According to Lowery, "or the first time the student's mental construct is comprehensive and has a rationale or logic to it. . . . Simple rules can be understood and generated by the student if given the opportunity."[11]

Less Trial and Error . . . More Mental Structuring

At this stage of brain development, students do less trial and error exploration and are more thoughtful about the actions they impose upon their environment; they create an internal mental structure of those manipulations.[12] An important aspect of students' actions is the rearrangement of the materials with which they work. Students also have the capacity to do things in reverse direction without distorting the concept, e.g., 3 + 2 = 5; 5 – 2 = 3. This is one of the powerful aspects of thinking at this stage.[13]

From an adult's perspective, there is a correct and an incorrect way to put things together or take them apart; the child at variance with this is thus seen as having done the job incorrectly. Rather than just judging the task, however, adults should also examine the reason why the student chose that particular response and then focus on what the answers reveal about the accuracy and depth of the student understands.

SECOND TO THIRD GRADE
Less Trial and Error . . . More Mental Structuring
Reversing Direction Without Distortion
Age-Appropriate Scientific Thinking Processes
Age-Appropriate Curriculum

MARY FROGGINS

For a genuine shock, compare the mental capabilities of these developmental stages with popular science textbooks. You'll find that much of the content is wholly age inappropriate. Look for areas which for firsthand experiences are not possible or the time frame is far from "here and now."

Typical examples:

FIRST GRADE
- *Earth as it looks from space*
- *Landforms around the world*
- *How water shapes the land*
- *Air*

SECOND GRADE
- *Climate changes creating extinction of prehistoric animals*
- *Matter*
- *Light waves*
- *Rotation of the Earth*

THIRD GRADE
- *Photosynthesis*
- *Particles in matter*
- *Forces: gravity, magnetism*
- *Tilt of the Earth causing the seasons*
- *Solar system*

To understand that numbers or ideas may be combined in any order, yet it is possible to return without distorting the starting place, is a really big deal for students in second and third grade.

Reversing Direction Without Distortion

According to Lowery, "The ability of the mind to do this—reverse direction without distorting the concept—is one of the powerful aspects of thinking at this stage. And the ability to think is this manner separates humans from computers (which cannot solve problems beyond a binary, comparing solution) and other primates (chimps, baboons, and orangutans can solve problems at the comparing stage but not at this stage)."[14]

This stage is variously described as the ability to put all objects together on the basis of a consistent, single property rationale or putting things together and returning things to the way they were.[15] Piaget's term is *early concrete operations.*

Age-Appropriate Scientific Thinking Processes

The scientific thinking processes appropriate for this developmental level are observing, communicating, and comparing but, at this developmental stage, using two or more properties at a time.[16] At this developmental level, content should become more conceptual, i.e., the study of big ideas that form a web that captures many related ideas. While exploration and wide-ranging experiences with the real world remain essential for high levels of sensory input, less concrete ideas can be explored.

Age-Appropriate Curriculum

Organizing concepts recommended for Grades 2-3 are these:[17]

For Second Grade—The physical characteristics of animals and plants vary greatly and determine what they can do and how they do it in order to meet their needs. Similarly, the physical characteristics of nonliving things vary greatly and determine what changes can occur in them and how they can be used.

For Third Grade—Things are changing around us all the time. Change can occur in a variety of ways (reversible, irreversible; controllable, not controllable; steady or repetitive and thus fairly predictable or not and thus unpredictable) and for different reasons. The rate and size of change may not be observable with human senses; tools to measure such change are needed. Change can be helpful, harmful, or neutral.

FOURTH TO SIXTH GRADE— SIMULTANEOUS IDEAS

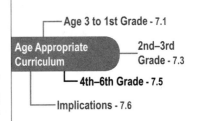

At about age 8 to 10, children develop the capacity to mentally coordinate two or more properties or concepts at a time. According to Lowery, when this capacity is in place—which may occur as early as age 8 or as late as age 10—students can comprehend place value in math, the need for controlling variables in a science experiment, and the use of similes and multiple themes in literature. They can begin to understand relationships in social studies such as free trade.[18] According to Lowery, "As with earlier capabilities, this new one integrates with those preceding it much like a new map of greater abstraction that can be overlaid upon other layers of maps."[19]

Multiple Properties

At this stage, students enjoy puns and can easily learn about homonyms. In their writing they shift to using multiple descriptors: "an old, bent, tired man." They shift from trial-and-error thinking to contemplating the effects of comparing two or more situations under different situations.[20] Arrangement of objects now indicates the intersection of multiple properties.

However, students at this developmental level are not yet ready to handle the traditional science "experiment" of stating a hypothesis, controlling the variables, and conducting the systematic testing of each variable individually while all others are held constant in order to determine which are relevant and which have no effect. Unfortunately, our traditional school curriculum treats elementary students as young adults. Yet for our young adults—high school students—the curriculum for the noncollege bound is a re-run of what students were given in elementary school and, thus, is unchallenging and often boring.

Piaget refers to this stage as late concrete operations; Lowery's term is *simultaneity of ideas*.[21]

Age-Appropriate Scientific Thinking Processes

The scientific thinking processes appropriate for this developmental level are observing, communicating, comparing, and organizing.[22] At this developmental level, content should be based in concepts which in turn are based in *being there* experiences.

FOURTH TO SIXTH GRADE

Multiple Properties

Age-Appropriate Scientific Thinking Processes

Age-Appropriate Curriculum

MARY FROGGINS

*More examples of age-**in**appropriate curriculum includes the following:*

FOURTH GRADE

- *Heat as particle activity*
- *How fossils are formed*
- *Causes of ocean tides and currents around the world*

FIFTH GRADE

- *Atoms, elements, compounds, molecules*
- *Nuclear fusion*

SIXTH GRADE

- *Photosynthesis*
- *The atom and its parts*

Most of the traditional sixth-grade curriculum should be moved to junior and senior high.

Age-Appropriate Curriculum

Organizing concepts recommended for Grades 4-6 are these:[23]

For Fourth Grade—Plants and animals interact with each other and their environment in ways that allow them to meet their basic needs. Keep in mind that humans are animals.

For Fifth Grade—All structures and systems, living and nonliving, are made up of smaller parts and/or processes.

For Sixth Grade—Both living and nonliving systems have situations in which they change in some way and other situations in which they remain essentially unchanged or constant. Why situations in such systems change and why they remain constant can be explained in terms of particular variables. Much change in our world is human-made; some is intended, some inadvertant.

IMPLICATIONS

The idea of age appropriateness is certainly not new. Montessori, Piaget, and countless others have addressed the issue quite clearly. Yet, it just gets pushed aside by tradition when textbooks and state frameworks are being created. A glance through textbooks from the past several decades shows tradition at its most mindless and blind adherence to "the way we've always done it."

So, what does all this mean for integrated curriculum? The closer the curriculum is to the real world, the more likely it will be age appropriate rather than abstract and calling for mental processing students don't yet possess.

The purpose of looking at what is appropriate at each age level is to make thoughtful decisions about curriculum content. Making "less is more" decisions requires us to emphasize the concepts that are age appropriate, to integrate through concepts so that we can group related concepts together across subject areas and thus save time, and to prioritize by deciding what to place "at the end of the list," knowing full well that it is impossible to cover everything on the list into one school year. We call this *selective abandonment,* an important tool in managing curriculum development.

It's important to note that although the age at which each capacity comes into place is accurate for most students, bear in mind that there will be some students who reach the developmental earlier and some who reach it later. For the late arrivals, if the mental scaffolding doesn't exist for learning a particular concept, they will need much more full sensory, *being there* experiences. A slower developmental timetable is usually due to fewer relevant, full-sensory experiences.

Another important lesson here is that just because some students can understand something doesn't mean that all students at that age can. Science content is too often selected on the basis of what a few precocious students are capable of understanding, not on what all students are developmentally capable of.

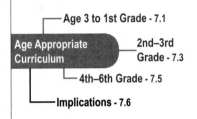

END NOTES

1 The pioneering work into the growth of intelligence was done by Swiss psychologist, Jean Piaget, 1896 to 1980. One of the most significant psychologists of the twentieth century. Since Piaget, others have studied these developmental stages, including Erickson, 1950, Bruner, 1966, Gagne, 1970, and Vygotsky, 1974 to 1997. Larry Lowery, formerly with the Lawrence Hall of Science and instructor at University of California, Berkeley, and principal author of the FOSS Science Kits provides one of the most practical explanations of developmental levels for those engaged in curriculum development.

2 Because Lowery applies the unfolding of developmental stages specifically to science curriculum and instruction, we have chosen to use his point of view. See Lawrence Lowery, *Thinking and Learning: Matching Developmental Stages With Curriculum and Instruction.* (Black Diamond, WA: Books for Educators, 1996).

3 Lowery, 17–19.

4 Lowery, 21.

5 Lowery, 19.

6 Lowery, 22.

7 Lowery, 22.

8 Lowery, 22.

9 Lowery, 19.

10 Karen D. Olsen, *Science Continuum of Concepts for Grades K-6* (Black Diamond, WA: Books for Educators, 2010), 8, 20.

11 Lowery, 33.

12 Lowery, 35.

13 Lowery, 36.

14 Lowery, 36.

15 Lowery, 34.

16 Lowery, 81–86.

17 Olsen, 30, 38.

18 Lowery, 43.

19 Lowery, 39.

20 Lowery, 40.

21 Lowery, 42.

22 Lowery, 40.

23 Olsen, 46, 54, 66.

CHAPTER 8

ASSESSMENT

It should be no surprise that the Effective First Teaching (EFT) approach to teaching science requires robust assessment—formative and summative.[1] Of the two, by far the most important arsenal of tools must reside in formative assessment.

Assessment for EFT has but one goal: Improving teacher effectiveness and student progress in the moment—as a lesson unfolds, not after the fact. The basis of accountability for student progress and teacher effectiveness should be viewed as a by-product of the processes and tools used to meet that goal.[2]

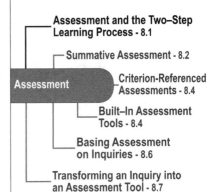

ASSESSMENT AND THE TWO-STEP LEARNING PROCESS

EFT demands that assessment be done primarily as an extension of instruction along each phase of the two-step learning process, in the moment as the lesson progresses, so that adjustments can be made immediately—to alter instruction, extend or alter a student's practice of a concept or skill, or to cycle back for reteaching before moving on.

At any moment during a lesson, teachers must be able to ask and answer two questions:

- Where in the Two-Step Learning Process is this student?

- Are there clues in his or her performance that will help me ensure that the student learns the first time?

The diagram below illustrates the relationship of assessment to how the new, brain-based definition of learning redefines assessment—its goals, tools, and processes. (See Chapter 13.)

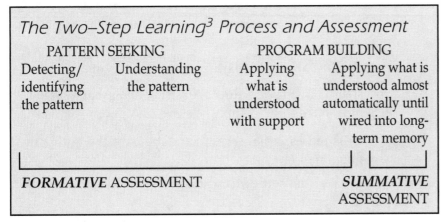

The Two–Step Learning[3] Process and Assessment

PATTERN SEEKING		PROGRAM BUILDING	
Detecting/ identifying the pattern	Understanding the pattern	Applying what is understood with support	Applying what is understood almost automatically until wired into long-term memory

FORMATIVE ASSESSMENT   *SUMMATIVE* ASSESSMENT

Figure 8A

MARY FROGGINS

Simply put, assessment for the new definition of learning is best done **as an extension of instruction** *in the classroom, providing in-the-moment feedback to the teacher as students practice applying what they understand in real-world situations.*

A WORD ABOUT SUMMATIVE ASSESSMENT

If your goal is to teach effectively the first time, use of summative assessment only is too little too late. However, used in conjunction with effective formative assessment tools and practices, summative assessment can be useful. It is best reserved for assessing completion of the last phase of the Two-Step Learning Process—whenever it might occur, rather than as an end-of-the-lesson or end-of-the-year snapshot.

Instruments for summative assessment range from standardized tests to criterion referenced instruments, from commercial to the homemade variety. Most fail to provide the kind of feedback that makes accountability a realistic goal.

The Inadequacies of Standardized Tests[4]

Standardized tests fail to test learning as defined by current brain research (see Chapter 13 for a discussion of the Two-Step Learning).

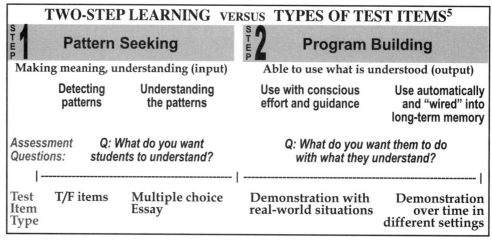

TWO-STEP LEARNING VERSUS **TYPES OF TEST ITEMS**[5]			
STEP 1 Pattern Seeking		**STEP 2 Program Building**	
Making meaning, understanding (input)		Able to use what is understood (output)	
Detecting patterns	Understanding the patterns	Use with conscious effort and guidance	Use automatically and "wired" into long-term memory
Assessment Questions:	Q: What do you want students to understand?	Q: What do you want them to do with what they understand?	
Test Item Type	T/F items Multiple choice Essay	Demonstration with real-world situations	Demonstration over time in different settings

Figure 8B

Our complaints about standardized tests are threefold:

- Most standardized science tests consist of items that test reading ability, not ability to apply science concepts and skills.

- Test items fail essential recommendations of the authentic assessment movement:

  - To use real-life settings and real-world levels of expectations

  - To assess what's worth assessing rather than what's easy to assess

- True/false and multiple-choice items, so typical in standardized tests because they are less expensive to score, only sample learning in the early stages.

Standardized Tests Versus Two-Step Learning. Although true-false and multiple-choice questions are less expensive to score, they do NOT measure learning as defined by brain research. The graphic on the next page illustrates what conventional kinds of test items really measure when compared to this new definition of learning.[6] (See Chapter 13 for a discussion of the brain research behind the Two-Step Learning process.)

An Inconvenient Truth. The inconvenient truth about standardized testing is this: [7]

- True-false items can be answered based on the barest of recognition, that little bell in one's head that says, "That choice sounds like something I've heard before." Understand it? No, not needed. One can ace a test composed of true-false and multiple-choice items without understanding the content. This source of the "sound of familiarity" is quickly dumped from short-term memory.

- Multiple-choice questions can also be correctly answered by a combination of bell ringing and cagey test-taking savvy. Understand the content? No, not necessary. Since real-life situations rarely provide us with multiple-choice options, test-taking savvy is of little value beyond school.

- As for essay questions, memorization can often carry one through the answer—the so-called "parrot back" exercise. In such instances, understanding the content isn't necessary and application is usually quite superficial, a memorized application in a limited sphere. Also, even if students do understand the content, and can talk and write about it, it doesn't necessarily indicate that they can use what they understand. And certainly it cannot determine if what they understand has been wired into long-term memory. For example, the country author can still remember her shock when her college Western Civilization blue-book exam was returned (the grading process took about three weeks). In her very own handwriting was information she'd never heard of before! The content she had "learned" lasted long enough in short-term memory to earn her an *A* on the exam but had completely evaporated shortly thereafter. Sound familiar?

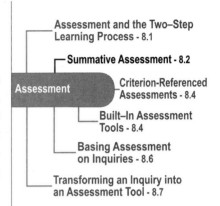

SUMMATIVE ASSESSMENT

The Inadequacies of Standardized Tests

THOUGHTS ON CRITERION-REFERENCED ASSESSMENT

The authentic assessment movement[8] has given us solid advice about assessment, perhaps the most important of which is to value norm-referenced assessment—for both formative and summative evaluation. When aiming at teaching effectively the first time using the *HET* (Highly Effective Teaching) model, norm-referenced criteria are drawn from real life, from what one needs to understand and be able to do as an employee, business owner, or visitor at the being there location that anchors the curriculum being studied. Nothing could be more authentic than that or more useful to students now and in their future lives. We call these norms real-life rubrics—they are embedded in what students experience in the real-world locations that their curriculum is based in and they represent the pass or fail reality of life itself.

The challenge with criterion-referenced tests, however, is ensuring that each item can provide a definitive yes/no answer—yes, the student has developed the ability to use a concept or skill and has wired it into long-term memory, or no, the student has not.

Fortunately, inquiries are an excellent source of criterion-referenced test items. If they meet the ABC + D^2 guidelines for writing an inquiry, you are ready to begin selecting and tweaking. With only a bit of tweaking, you can make them objective and allow for a clear-cut yes/no judgment.

BUILT-IN ASSESSMENT TOOLS

Fortunately, curriculum developed for the *HET* model contains the assessment tools[9] needed for formative and summative assessment:

- *What we want students to understand* is clearly stated in the key points—concepts, significant knowledge, and skills.

- *What we want students to do with what they understand* is specifically described in the inquiries.

The Role of Key Points in Assessment

Before investing time and effort to assess what students are learning, make sure that what you're asking students to learn is worth measuring. Authentic assessment of inauthentic curriculum is simply not possible.

To ensure that the time spent on teaching and assessing is well-spent, review Chapter 3 on Key Points and carefully rate each of

READ ALL ABOUT IT!

Mysterious Cause of Science Failure Discovered on Friday!

MARY FROGGINS

Refer to Caine and Caine's four relevant indicators for determining mastery:[10]

- *The ability to use the language of the discipline or subject in complex situations and in social interaction.*

- *The ability to perform appropriately in unanticipated situations.*

- *The ability to solve real problems using the skills and concepts.*

- *The ability to show, explain, or teach the idea or skill to another person who has a real need to know.*

your key points against the rubrics provided. Use the GUTS criteria for your conceptual key points and the STUDENTS criteria for significant knowledge and skill key points. Revise all key points that don't measure up. The better your key points, the easier the tasks of teaching and formative assessment and the more useful the results in terms of guiding your ongoing lesson planning and selection of instructional strategies.

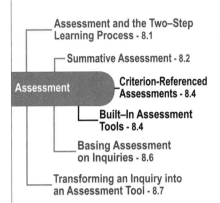

Key points are a source of accountability for multiple audiences.

- *For the classroom teacher*, key points make explicit the real curriculum of the classroom; in so doing, it's possible to determine the degree of alignment of the classroom curriculum with state and district standards. Key points are the foundation for lesson planning and for both formative and summative assessment.

- *For students*, key points clarify expectations, stating exactly what students are to learn and thus allow them to direct their own learning. With a clear sense of what they are to learn—and how it is to be applied (as described in the inquiries)—students can begin to find their ways to practice applying concepts and skills until those concepts and skills become wired into long-term memory.

- *For parents*, key points provide a clear understanding of the content being taught as well as the focus for teacher-parent conferences (thus allowing students to be active participants in such discussions).

- *For colleagues*, key points communicate exactly what you will be teaching and thus how your curriculum fits with your grade level and preceding and subsequent grade levels.

- *For administrators*, key points state the real curriculum of the school (as compared to the overfilled wish statements of textbooks and many state standards); in doing so, they make it possible to determine if the real curriculum of classrooms aligns with state and district standards. They also provide a clear focus for curriculum leadership and assessment.

Clearly, well-written key points are multi-purpose and worth the time and effort to make them as effective as possible.

The Role of Inquiries in Assessment

Inquiries call forth the kinds of observable actions by students that allow the teacher, as well as the student, to determine whether progress through the Two-Step Learning Process is occurring and, if not, where the student is stuck. And, because inquiries are based in

BUILT-IN ASSESSMENT TOOLS

The Role of Key Points in Assessment

The Role of Inquiries in Assessment

real-world applications, they contain within them the standards of performance expected of the real world—the workplace of the *being there* location in which the curriculum is based.

These norms, what we call real-life rubrics, are inherent in *being there*-based inquiries and provide the benchmarks for norm-referenced, sometimes called criterion-referenced assessments. This is true for both formative and summative assessment. They take the guess work out of making judgments about whether learning is progressing through the Two-Step Learning process.

In addition, because inquiries call for skills needed to apply the concepts of key points, they are also useful curriculum niches for skills outlined in standards and benchmarks.

BASING FORMATIVE AND SUMMATIVE ASSESSMENT ON INQUIRIES

Using inquiries for constructing formative and summative assessment items provides the best possible platform for accountability. Why? Because they test student mastery and teacher effectiveness on content actually taught to students. In contrast, externally designed assessment instruments present a smorgasbord of items across the broad range of content included in state standards—content so ambitious in scope that no teacher in the country can possible teach it all to mastery. Thus, rather than berating teachers whose student fail to learn what wasn't even taught, using inquiries from teachers' curriculum allows for true assessment of teacher effectiveness.

Why Use Inquiries as Assessment Tools?

Any inquiry that meets the ABC + D^2 rules for writing an inquiry is a strong candidate for formative assessment.[11]

MARY FROGGINS

Inquiries call for skills needed to apply the concepts of key points; they are also useful curriculum niches for skills outlined in state educational standards and benchmarks.

The ABC + D^2 Rules for Writing Inquiries

- **A**lways start with the action in mind. What are students to do? How can they practice applying what they understand to real-world situations?

- **B**e specific with your directions so that students can see the outcome or finished product in their minds' eye. What is the inquiry telling them to do?

The ABC + D² Rules for Writing Inquiries (continued)

- **C**onnect to the key point. Will doing this inquiry help students both understand and be able to apply the concept, significant knowledge, or skill described in the key point?

- Require **d**eep thinking and real-world applications.

- **D**on't stop writing until you have enough inquiries for each key point to take students through mastery to long-term memory. Also ensure that the set of inquiries for each key point utilizes all of the multiple intelligences.

Figure 8C

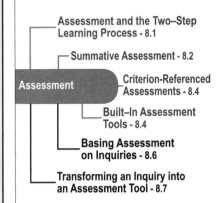

Key to Reliability and Validity

Reliable and valid assessment is assessment that measures what one wants measured and provides results one can trust. EFT demands that we know if students are learning and applying the content of the key point to be assessed. To do so, formative assessment must be built in throughout the teaching/learning process.

The "C" in the ABC + D² rules for writing inquiries ensures reliability because it demands that all inquiries for a key point do in fact relate to that key point; they are not just engaging tasks, they are important applications of the key point. It is this key point-inquiry relationship that makes inquiries useful, reliable, and valid assessment items. In other words, if each key point describes an agreed-upon content (a concept, significant knowledge, or skill from the state and district standards), then student performance on the inquiries for that key point are precisely what should be measured.

HOW TO TRANSFORM AN INQUIRY INTO AN ASSESSMENT TOOL

Whether for formative or summative assessment, the process for transforming an inquiry into an assessment tool is the same:

First, select the inquiry that asks for the most authentic real-world application of the content or skill you wish to assess.

Second, sharpen the focus.

Third, tweak that inquiry so that it can provide a definitive yes/no determination.

ASSESSING USING INQUIRIES

Why Use Inquiries as Assessment Tools?

Key to Reliability and Validity

MARY FROGGINS

A system is a collection of parts and processes that interact to perform some function. We encounter many systems in our lives.

Selecting an Inquiry for Assessment

The most important question to ask is which inquiry demands the most authentic real-world application of the content or skill to be assessed? Not the least expensive or easiest to administer but one that would be the most convincing proof of ability to apply what is understood and if it has been wired into long-term memory.

For example, the following inquiries for this fifth-grade key point provide a typical foundation for creating an inquiry to carry the load of summative assessment.

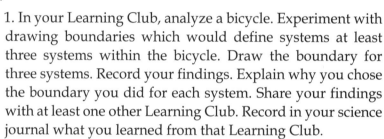

Conceptual Key Point: A system is a collection of parts and processes that interact to perform some function. Many things can be looked at as a system or as part of a system. To study a system, one must define its boundaries and parts.

Inquiries:

1. In your Learning Club, analyze a bicycle. Experiment with drawing boundaries which would define systems at least three systems within the bicycle. Draw the boundary for three systems. Record your findings. Explain why you chose the boundary you did for each system. Share your findings with at least one other Learning Club. Record in your science journal what you learned from that Learning Club.

2. Select one of the systems identified in Inquiry 1. Analyze the structures and describe the parts and processes that interact to perform some function. Identify the function performed. Record your findings in your science notebook. Share your findings with other members of your Learning Club.

3. Based on what your Learning Club now knows about parts and processes of structures and systems, work together to complete the U column of the KWU chart (_k_now before study, _w_ant to learn, now _u_nderstand) that was begun as a whole class task. After you complete your work as a Learning Club, contribute your group's ideas to the class discussion to complete the U column for the class KWU chart.

Question: Which inquiry provides the most authentic assessment of the key point?

Opinion: We would choose the first one. It's the most direct assessment of the concept in the key point.

Question: Could the inquiry be made more reflective of real life, more of a real-world test of understanding and ability to apply the concept?

Opinion: Yes. For example, the student could be asked to analyze the systems in terms of a bicycle repair person looking for the source of brake failure or a propulsion problem.

Reminder: From third grade upward, students are quite capable of designing and writing inquiries. And they are very good at it. The actual process of writing an inquiry is another way of applying what they have learned. Like the TV game show *Jeopardy*, if they know the answer, they can write a doozy of a question. As in math, understanding both sides of the equation enhances the likelihood of solving it.

Also remember that assessment shouldn't be a surprise or a mystery. The learner as well as the teacher should know from the beginning what kinds of applications of a concept or skill are to be mastered — a known goal to work toward.

Sharpening the Focus

If you find yourself still in doubt about whether a student has completed a stage in the Two-Step Learning Process, there are two remedies: Clarify the expected performance (what is to be done) and add or clarify the criteria or standards by which performance will be judged (how well something is to be done).

Clarify the Expected Performance. Trying to apply criteria or standards to a performance that was poorly or inaccurately understood is a waste of time. First, make clear in the inquiry **what is to be done.** Be specific. Review "B" and "C" of the ABC + D^2 rules for writing inquiries. For good measure, toss in "D" as well.

Clarify the Standards of Performance. Uncertainty when judging whether or not a student is progressing through the Two-Step Learning process is usually the result of unclear or even unknown standards of performance. Such standards — be they rubrics specific to a particular inquiry or a generic yardstick such as the 3Cs (see next page) or anything in between — make assessment possible.

Standards from *being there* locations. Whenever possible, use what an employee or visitor to the *being there* location must know and be able to do — and how well they must know it and perform it.[12] Many of these standards are well known; others are not.

If in doubt, use the interview process with the on-site resource person to help clarify those standards. Also, make them the subject of questions asked of the classroom resource person.

Classroom rubrics. Rubrics designed for classroom use are another useful assessment tool because they specifically describe the successful attributes of performance for a specific action or product. For

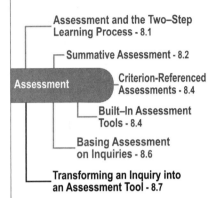
TRANSFORMING AN INQUIRY INTO AN ASSESSMENT TOOL

Selecting an Inquiry for Assessment

Sharpening the Focus

Reaping the Rewards — Competence and Confidence

Tweaking for a Definitive Yes/No Determination

example, assessing essays or short stories, assessing the planning process for carrying out a Celebration of Learning. Such rubrics provide guidance to students before they begin their task and thus help students direct their own learning process as well as make teacher judgments less subjective.[13] A useful source of rubrics can be found at Rubistar.com.[14] Find ready-to-use rubrics or ideas with which to build your own.

Some of these rubrics are generic, such as for assessing a business letter. The best rubrics, however, are those unique to the content of the task and built into the task itself so that feedback for students occurs throughout performance of the task when it is most needed — and with only occasional involvement by the teacher. Obvious examples are learning to ride a bike, how to connect to the Internet, or borrowing in subtraction, and so forth. More challenging assessment examples include learning to write an effective business letter (the mayor is persuaded to take action as a result of the letter you wrote), speak effectively (you win the election for student body president/ mayor) or computing various profit margins for the class business (you strike a good balance between customer perception of value and the profit needed to keep in business).

The 3Cs of assessment. Learning in life is largely a self-driven, self-analyzed pursuit. Key to this is developing a sense of when we know and when we don't know. Part of this capacity is developing a sense for how much about a topic needs to be understood before one can begin to rely on what one knows as being accurate, then fairly complete, and, finally, comprehensive and therefore trustworthy. Without this sense, life continues to be a trial-and-error affair, with far more error than success.

The 3Cs of assessment are useful when real-life standards are not known and specific rubrics are unavailable.

MARY FROGGINS

Don't try to dodge subjectivity; embrace it; school it.

It's an essential skill for lifelong learning as well as teaching.

> ## The 3Cs of Assessment
>
> * **Correct** — conforming to fact or truth; free from error; accurate
>
> * **Complete** — having all parts or elements
>
> * **Comprehensive** — of large scope; inclusive; extensive mental range or grasp

Figure 8D

The 3Cs are a generic rubric, easily used by both teacher and students, and designed to spark that lifelong conversation with the small voice in the back of our head that directs lifelong learning.

Examples of useful applications of the 3Cs of Assessment come from all facets of life.

When washing a car:

Correct — The outside of the car has been washed and rinsed.

Complete — The outside has been washed and rinsed; windows have been wiped inside and out.

Comprehensive — The outside has been washed and rinsed; windows have been wiped inside and out; mats have been washed and the floor has been vacuumed; "stuff" has been cleared, the trunk has been organized, and receipts have been collected.

When doing the dishes:

Correct — Dishes are in the dishwasher.

Complete — Dishes are in the dishwasher; pots and pans are washed and put away.

Comprehensive — Dishes are in the dishwasher; pots and pans have been washed and put away; the stove and counter area has been wiped, the table cleaned and place mats shaken; the sink is scrubbed; floor is swept and the garbage taken out.

When assigned to define **egg**:

Correct — Female cell of reproduction

Complete — Female cell of reproduction in all species, large and small, delicate and robust; can vary in size and color

Comprehensive — Female cell of reproduction across all species, large and small, delicate and robust; can vary in size and color; can develop inside and outside of the body. Can have different size, shape, and strength of shell, i.e., from very hard, ostrich, to very delicate, frog; can be fertilized in a petri dish; can be harvested and frozen for future use

Reaping the Rewards— Competence and Confidence

The reward for success meeting the 3Cs is competence, which leads to confidence which births a rock-solid concept of self and opens a sense of possibilities. Make no mistake about it, competence precedes positive self concept.

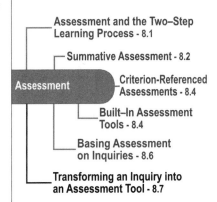

TRANSFORMING AN INQUIRY INTO AN ASSESSMENT TOOL

Selecting an Inquiry for Assessment

Sharpening the Focus

Reaping the Rewards— Competence and Confidence

Tweaking for a Definitive Yes/No Determination

MARY FROGGINS

Competence is its own reward and precedes a learner's view of seeing him- or herself in a positive manner.

Asking students to assess their own work using the 3Cs begins the journey to competence and confidence. Ask it regularly—individually, with a partner, or as a Learning Club. At least once a week, ask each student to select one of his or her inquiries that best represents their performance of correct, complete, and comprehensive. And have them describe why they think so. Their answer can be shared with the teacher, a partner, their Learning Club, or a parent. Or it can be recorded in their Science Journal.

Your goal is to create students who have a strong desire to dig beneath the surface and citizens who have the confidence they can ferret out information vital to judging complex issues in the voting booth and the competence to cast an informed vote.

Tweaking for a Definitive Yes/No Determination

Successful assessment is relatively straightforward. It must answer the basic question: Who will do what, how well, as measured by what, and when?

Elements. The elements of a measurable test item are:

- Who—all students (not just the advanced students)

- What students should know and be able to apply (the concept or skill described in the key point and the application described in the inquiry)

- How well—framed by the inquiries and judged against the real-life standards of the *being there* location, by classroom rubrics, or by the more generic 3Cs of Assessment

- When—as described in the inquiry (for example, within the next 15 minutes, by the end of the day, by tomorrow morning, by the end of the week or month)

There are several questions you might ask about an inquiry in order to ensure that both teacher and student can say with conviction, "Yes; the student has completed Two-Step learning for this key point" or "Not yet."

Let's revisit Inquiry 1 as an example:

1. In your Learning Club, analyze a bicycle. Experiment with drawing boundaries which would define systems at least three systems within the bicycle. Draw the boundary for three systems. Record your findings. Explain why you chose the boundary you did for each system. Share your findings

with at least one other Learning Club. Record in your science journal what you learned from that Learning Club.

Thinking Process. The thinking process might look like the following:

Q1: Is the action required observable and specific?

Answer: Mostly yes but the action required needs tweaking. For example, the "what" is incomplete. Add something like "Describe the parts and processes of each of the three systems and the functions these parts and processes create."

Q2: Would this inquiry as written tell you if each member of the Learning Club understood and could apply it?

Answer: Probably not. Tweak it to make it an individual task.

Q3: Does this inquiry provide a time frame for completion?

Answer: No.

Result. Once tweaked as a result of asking the above questions, the inquiry might look like this:

"Working alone, analyze one of the bicycles in the classroom. Then:

a. Sketch the bicycle.

b. Draw the boundaries for three systems: one which would help you analyze a customer's complaints about brake failure, a second that would help you analyze a customer's propulsion problems, and a third system of your choice. Use a different color ink or pencil for each system.

c. Diagram the parts and processes of each system. Describe on the diagram the functions that those parts and processes perform together. Check your work by physically moving the bicycle and comparing its movement to the boundaries you have drawn for each system.

d. Identify what you believe to be the part and/or process that is the most common cause of failure of that system. Add this information to your sketch. Add your work to your science journal.

e. Before submitting your science journal to the teacher to review, look over your work. Analyze it using the 3Cs of Assessment and make sure it represents your personal best. Complete all work within 90 minutes. "

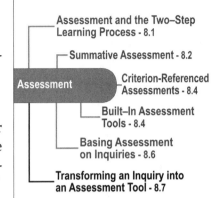

TRANSFORMING AN INQUIRY INTO AN ASSESSMENT TOOL

Selecting an Inquiry for Assessment

Sharpening the Focus

Reaping the Rewards—Competence and Confidence

Tweaking for a Definitive Yes/No Determination

MARY FROGGINS

Remember, learning is the acquisition of useful programs—long-term memory of how to apply what we understand.

Therefore, assessment needs be action-based and interested in assuring that learning has reached long-term memory, not just the test-taking, short-term memory bank info that is lost within a few days.

Validity. Such tweaking now allows you to definitively answer the question who will do what, how well must they do it, and within what time allotment:

- Who—a student working alone

- What the learner will know and be able to apply—define boundaries of three systems

- How—by analyzing and identifying three systems of a bicycle and describing the parts and processes of each of those systems and the function the parts and processes create

- How well—framed by the inquiries and judged according to real-life standards, specific rubrics, and/or 3Cs of mastery

- When—within an hour and a half

You now have an assessment tool that will allow you to say quite objectively, "Yes; the student understands and can apply this concept." Or, "No, this student needs more practice applying this concept."

The ultimate question is this: Has the student truly mastered this concept and wired it into his or her long-term memory? Understanding and applying are the beginning steps. But, in your professional judgment, has the student developed a mental program for long-term memory? If in doubt, ask the student to select his or her favorite toy (must have moving parts). Have him or her do the same inquiry but substitute this toy for the bicycle. Still in doubt, you select a toy or machine and have the student do the same inquiry again. To quote Leslie Hart: "Learning is the acquisition of useful programs."[16] Make sure mastery becomes embedded in long-term memory.

Tweaking and Team Work. Clearly such tweaking to transform an inquiry into a criterion-referenced test item can be done by any teacher working on his or her own and with or without help from students. However, when it comes to summative assessment, it's a task best done as a grade-level team and the item then utilized for summative assessment by each member of that team in his or her own classroom.

Such team work and consistent use lightens the workload and greatly improves coherence of curriculum and usefulness of assessment.

SCIENCE ASSESSMENT RESOURCES

Performance-Based Curriculum for Science: From Knowing to Showing by Helen L. Burz, and Kit Marshall (Thousand Oaks, CA: Corwin, 1997).

Provides explicit guidelines for organizing and thinking about information using "performance designers." Students are provided with clearly stated actions such as, Do what? With what? How well? Includes reflective questions and lits skills and abilities for Grades 3, 5, and 8.

Reading and Writing in Science by Marcia Grant and Fisher Douglas (Thousand Oaks, CA: Corwin, 2010).

An excellent guide to understanding the necessity of building science vocabulary in an organized and effective way using word walls, word cards, and how to read a scientific text for understanding. This resource will assist a teacher in building a solid foundation for understanding science inside and outside the course of study.

Science Formative Assessment: 75 Practical Strategies for Linking Assessment, Instruction and Learning by Paige Keeley (Thousand Oaks, CA: Corwin, 2008).

Suggests a variety of classroom configurations that support learning: learner-centered environment, knowledge-centered environment, assessment-centered environment, community-centered environment; all of which contribute to a learning community providing multiple ways to collaborate and understand science.

Formative Assessment for Secondary Science Teachers by Erin Marie Furtak (Thousand Oaks, CA: Corwin, 2009).

The guidelines in this book can be useful in teaching science at any grade level. Students are expected to respond to the three steps in the feedback loop: Where are you going? Where are you now? How are you going to get there? Formats for gathering information include big idea, concept maps, predict-observe-explain, evidence-to-explanation and multiple-choice questions.

The goal is to assist and support learners while they are processing new information and connecting it to what they already know. Includes examples.

END NOTES

1   Although both formative and summative assessment have a long history, the two terms were first coined by Michael Scriven in 1967 to emphasize the difference between the two. Formative assessment is generally seen as a bidirectional process between teacher and student to improve instruction and learning. Summative assessment on the other hand is designed to make judgments about student performance to produce grades or to predict student performance on other tests.

Formative assessment is intimately connected to instruction. Its goal is to use the information obtained to adapt teaching to meet the learner's needs throughout the period of learning through the Two-Step Learning Process). Research indicates that formative assessment has a much more powerful effective on student learning than summative assessment, especially for students who have not done well in school, thus helping narrow the gap between low and high achievers while raising overall achievement. Furthermore, research by Black and William supports the conclusion that summative assessments tend to have a negative effect on student learning

In an EFT environment where the goal is to teach effectively the first time, summative assessment is of little value. Thus, one is forced to conclude that resources for assessment Under No Child Left Behind were ill-spent. For a brief and succinct overview of formative and summative assessmen, see Wikipedia, www.wikipedia.com.

2   Without question, accountability is essential. However, too often it serves to coerce rather than to improve student progress and teacher effectiveness. Under No Child Left Behind, the instruments used and their timing resulted in bludgeoning after the fact and did nothing to improve student learning and teacher effectiveness in the moment—during lessons as they were occurring. Having and using feedback throughout the learning process is essential if one's goal is to prevent the need for remediation and enable teachers to teach effectively the first time.

3   Of all the areas of classroom life, the new brain-based definition of learning impacts assessment most strongly (see Chapter 13). Nothing short of a radical reenvisioning of assessment will suffice.

4   Like it or not, the standardized test format—with its true-false and multiple-choice questions—plagues us throughout our lives. Driver's license,

career license (plumber, lawyer, teacher), college entrance exams, military service exams, contestant on *Are You Smarter Than a Fifth Grader?* and on and on. Standardized tests, although we believe their failings far outweigh their benefits, should be addressed in the *HET* classroom—not because they provide the teacher valuable information with which to improve student learning but because knowing how to navigate them is a survival skill.

Linda Jordan, an *HET* associate and Associate Professor at Hope College, Holland, Michigan, taught her intermediate grade students how to write multiple-choice test items. For selected key points, her students developed a correct response, one that was close, one that was wrong, and one that was tricky. They then tried each other's test items.

For example:

Item 1: Which of the following is a plant part?

(a) dirt *(close)*   (b) roots *(correct)*   (c) wing *(wrong)*   (d) ring *(tricky because it starts with "r" and is correct only in some plants, such as trees with annual growth rings)*

Item 2: Find the answer of 54 + 21 =

(a) 32 *(tricky; correct if one mistakenly subtracted instead of added)*   (b) 76 *(close)*   (c) 75 *(correct)* (d) 16 *(wrong)*

The importance of knowing the vocabulary of the test, gave them skill in ferreting out the correct answers, and built the confidence needed to perform at their best. In short, they learned to play the testing game.

5   The Two-Step Learning Process is based on the work of Leslie A. Hart; see *Human Brain and Human Learning*, 3rd ed. (Black Diamond, WA: Books for Educators, 2002). The comparison os the Two-Step Learning process and types of tests is taken, with written permission by the author, from *What Brain Research Can Tell Us About Cutting Budgets* by Karen D. Olsen, 10.2.

6   For a discussion of how to analyze test items against the new brain-based definition of learning used in this book, see pages 10.2–10.11 in *What Brain Research Can Teach Us About Cutting School Budgets* by Karen D. Olsen (Thousand Oaks, CA: Corwin, 2010). Content from this book is used here with the written permission of the author.

7   Olsen, 10.2–10.3.

8   Fred Newman, one of the early leaders of the authentic assessment movement, states, "The idea of authentic achievement requires students to engage in disciplined inquiry to produce knowledge that has value in their lives beyond simply proving their competence in school." Also see the work of Grant Wiggins. Their ideas are sound and lucidly described. We believe that failure to implement their ideas is largely because teachers have lacked tools that could be readily converted into useful assessment items. Inquiries, as described here, fill that void in teachers' tool boxes.

9   The *HET* tools for developing curriculum, especially inquiries can be easily adapted for developing assessment tools. See Kovalik and Olsen, *Exceeding Expectations: A User's Guide to Implementing Brain Research in the Classroom*, 5th edition (Federal Way, WA: The Center for Effective Learning, 2010), especially Chapter 19.

10 Caine and Caine's four relevant indicators for determining mastery. See *Making Connections: Teaching and Learning and the Human Brain* by Renata and Geoffrey Caine (Thousand Oaks, CA: Corwin, 2008), 166.

11 Susan J. Kovalik and Karen D. Olsen, *Exceeding Expectations*, 19.2–19.8.

12 Every field of intellectual endeavor—be it auto mechanics, aerodynamics, law, or history—has its way of thinking and reasoning necessary to the discipline. Historians aren't historians just because they read history; they share a way of looking at events and human nature that is unique to their field. Implicit in this is an ingrained sense of standards of performance. Again, this is true of all jobs at a *being there* location which a teacher chooses as a base for curriculum. For example, good customer service reps have a different way of looking and thinking about defective merchandise than the salesperson that sells them. Managers have a different way of thinking about business problems than a stock boy or customer.

13 For a fascinating and useful look at developing rubrics to fit the purpose at hand, see *Performance-Based Curriculum for Science: From Knowing to Showing* by Helen L. Burz and Kit Marshall, 1997.

14 For an array of rubrics, see rubistar.com.

15 Hart, 165.

CHAPTER 9

FOUNDATIONS OF BODYBRAIN-COMPATIBLE LEARNING

It's one thing to read and learn about the advances made in neuroscience, it's another to know what to do with the information. Intuition has led many educators to bodybrain-compatible teaching long before the neuroscience was available to the public at-large. The list is a long one: Montessori's insistence on individualized and independently pursued projects (early 1900s), a century of the various faces of progressivism in America—John Dewey's "learn by doing" (late 1800s to early 1900s), the many contributors to constructivism and the Whole Child and Open Classroom movements, and so on.

However, and this is a huge *however,* using intuition alone has never been possible to intuit how to combine the best of these elements into a seamless whole. Fortunately, brain research allows us, by using a common vocabulary, to do just that—to identify, analyze, and discuss why some things work and others don't, and then to modify our actions as needed.

The city author, for example, believed she was a successful teacher because she was Italian! She met all 1,200 students at the door of her Mini Science Observatory, gave them a hug, brought food on a regular basis, had all the life science critters living in the room, and took students to visit fascinating and meaningful locations. And, of course, creating relationship was at the heart of the classroom. She later found that it wasn't about being Italian, but was about being a learner herself and creating a classroom that she would have liked while a student in school. Many teachers have had similar experiences and yet couldn't necessarily put into words why the lesson/day/week/year went so well.

The city author began her research in the early 1970s while teaching students in California's Gifted and Talented program. At the time, Dr. Marion Diamond, University of California, Berkeley, was doing groundbreaking research into the impact of an enriched environment on mice. This research found that an enriched environment changed the physical structure of the brain (and a sterile environment caused the brain to shrivel). That was the beginning for the city author. She began looking for additional information about the brain and personality. In 1983, she found Leslie Hart's book *Human Brain and Human Learning,* which tied together all that she had read during the previous 10 years and gave foundation to her intuitions. Since that time, hundreds of books and tens of thousands of articles have appeared.

The more that is known, the more it resonates with our experiences as educators, parents, and learners.

Meanwhile, the country author found herself training mentor teachers—7,000 of the top three percent, peer-selected teachers in California. The dilemma many of these talented teachers faced was difficulty articulating why what they did worked and how to explain to other how to replicate it. Some operated so fully on intuition that they couldn't even put into words what they were doing and were forced to rely on asking teachers to come visit their classroom. To the country author, only brain research could answer the challenge of transforming individual intuition into team tools.

As daunting as the task first seemed, it proved doable. And became a 25-year journey ending in the book you hold in your hands.

SCIENCE VERSUS INTUITION AND OUR OWN EXPERIENCES

Without question, the technology now being used to study the brain reads like the science fiction we would expect in the year 2050. But the findings themselves often ring with our own experiences, validating or explaining our own successful learning opportunities and experiences.

For example, think of a time when you

- Learned a great deal

- Caught on very quickly

- Had a terrific time doing it

- Could readily apply it

- And you still vividly remember what you learned.

Take time to jot down the learning event that comes to mind. Mull it around in your mind for a moment.

How did you feel as a learner? For example, excited, enthusiastic, empowered? Note your own descriptors:_____.

How did you learn it? What was the instructional process? For example, hands-on, trial and error, an "experience" that got your imagination flowing, learned it with a friend(s), time was under your control, got immediate feedback telling you if you were hot or cold? Again, recall and record your own experience so you can compare your everyday experience descriptors with brain research findings:

_____.

MARY FROGGINS

The next four chapters are about the science of teaching science. The information makes for fascinating reading in its own right.

To make it your own, think about your personal journey as a learner and teacher and the students that illustrate these principles.

I urge you to take the GEICO challenge: 15 minutes of time invested in this analysis can save you 15 percent or more when reading Chapters 10-13.

What was it? How was it organized, how did it get presented to you? For example, you chose it because it was meaningful to you, it was the real version with all the richness and complexity of the real world, and you had to either "get it" (the whole thing) or understand nothing. *OR,* you went from piece to piece first and then understood the whole thing, someone else chose it, and it was shaped by others as you went along.

Once you've chosen a powerful learning experience to examine, keep a record of your responses. If you do, you'll soon realize that you already know a great deal about what current brain research says about how the human brain works. And, your everyday labels will be very useful to you later on as you prepare to make your classroom learning environment more brain-compatible.

Refer to your responses while viewing the following diagram. Analyze your findings and compare them to the brain research principles discussed in Chapters 10-13 and you can see why we believe that science is the most brain-compatible of all subjects. The most powerful learning experiences are those that allow the student to learn as the brain naturally learns. This is true bodybrain-compatibility.

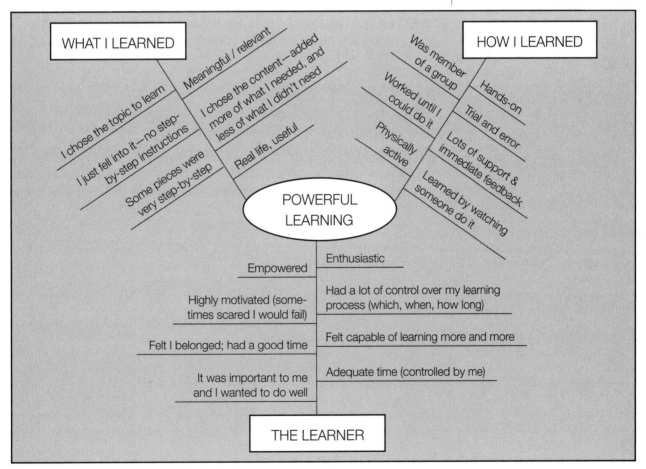

Figure 9A

MARY FROGGINS

Achieving bodybrain-compatibility for your students is not the result of following a checklist. The concepts from brain research cannot be implemented by a few simple strategies. Effective implementation will only come through full understanding of the brain research and the richness of its implications.

MOUNDS OF BRAIN RESEARCH . . . FOUR CONSISTENT THEMES

Chapters 10 through 13 provide an overview of four important principles from brain research that—when taken as a whole—provide a comprehensive, integrated, singular view of what should be happening in the classroom—in terms of both instructional strategies and curriculum development.

These principles about how the human brain learns are

- Learning as a function of experience (Chapter 10)

- The inseparable bodybrain learning partnership (Chapter 11)

- Multiple intelligences (Chapter 12)

- Learning as a two-step process of pattern seeking and program building for long-term memory (Chapter 13)

For a brief summary of each of these principles, see Chapter 1. For a more in-depth view of the Principles of Learning, see *Exceeding Expectations: A User's Guide to Implementing Brain Research in the Classroom*, 5th ed., by Susan J. Kovalik and Karen D. Olsen (Federal WAy, WA: The Center for Effective Learning, 2010).

CHAPTER 10

LEARNING PRINCIPLE 1— INTELLIGENCE AS A FUNCTION OF EXPERIENCE

Learning is the result of real, observable physiological growth in the brain[1] that occurs as a result of sensory input and the processing, organizing, and pruning it promotes. The richer the sensory input, the greater the physiological growth in the brain and thus the greater the learning that will be wired into long-term memory. This factor is the important issue in the great nature versus nurture debate about intelligence. It now appears that there is plenty of scientific evidence to establish the power of both.[2] Genetics was once thought to be an immutable determiner of intelligence—what you were born with was what you would end up with. Not so.

The work of Marian Diamond, University of California, Berkeley; Reuven Feurstein, Israel; and many others refutes the long-held beliefs that intelligence is a genetically fixed, singular quality. Feurstein and his associates have even gone so far as to stipulate that "Genetics is no barrier to learning.[3] Marian Diamond's work[4] shows that an enriched environment results in measurable physiological growth in the brain. In short, if we know how the brain learns—what happens physiologically when learning occurs—we can assist a learner to create new "hardwiring" in the brain to carry new learnings. Intelligence, the capability to solve problems and create products, is significantly influenced by environment and experience.

The brain, whether child or adult, is both plastic and resilient and is always eager to learn. What it encounters—experiences, thoughts, actions, and emotions—literally changes its structure.[5] Everything affects brain development, and development is a lifelong process.

PHYSIOLOGICAL CHANGES

While the story of the physiological changes that result in learning is fantastically more complex than we need to delve into here, a simplified accounting of the biology of learning provides, we believe, valuable images that can help teachers enhance student learning. The basic building blocks of learning are neurons, brain organization, and information substances.

Neurons, Dendrites, and Axons

There are, by conservative estimate, 100 billion brain cells (neurons). Each neuron has one axon and as many as 100,000 dendrites.

PHYSIOLOGICAL CHANGES

Neurons, Dendrites, and Axons

Communication Among Neurons via Information Substances

The resulting intertwining forms 100 trillion constantly changing connections. Just to catch your attention here, it's said that here are more possible ways to connect the brain's neurons than there are atoms in the universe.[6]

How neurons organize themselves and how they connect with each other results in the outward manifestations of learning and the quality we call intelligence. For example, this graphic illustrates the increase in complexity of dendrites and axons from birth to age two. As a result, the brain becomes measurably denser and heavier (during infancy, the overall size of the skull increases as well, reaching full size by age five).

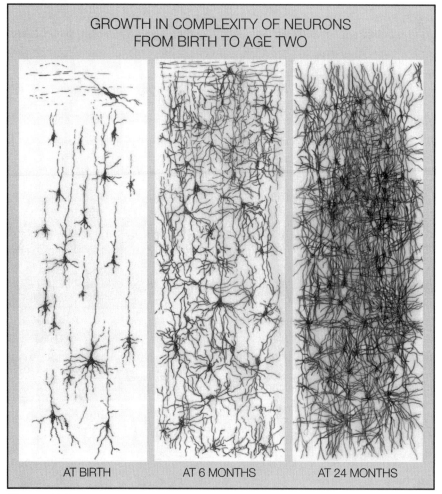

GROWTH IN COMPLEXITY OF NEURONS
FROM BIRTH TO AGE TWO

AT BIRTH   AT 6 MONTHS   AT 24 MONTHS

Figure 10A

Such growth—multiple branching of the dendrites, myelination of axons, enlargement of synapses and overall size of the neurons—is the brain's response to rich sensory input from an enriched environment. In contrast, sterile, boring environments not only result in significantly less growth but also in actual shrinking of existing dendrites. A period of drastically reduced enrichment, even as short as four days, can result in measurable shrinkage of dendrites.[7] "Use it or lose it"[8] is a univer-

---

MARY FROGGINS

Learning is the result of real, observable physiological growth in the brain that occurs as a result of sensory input and the processing, organizing, and pruning it promotes. The richer the sensory input, the greater the physiological growth in the brain and thus the greater the learning that will be wired into long-term memory.

sally acknowledged premise among neuroscientists and is powerful advice when it comes to growing and maintaining a healthy brain. The job of parents and teachers is to help children (and fellow adults) grow dendrites[9] and to nurture continued use of what is grown.

Exactly how learning occurs is still a mystery, hidden at the molecular level. But the story is rapidly unfolding. In simple terms, there are two ways that neurons in the brain communicate with each other.

Communication of Neurons Across the Synaptic Gap. The means of communication that has been understood for decades is an electrical-chemical process. The sending neuron transmits an electrical signal down its axon to its tip which is very close to the bulbous ending on the dendritic spines of the receiving cell. Chemical messengers, neurotransmitters, travel from the axon to the dendrite across the synaptic gap. If the information is compelling enough[10] to the receiving neuron, it in turn will spark an electrical transmission down its axon to the dendrites of another cell and on and on until the communication is complete, all at the rate of up to a billion times a second.[11] This means of communication carries the bulk of academic learning, particularly symbolic and abstract content, and is heavily influenced by emotion.

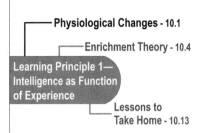

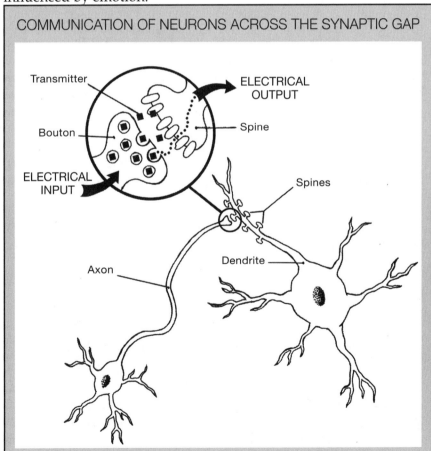

COMMUNICATION OF NEURONS ACROSS THE SYNAPTIC GAP

Transmitter

ELECTRICAL OUTPUT

Bouton

Spine

ELECTRICAL INPUT

Spines

Axon

Dendrite

PHYSIOLOGICAL CHANGES

Neurons, Dendrites, and Axons

Communication Among Neurons via Information Substances

Figure 10B

Communication Among Neurons via Information Substances

The previous description of neurons, dendrites, and axons has been bedrock knowledge for some decades. Recently, however, the story has expanded quite dramatically. In short, it seems that the Greeks were on to something 2,000 years ago when they emphasized the importance of educating and training both mind and body.

Another means of communication among neurons, and one that interconnects the entire body, is wholly chemical. These chemicals, often called "information substances,"[12] include transmitters, peptides, hormones, factors, and protein ligands. They carry information throughout the body. Some of these substances are created in other organs in the body but, wherever they are produced and wherever else they are received (the heart and respiratory center are major hot spots), all are received by neurons in the brain. These information substances are fundamental to the bodybrain learning partnership.

ENRICHMENT THEORY

The story of neurons, axons, and dendrites and how to make them develop and grow leads us to the field of brain enrichment pioneered by Dr. Marian Diamond 30 years ago. Dr. Diamond suggests that the plaintive question "Why can't Johnny read?" should be rephrased: "How do I best stimulate Johnny's brain to make it grow, to increase the number and strength of connections being made, and to hard-wire learning into long-term memory?"

Answer: **The best way to stimulate the brain is to provide massive amounts of sensory input that activate all our senses**, not just the traditional five (sight, hearing, touch, smell, and taste). At last count, we have at least 20 senses.

To illustrate these senses, consider two learning events told by the country author.

Story 1 — A Day at the Creek. Half a century later, here is what the country author remembers of the day at the creek:

> Age eight, with my older brother (and only sibling), engaged in the thoroughly hopeless but intriguing task of attempting to dam up the creek south of the family home; sunshine on our backs, reflections dancing on the water; bare feet scrunching in the pebbly gravel and gooey mud; the tepid, slow-moving water with darting minnows disturbed by rearranging rocks and the shovels full of smelly mud; the sweat from our efforts

MARY FROGGINS

An undeveloped potential is just that, an undeveloped brain capable of less intelligent behaviors. It is our responsibility as educators to provide the kinds and amounts of sensory input that will ensure that each student's brain is developed to the full range of its capacity.

dripping down our faces; our laughter rippling across the creek; my brother's nearness; his patience with a little sister who "never stayed home like the other girls did" . . . the lessons of that day, the wonder of the creek, the beauty of family relationships.

The chart on the next page analyzes the sensory input behind this story. This learning experience has stayed vivid for 50 years and will likely remain so until death. The vividness—the richness of the memory and its tenacity—can be replicated in our school programs

In stark contrast, consider this next instructional event.

Story 2 — Hello, Computers! This is a story about how inadequate sensory input failed to move new learning from short-term memory to long-term memory, despite the learner's high level of motivation and need to know.

A colleague and his wife offered computer literacy classes in their home (at the time, they had more computers in their spare bedroom for such a class than the local university did). I was thrilled at the opportunity, paid my $30, and sat in the front row. My instructor-friend dove right into "what goes on inside the box." "Wow," I thought, "If I understood how things work, program writing, never mind word processing, would be a piece of cake. This is the class for me!"

The story that unfolded boggled my mind. Whoever thought up this stuff in the first place? If I didn't understand something, I raised my hand and kept it there until I got an explanation I understood. The night was fascinating. I left the class thrilled to my toes. It was, after all, quite understandable conceptually despite its sci-fi veneer.

The next morning, my mother, who was visiting me at the time and whom I tried to talk into coming with me to the class, asked reasonably enough, "Well, what did you learn last night?"

"Holy moley, Mom! You should have come. You would've loved it. It was our kind of workshop. He explained what goes on inside the box. It was fabulous!"

"Oh," she said, "just what does go on in there?"

"Well, when you plug it in and turn it on, it . . . ah, er. Let's see, now, when . . . when you plug it in and turn it on, it. . . ."

Egad, how is this possible? Zero! Nada! I couldn't remember a thing except for my very clear recollection that I understood it all at the time. But nothing else stuck in my brain over night! What a waste!

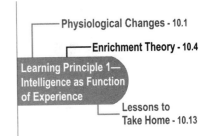

ENRICHMENT THEORY

More About Sensory Input

Six Kinds of Sensory Input

Why *Being There* Experiences?

THE 20 SENSES		
SENSES	**KIND OF INPUT**	**EXAMPLES OF SENSORY INPUT FROM STORY**
Sight	Visible light	Reflections dancing on the water; darting minnows; dams breaking, etc.
Hearing	Vibrations in the air	Laughter, gravel scrunching; mud sucking; rocks clashing, splashing
Touch	Tactile contact	Bare feet scrunching in the pebbly gravel; tepid, slow-moving water
Taste	Chemical molecular	Sweat dripping down their faces; an occasional splash of creek water
Smell	Olfactory molecular	Smelly mud
Balance	Kinesthetic geotropic	Keeping balance wading in the deep gravel; moving rocks/mud
Vestibular	Repetitious movement	Re-arranging rocks and shoveling smelly mud
Temperature	Molecular motion	Warm summer day
Pain	Nociception	Thankfully, none!
Eidetic imagery	Neuroelectrical image retention	The vivid picture of the scene and its details
Magnetic	Ferromagnetic orientation	The location of creek – south of family home
Infrared	Long electromagnetic waves	The warmth and power of the sun's rays
Ultraviolet	Short electromagnetic waves	The warmth and power of the sun's rays
Ionic	Airborne ionic charge	The refreshing feeling from being around water
Vomeronasal	Pheromonic sensing	Primal sense of smell – body odors, sweat, rotting vegetation
Proximal	Physical closeness	The nearness of the brother
Electrical	Surface charge	The humidity of the creed eliminated any perceivable static electricity
Barometric	Atmospheric pressure	The steady, unchanging atmospheric pressure on a calm summer day
Proprioception	Sensation of body in space	Shoveling mud (shovel as extension of body)
Geogravimetric	Sensing mass differences	Density (weight to mass) of material – firm, pebbly gravel versus gooey mud

Figure 10C

Clearly, the only sensory input during this learning experience was hearing and sight (and that was limited to the exterior of the computers). Limited sensory input, coupled with little to no prior experience (and thus no post office address in the brain to capture and help organize the new information), conspired to create that all too familiar short-term memory dump.

More About Sensory Input

As indicated on the chart on the previous page, humans have at least 20 senses, not just five. The more that are activated, the greater the physiological change in the brain, and, therefore, the greater the learning. Therefore, the amount of sensory input in each and every lesson is critical.

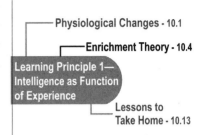

Physiological Changes - 10.1

Enrichment Theory - 10.4

Learning Principle 1— Intelligence as Function of Experience

Lessons to Take Home - 10.13

SIX KINDS OF SENSORY INPUT

Being there input occurs when ideas/concepts are studied in their real-world context, such as a pond, lake or wetlands area, a mall, a factory, or a neighbor's backyard—literally "being there." All 20 senses are activated, producing maximum electrical and chemical activity in the brain. Input is rich, varied, and plentiful.

Immersion input replicates the real world context of the being there experience in the classroom as fully as possible. For example, if a pond is the being there site, a classroom pond (a child's swimming pool with a black plastic drape) is created with as many real pond critters and plants as possible. The classroom itself is then made to look like a pond with the water line slightly above the teacher's head when standing. Blue film covers the windows to simulate the water line of the pond. Replicas of animals and plants at the water's edge and underwater cover the walls. The tape deck plays water sounds and pond animal sounds. At least 50 resources fill the room—books and other printed materials about ponds plus Internet and multimedia resources. Models and pictures of pond animals and plants are available for close analysis and exploration.

Hands-on of the real thing provides input through examination of real world things but without the context of being there or immersion. In the case of the pond, there would be frogs and polliwogs, cattails, and so forth for students to handle and examine closely.

Hands-on of representational items provides input from models of real things such as plastic frogs and polliwogs. Without the context of being there or immersion or the experience of the real items, hands-on of representational items elicits little response. Such limited sensory input reduces pattern-seeking capabilities for many learners. Program-building opportunities are all very limited because real world applications are so difficult to create with only representational items.

Secondhand input can be found in books, computers, videotapes, and other multimedia presentations which can activate only sight, hearing, and eidetic imagery. Such limited input makes pattern-seeking difficult and provides no opportunities for program-building.

Symbolic is the most difficult input to process. Fewer than 20 percent of students can learn well through this type of input which includes such things as mathematical sentences and parts of speech. High linguistic and spatial intelligence is needed to make use of symbolic input, plus prior being there experiences related to the new learnings.

Figure 10D

Six Kinds of Sensory Input

When lesson planning, the 20 senses can be grouped into six input pathways as shown below.

The two kinds of input least used in classrooms, *being there* and *immersion*, provide the most sensory input. Conversely, the two most commonly used, *secondhand* and *symbolic*, provide the least sensory input. Your goal is to flip those percentages so that 90 percent of the sensory input during initial learning is from being there and immersion experiences and 10 percent from hands-on experience with the real thing.

Secondhand input—principally reading, Internet, and video— becomes a useful way to extend what has been learned only when sufficient sensory input through being there experiences supplemented with immersion have created an accurate and rich understanding of the thing to be learned.[13]

Input Pathways Toward Understanding. There is no shortcut to the brain. All input must come through the senses. When it comes to the 20 senses, "less is more" is emphatically ***not*** true. More is better, and 20 senses fully engaged is a must.

MARY FROGGINS

The best way to stimulate the brain is to provide massive amounts of sensory input that activate all our senses, not just the traditional five (sight, hearing, touch, smell, and taste).

Figure 10E

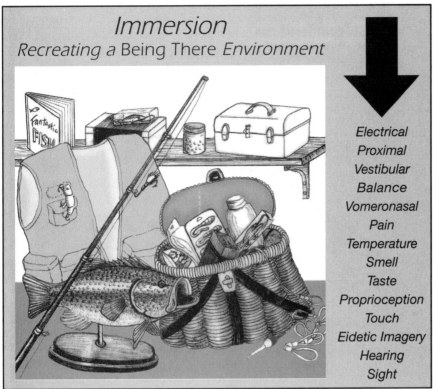

Figure 10F

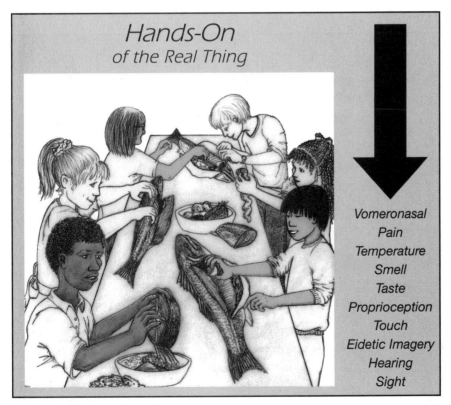

Figure 10G

ENRICHMENT THEORY

More About Sensory Input

Six Kinds of Sensory Input

Why *Being There* Experiences?

MARY FROGGINS

Our window on the world is far more powerful than conventional thinking indicates. Human beings have at least 20 senses, not five. And, not surprisingly, there is a direct correlation between the number of senses activated and the amount and locations of brain activity. Quite simply, the greater the range of sensory input, the greater the physiological activity and growth in the brain. The result is more learning and a greater likelihood that such learning will be retained in long-term memory.

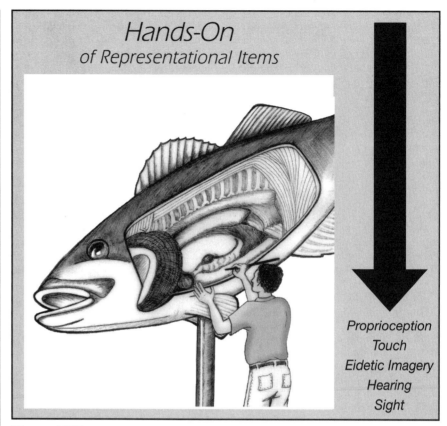

Figure 10H

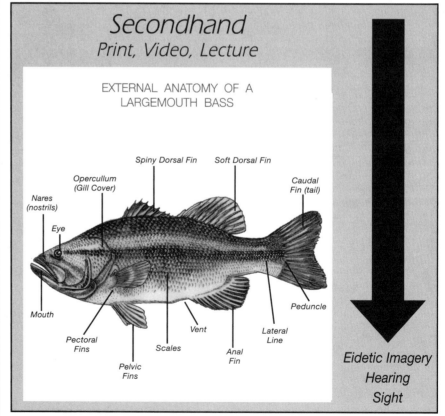

Figure 10I

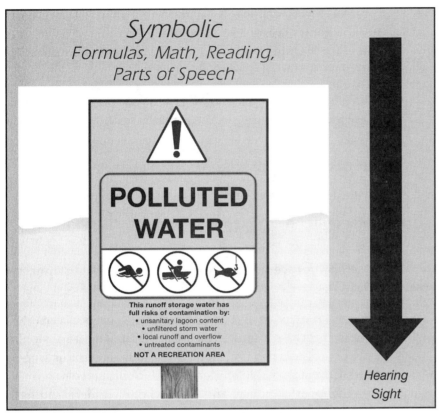

Figure 10J

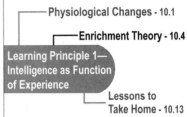

Why Being There *Experiences?*

Using *being there* experiences to engage all 20 senses and make learning come alive is powerful because they:

- Provide the massive sensory input needed to create physiological changes in the brain that wire learning into memory

- Demonstrate how and why concepts and skills are used in the real world

- Remind students of previous related experiences (and knowledge) and illustrates future possibilities for work or hobbies

- Clarify and correct misconceptions

- Overcome inequities in student experience

- Provide a base for second-language acquisition

The power of being there experiences as the basis for curriculum development and instruction is well documented. The States' Education and Environment Roundtable study, *Closing the Achievement Gap: Using the Environment as an Integrating Context for Learning,* is one of many studies documenting a wide range of benefits. According to

ENRICHMENT THEORY

More About Sensory Input

Six Kinds of Sensory Input

Why *Being There* Experiences?

MARY FROGGINS

The two kinds of input least used in classrooms, being there and immersion, provide the most sensory input. Conversely, the two most commonly used, secondhand and symbolic, provide the least sensory input.

this study involving 40 schools K-12 and more than 250 educators in 13 states, the general results of using the environment as an integrated context for learning improved science and general outcomes. General outcomes included the following:[14]

- Better performance on standardized measures of academic achievement in reading, writing, math, science, and social studies

- Reduced discipline and classroom management problems

- Increased engagement and enthusiasm for learning

- Greater pride and ownership in accomplishments (for students and staff)

The specific improvements in science were particularly impressive, including:[15]

- Increased knowledge and understanding of science content, concepts, processes, and principles (99%). The hands-on, minds-on approaches typical of EIC (Environment as Integrating Context) enable students of all ability levels to improve their performance, and gain a better understanding and appreciation for science.

- Better ability to apply science to real-world situations (99%). Involvement in real-world, project-based activities seems to help students refine their abilities in scientific observation, data collection, analysis, and formulating conclusions.

- Greater enthusiasm and interest in learning science (98%).

The impact on the brain of an enriched environment, particularly being there supplemented with immersion and hands-on of the real thing, is equally well documented. According to Dr. Diamond, a number of physiological changes occur when the brain is immersed in an enriched environment:[16]

1. Dendritic spines grow, change shape, or shrink as we experience the world. Neurons grow larger. The brain becomes denser and heavier. Therefore, choose the types of input that will produce the greatest physiological change in the brain.

2. The stimulation of an enriched environment results in significant physiological change in the brain—as much as 20% compared to brains in sterile, boring environments.

3. There is a correlation between brain structure and what we do in life—what we spend time doing and not doing.[17] In other words, how we spend our time—what we ask our brain to do on a daily basis—actually alters its physical

structure. Vast amounts of time spent on television and/or video games (4-6 hours daily) wire the brain to do television and video games and does not wire the brain for other things such as physical exploration or high facility for initiating and processing language.

4. Much of the increase in the physical size of the brain (at birth, the brain is one-quarter of its eventual adult size) is due to myelination, a process by which fatty tissue forms around the axons of frequently firing neurons which act like rubber insulation on electrical cords. This allows for speedier and more reliable transmission of electrical impulses. While much of this process occurs with the unfolding maturation of the brain[18] much can be deliberately enhanced through ample practice in using the knowledge or skill being learned, particularly in real-world settings which allow for rich sensory input and feedback.

5. Use it or lose it is a maxim for all ages—birth through old age. "Brains don't just steadily make more and more connections. Instead, they grow many more connections than they need and then get rid of those that are not used. It turns out that deleting old connections is just as important as adding new ones."[19] This is especially important when the previous learning is wrong or incomplete.

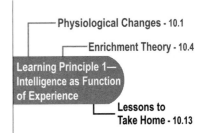

Physiological Changes - 10.1

Enrichment Theory - 10.4

Learning Principle 1—
Intelligence as Function
of Experience

Lessons to
Take Home - 10.13

LESSONS TO TAKE HOME WITH YOU

1. Eliminate or drastically reduce low-sensory input materials and processes such as textbooks, worksheets, and working in isolation. Use being there experiences outside your classroom to provide large amounts of sensory input. Remember, dittos don't make dendrites!

2. Design curriculum and instructional strategies that encourage practice and mastery in everyday situations, rather than aiming at quick quiz responses that usually stop at the ability to recognize content but don't demand students understand and and are able to use it. Using knowledge and skills greatly increases development and maintenance of neural connections.

END NOTES

1   See Marion Diamond with Janet Hopson, *Magic Trees of the Mind: How to Nurture Your Child's Intelligence, Creativity, and Healthy Emotions from Birth to Adolescence* New York: Penquin, 1998) and Frank Smith, *to think* (Teachers College Press, New York, 1990), 105–108.

2   The early work leading up to the now established field of epigenetics hit the popular press in a Pultizer Prize winning series by Ron Kotulak in the *Chicago Tribune* in 1995, then released as a book in 1996. See *Inside the Brain: Revolutionary Discoveries of How the Mind Works* (Andrews McMeel Publishing, Kansas City, MO, 1996). Kotulak reported that elements in one's environment trigger (or don't trigger) genes to express themselves. This results in differences in structural wiring which in turn makes for differences in behavior. Shocking in its time, the research has been confirmed and expanded. For a layman's introduction to the exploding field of epigenetics, see *Ghost in Your Genes*, a DVD produced by the BBC, expanded in 2008 by WGBH Educational Foundation, and shown on *NOVA*.

3   An eminent cognitive psychologist known for his groundbreaking research in cognitive mediation and practice, Reuven Feurstein established the principle that "all children can learn" while working with culturally deprived, retarded, and autistic children. His classroom curriculum, designed to build the cognitive functions of students diagnosed by others as incapable of learning, provides students with the concepts, skills, strategies, operations, and techniques necessary to become independent thinkers. The program is called Instrumental Enrichment.

4   If teachers and administrators took Marian Diamond's Enrichment Theory to heart, workbooks and dittos would have to go. As Susan Kovalik has often said, "Dittos and worksheets don't make dendrites."

5   This is not a new idea. Jane Healy in *Endangered Minds: Why Our Children Don't Learn* weighed in on this issue in 1990; John Ratey expanded the information in 2001, Elkhonon Goldberg in 2001 and 2005, John Medina in 2008, to mention but a few. It is now a well-established scientific fact. See also the field of epigenetics.

6   John Ratey, *A User's Guide to the Brain: Perception, Attention, and the Four Theaters of the Brain* (New York: Pantheon Books, 2001), 19–20.

7   Marian Diamond observed the impact of boredom on young and adolescent rats: "A boring environment had a more powerful thinning effect on the cortex than an exciting environment had on cortex thickening. Young rats are obviously very susceptible to losing mental ground when not challenged, and that shrinkage shows up after just four days. In rodent teenagers, at least, the shrinkage can begin to be reversed again after four days of enrichment." Given the number of parallels between the effects of enrichment and boredom on the brains of rats and humans that have proven true, this is quite disturbing. Among many things, it should cause us to reexamine the school calendar. It would appear that the traditional agrarian calendar with three months of summer vacation works strongly against those who most depend upon the public schools for learning. See Diamond and Hopson, 31.

For an discussion of how this brain fact applies to the classroom, see *Exceeding Expectations: A User's Guide to Implementing Brain Research in the Classroom,* 5th ed., by Susan J. Kovalik and Karen D. Olsen (Federal Way, WA: The Center for Effective Learning, 2010), especially Chapters 1 and 12.

8   "Use it or lose it" is more than a catchy phrase or metaphor. It applies to the brain "directly and literally." See Elkhonon Goldberg, *The Executive Brain: Frontal Lobes and the Civilized Mind* (Oxford: University Press, 2001), 209; John Ratey, *A User's Guide to the Brain: Perception, Attention, and the Four Theaters of the Brain* (New York: Pantheon Books, 2001), 24; and Diamond and Hopson, , 31.

9   For a powerful, electrifying image of how dendrites grow and connect in the brain, see Diane Sawyer, "Your Child's Brain," *ABC News Prime Time* (January 25, 1995).

10 William Calvin, author of *How Brains Think: Evolving Intelligence, Then and Now,* talks about competing choruses, each singing its own message or answer and trying to get others neurons to agree. The chorus best able to recruit neighboring neurons into singing its song determines which competing message wins out. An example of this is when we "can't make up our mind." Choice A or B, is it a cheetah or a leopard? (Conversations with William H. Calvin, January, 1997, Covington, Washington.)

11 Diamond and Hopson, 26. We strongly recommend this book to parents who are committed to helping their child reach his or her potential.

12 *Molecules of Emotion: Why We Feel the Way We Feel* (New York: Scribner, 1997) by Candace Pert gives an extraordinary glimpse into the molecular basis of emotion. It provides the scientific underpinings for Robert Sylwester's comment that "Emotions drive attention which drives learning, memory, problem solving, and just about everything else."

13 One can't overstress the importance of full sensory input through *being there* experiences in building the necessary neural wiring for understanding the concepts involved. Once understanding through sensory input and prior experience is brought together, secondhand input allows the learner to extend and expand learning.

14 Gerald A. Lieberman and Linda I. Hoody, *Closing the Achievement Gap: Using the Environment As an Integrating Context for Learning*, Executive Summary (Poway, CA: Science Wizards, 1998), 7.

15 Lieberman and Hoody, 46.

16 Diamond and Hopson, 48.

17 Also noted by Jane Healy in 1990 and Jeff Hawkins in 2004 (see *On Intelligence: How a New Understanding of the Brain Will Lead to the Creation of Truly Intelligent Machines* with Sandra Blakeslee. New York: Times Books/Henry Holt and Company, 2004).

18 Diamond and Hopson, 48. See also Piaget and Larry Lowery on age appropriateness, Chapter 7.

19 Another method of brain organization is pruning, the result of a chemical wash of neurons that are not connected. The synapses that carry the most messages get stronger and survive, while weaker synaptic connections are cut out. Experience determines which connections will be strengthened and which will be pruned: connections that have been activated most frequently get preserved. Between about age 10 and puberty, the brain will ruthlessly destroy its weakest connections, preserving only those that experience has shown to be useful. See A. Gopnik, A. Meltzoff, and Patricia Kuhl, *The Scientist in the Crib: Minds, Brains, and How Children Learn* (New York: William Morrow and Company, 1999), 189. For an electrifying description of how the fetal brain forms, connects, organizes, prunes, and operates, see Ratey, 25–26.

NOTES TO MYSELF

CHAPTER 11

LEARNING PRINCIPLE 2 — THE INSEPARABLE BODYBRAIN LEARNING PARTNERSHIP

Given the Western world's love affair with rational, logical thought and the underpinnings of science and technology, investigating the biological basis of emotion has been slow in coming. But once begun, brain research in this area has exploded, especially in the last 15 years of the 20th century and early 21st century. Today we must talk in terms of a bodybrain partnership, an inseparable partnership running parallel, complementary information systems. This partnership is a combination of an electrical and chemical system and a system that's wholly chemical carrying the molecules of emotion.[1]

A BRIEF HISTORY

One of the earliest attempts to analyze the role of emotion in brain function emerged from Dr. Paul MacLean's work at the National Institute for Health in the 1950s. MacLean was the first to make clear that emotions significantly affect brain functions and thus learning, memory, and behavior. However, MacLean mistakenly perpetuated the assumption that we mostly operate from our cerebral cortex, known for its logic and rational thinking and the home of academic learning, and only occasionally downshift into our limbic system. Now we know that emotions are a function of the entire bodybrain partnership and are with us all of the time. Emotions, in fact, filter incoming sensory input, modulating what the cerebral cortex attends to, processes, and stores in long-term memory. Emotions truly are the gatekeeper to learning and performance.

Somewhat to our surprise, we have discovered that emotions are processed throughout the entire brain and all of its structures not just the interconnected structures of the amygdala, hippocampus, thalamus, hypothalamus, and cingulate gyrus, an area once referred to as the limbic system.

EMOTION—GATEKEEPER TO LEARNING AND PERFORMANCE

What happens in our brains when emotionally charged sensory data comes in? A great deal. Here's the brief version of what happens within the limbic structures:[2]

MARY FROGGINS

This chapter is about the science of teaching science. It sinformation makes for fascinating reading in its own right.

To make it your own, think about your personal journey as a learner and a teacher and the students who illustrate these principles.

- The walnut-sized thalamus, located in the center of the brain, receives, sorts, and forwards almost all input from the sensory organs. It is the relay station for all of the 20 senses, except the olfactory or sense of smell, which goes directly to the cortex. Some sensory information from the thalamus travels to the amygdala, which is essential to decoding certain emotions, particularly those related to potential dangers in the environment.

- The almond-shaped amygdala is located close to the hippocampus, in the frontal portion of the temporal lobe. Sensory information arrives at the amygdala via either the short, fast, but imprecise route directly from the thalamus or the long, slow, precise route from the various sensory cortexes. Information coming to the amygdala directly from the thalamus arrives very quickly and helps us prepare for potential danger before we even know exactly what it is. After receiving the information from the thalamus, the amygdala sends signals to the hypothalamus, informing it of potential danger.

- The hypothalamus, a pecan-sized structure below the thalamus, unleashes a host of chemicals that raise blood pressure, increase heart rate, release fat into the bloodstream and in many other ways prepare the body to fight, flight, or freeze.[3] This rapid automatic response often means the difference between life and death.

- The hippocampus, Greek for seahorse because of its shape, seems to be primarily responsible for helping form and find long-term memories which are actually stored elsewhere in the cerebral cortex.

- The cingulate gyrus, located on top of the corpus callosum that connects the two hemispheres of the brain, helps resolve ambiguous situations. The cingulate gyrus reviews incoming sensory data from the 20 senses and determines whether the data has emotional significance. It then coordinates the retrieval and analysis of memories about previous similar situations and relays information to the prefrontal cortex for a decision about what to do.

The prefrontal cortex acts like the CEO of the brain, coordinating and integrating almost all basic brain functions. Unlike most other animals that can primarily react to sensory input, humans have a large prefrontal cortex that permits proactive behavior that anticipates and prepares for challenges. When there is sufficient time, it's the prefrontal cortex that analyzes possible choices and makes the decision as to the best action for the bodybrain to take.[4]

Sensory information sent directly from the thalamus to the amygdala and then on to the hypothalamus for the appropriate fight, flight, or freeze response helps get us out of danger fast. Information sent via the long, slow, precise route from the sensory cortex to the amygdala arrives after the brain has had a chance to process the input and decide if it really is threatening. The prefrontal cortex also seems to be involved in the final phase of confronting a danger, where, after the initial automatic, emotional reaction, with input from the cingulated gyrus, the brain must react and choose the course of action to move us out of the dangerous situation. The connections between the prefrontal cortex and the amygdala help the amygdala store additional information such as perceptions of sight and sound to create an automatic response the next time a similar dangerous situation is perceived. Meanwhile, our memory immediately stores details of where we are, what we are doing, who we are with, what we are feeling, and when this is happening in the hippocampus.

The connections between prefrontal cortex and amygdala are also involved with anxiety. At times, the prefrontal cortex can gain some control over anxiety, but at other times our creative prefrontal cortex generates anxiety through imagination of failure or presence of dangers that do not actually exist. When students are anxious or fearful for either real or imagined reasons, the amygdala may begin its automatic response and hijack the thinking, reasoning prefrontal cortex.[5] The only learning that takes place during this time is the amygdala's recognition of another potential danger to add to its list of automatic responses to remove the body from danger. Reflective thinking and long-term learning do not take place during times of real or perceived threat.

Emotions and Learning

According to Goldberg, the prefrontal cortex becomes particularly active during emotional experiences. "The function of the prefrontal cortex is to calculate 'what is good for the organism,' more than to calculate 'what is true' in an abstract, dispassionate sense."[6] Engaging the prefrontal cortex in determining what's good for the organism seems to be critical for the formation of new cognitive routines and patterns so that learning can take place.

The sensory data gathered from constantly scanning the environment for patterns in the form of sensory data is stored throughout the brain and is then available to help form neural connections as further learning takes place. However, we can't take in all of the sensory information available to us. If every bit of the sensory data available to us came into the brain all at once, we would suffer sensory overload. The brainstem, the thalamus, and the sensory cortex together form

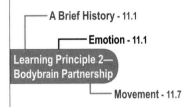
EMOTION—GATEKEEPER TO
LEARNING AND PERFORMANCE

Emotion and Learning

Information Substances:
The Rest of the Story

the RAS, or reticular activating system. The RAS acts somewhat like a dimmer switch or volume control to filter the amount of sensory input that makes it to our cortex. Important data that we are paying attention to makes it past the filter to the cortex where the patterns are manipulated, processed, combined with other future learnings, and turned into programs and long-term memories.[7]

When classrooms are safe and free from threats, the thalamus allows life to go on in a normal pattern and learning is possible. Providing relevant and meaningful curriculum that students can experience both emotionally and cognitively encourages involvement of the prefrontal cortex and helps it to determine what is good for the organism and what can and should be moved to long-term storage. Lack of engagement often happens when information and skills are broken down into small discrete parts that do not allow students to see patterns and search for novel solutions. Using instructional strategies that tap the power of emotion such as collaborative learning, simulations, music, and drama enable students to engage more systems in their brains and make learning powerful and memorable.

So it would seem that the structures of the brain make learning and performance an emotionally driven function.[8]

Information Substances: The Rest of the Story

For 100 years, scientists have understood the basic electrical-chemical building blocks of learning in the brain: Nerve cells (neurons) grow dendrites (structures that receive information from other neurons) and axons (structures that send information to other neurons and then send electrical impulses down the axon to the synapse. At the synapse, chemical messengers jump (actually float across) the tiny gap of synapse to the dendrites of the next neuron.

However, the neurotransmitters in the brain responsible for the synaptic leap are but one category of information substances found throughout the body and brain that carry out the process we call learning. The term "information substances" was coined initially by Francis Schmitt, elder statesman of neuroscience from the Massachusetts Institute of Technology, to describe a variety of transmitters, peptides, hormones, factors, and protein ligands that make up a second system. In this system, chemical information substances travel the extracellular fluids circulating throughout the body to reach their specific receptors on cells located not just in the brain but throughout the body.[9] Candace Pert, in *Molecules of Emotion: Why We Feel the Way We Feel*, provides a stunning, layman-friendly account of this system in action.

MARY FROGGINS

Achieving bodybrain-compatibility for your students is not the result of following a checklist. The concepts from brain research cannot be implemented by a few simple strategies. Effective implementation will only come through full understanding of the brain research and the richness of its implications.

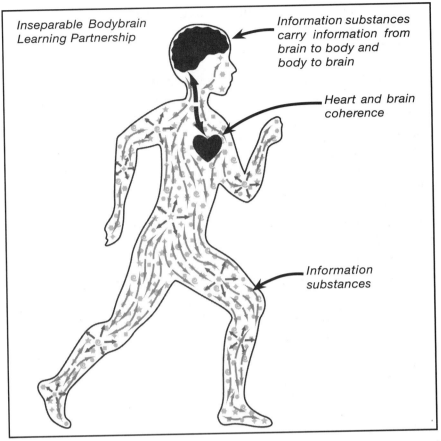

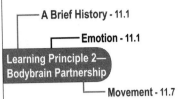

Figure 11A

Some neuroscientists now speculate that less than two percent of neuronal communication actually occurs at the synapse.[10] Less than two percent! Most of the information received by a neuron is taken in by the receptors at the cell's surface. And no wonder. The number of receptors on a neuron is staggering; current estimates are tens of thousands to a million plus per neuron.[11] That's a lot of potential for conversation! It would appear that the ability to perceive understandable patterns and learn from them is so important to survival that it cannot be posited only in one place or with one method of communication—not just one part of the neuron (at the synaptic gap) nor just in the brain. The entire body is involved.[12]

So just what are these information substances and what is their role in learning? These molecules, or ligands, are the basic units of a language used by cells throughout the organism to communicate across systems such as the endocrine, neurological, gastrointestinal, and even the immune system. As they travel, they inform, regulate, and synchronize.[13] Peptides are the largest category of information substances; one kind or another is produced in every cell in the body, not just by cells in the brain. Furthermore, every peptide now known to be produced within the body has receptors in the brain, thus quali-

EMOTION—GATEKEEPER TO
LEARNING AND PERFORMANCE

Emotion and Learning

**Information Substances:
The Rest of the Story**

MARY FROGGINS

An undeveloped potential is just that, an undeveloped brain capable of less intelligent behaviors. It is our responsibility as educators to provide the kinds and amounts of sensory input that will ensure that each student's brain is developed to the full range of its capacity.

fying each peptide to be considered a neuropeptide. This means that the body talks to the brain, giving it information that alters its messages back to the body and vice versa.

Emotions are the result of multiple brain and body systems that are distributed over the whole person in reaction to external and internal input. Emotions are; we don't consciously create them. We cannot separate emotion from cognition or cognition from the body.[14]

The Molecules of Emotion. The effect of such conversations on the organism is to change physical activity cell by cell and as a total organism, "including behavior and even mood—the closest word to emotion in the lexicon of hard science."[15] Examples of outward manifestation of such inner "conversations" include a gut feeling about something; a first impression of someone as untrustworthy; a physical restlessness that something is wrong before you can put your finger on it; a spark in the eye that says, "I get it even though I can't yet explain it"; a passion for one's hobby; deep love for the beauty of nature; the contentment of a quiet hour spent with a special friend. As was foreseen by the now virtually abandoned triune brain theory,[16] core limbic brain structures such as the amygdala, hippocampus, and hypothalamus—which were long believed to be involved in emotional behavior—contain a whopping percent of the various neuropeptide receptors studied to date, perhaps as high as 85 to 95 percent.[17] Now add to that the startling finding that several of the key emotion molecules such as endorphins can be found in single-cell animals as well as on up the evolutionary trail. Peptides, it appears, have been carrying information since before there were brains, leading researchers such as Antonio Damasio to assert that "emotion is the highest part of our mindbody survival kit."[18] One of their key roles is to tell the brain what's worth attending to and the attitude with which one attends.

Emotion as Filter. Another important piece of this new view of learning as a bodybrain partnership is the discovery that there are other locations in the body where high concentrations of almost every neuropeptide receptor exist. One example is the dorsal horn (the back side of the spinal cord) which is the first synapse with the nervous system where all somatosensory information is processed. In fact, in virtually all locations where information from the senses enter the nervous system, there are high concentrations of neuropeptide receptors. Such regions, called nodal points or hot spots, seem to be designed so that they can be accessed and modulated by almost all neuropeptides as they go about their job of processing information, prioritizing it, and biasing it to cause unique neurophysiological changes. Thus, peptides filter the input of our experiences, significantly altering our perception of reality and the input selected and allowed in during any learning situation.[19] According to Dr. Candace Pert, author of *Molecules of Emo-*

tion: Why You Feel the Way You Feel, "Emotions and bodily sensations are thus intricately intertwined, in a bidirectional network in which each can alter the other. Usually this process takes place at an unconscious level but it can also surface into consciousness under certain conditions or be brought into consciousness by intention."[20]

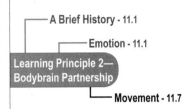

Implications. In summary, this wholly chemical system of learning, that parallels the electrical-chemical system of neurons, dendrites, axons, and synapses, expands our definition of learning in multiple ways. We now know the following:

- The body and brain form an inseparable learning partnership. Each sends messages out to the other which alters the messages that are sent back. Most sensory input (if not all) is filtered through and modulated by our emotions which direct our attention. What we attend to then drives learning, problem solving, and memory. Conversely, if we do not attend, learning and memory cannot occur.

- Therefore, the environment of the body is critical—the physical surroundings and the quality of interrelationships of those in it (student to student and student to adult). Consequently, brain compatibility begins with ensuring that the classroom and schoolwide environment enhance rather than impede students' ability to focus on the learning at hand. Two essential aspects are an absence of threat (real and perceived) and the creation of a sense of community.[21]

MOVEMENT TO ENHANCE LEARNING

During the 1980s and 1990s, the wellness movement extolled and sold the virtues of physical fitness as a means increasing mental sharpness and reducing stress, to overall health and well-being. But the story now emerging from brain research is amazing. As Carla Hannaford is fond of saying, "The body grows the brain."[22] Indeed, animals that don't move, don't have a brain. And those like the sea squirt that move early in its life cycle, later reabsorb their brain when they permanently affix themselves to a stationary object.[23]

Brain Research

Brain research into the relationship between movement and cognition is startling. The major findings that we believe are key for classroom teachers are the following:

- Movement is fundamental to the very existence of a brain.

MOVEMENT TO
ENHANCE LEARNING

Brain Research

Implications

MARY FROGGINS

An undeveloped potential is just that, an undeveloped brain capable of less intelligent behaviors. It is our responsibility as educators to provide the kinds and amounts of sensory input that will ensure that each student's brain is developed to the full range of its capacity.

Only an organism that moves from place to place requires a brain.[24]

- The entire front half of the brain—the newest in evolutionary terms—is devoted to organizing action, both physical and mental.[25] "Higher" brain functions have evolved from movement and still depend on it.

- Movement is crucial to every brain function including planning and executing plans, memory, emotion, language, and learning.[26]

- The ability to mimic, one of young human's most powerful avenues for learning, is movement based.[27]

- Aerobic exercise, a minimum of 35 minutes a day, unleashes a torrent of neurotransmitters that goad the brain into getting prepared to learn, speed procesing, and wire learning into long-term memory.[28]

Implications

When planning *being there* visitations, design as much action and activity into them as you possibly can. Keep students focused but keep them active.

Movement enhances powerful learning opportunities. The brain and the body are an inseparable partnership. When the educational environment demands that the students sit down and be still, the learning process is immediately affected. The body and brain are always talking and working together. Learning can be greatly enhanced when the bodybrain partnership is allowed to process motor and mental functions simultaneously.

For an in-depth discussion of the importance of movement and how to incorporate it into your curriculum and instructional strategies, see Chapter 14, pages 14.10–14.17.

END NOTES

1   See Candace Pert, *Molecules of Emotion: Why We Feel the Way We Feel* (New York: Scribner, 1997).

2   Robert Sylwester, *How to Explain a Brain* (Thousand Oaks, CA: Corwin, 2005), 160–161, 18, 85–86, 82, 46, 69–70.

3   Recent research suggests that the female brain responds to threat differently than the male brain. It is interesting to note that almost all brain research has been done with men. When studies are done with women, the results are quite interesting.

4   See *A User's Guide to the Brain: Perception, Attention, and the Four Theaters of the Brain* (New York: Pantheon Books, 2001) by John Ratey.

5   Synthesized from information found under the topic of "Emotions and the Brain" on the website titled "The Brain from Top to Bottom," located at http://www.thebrain.mcgill.ca/flash/index_i.html. Material was developed by Bruno Dubuc in conjunction with Douglas Hospital Research Center in Quebec and the Canadian Institutes of Health Research: Institute of Neurosciences, Mental Health and Addiction. Hosted by McGill University, all material on the website is copyright free.

6   Elkhonon Goldberg, *The Wisdom Paradox: How Your Mind Can Grow Stronger as Your Brain Grows Older* (New York: Gotham Books/Division of Penquin Books, 2005), 229.

7   Patricia Wolfe, *Brain Matters: Translating Research into Classroom Practice* (Alexandria, VA: ASCD, 2001), 76–86.

8   Robert Sylwester has synthesized a good deal of research into a very useful and memorable phrase: "Emotion drives attention, attention drives learning/memory/problem solving/just about everything else." See "The Role of the Arts in Brain Development and Maintenance," 6. Available at http://ode.state.or.us/teachlearn/subjects/arts/resources/rolesbraindevelopment.pdf. Also see Sylwester *A Biological Brain in a Cultural Classroom* (Thousand Oaks, CA: Corwin, 2003), 126 and *A Child's Brain:The Need for Nurture* (Thousand Oaks, CA: Corwin, 2010).

9   Pert, 139.

10 Pert, 140.

11 Conversations with Dr. Candace Pert, Best of the Best Invitational sponsored by Susan Kovalik & Associates, Tukwila,WA, May, 1998.

12 An amazing but still mysterious discovery is the presence of cells through the digestive track—from mouth to anus—that are identical to neurons in the brain. Dr. Candace Pert and other scientists wonder aloud if these cells may be the source of our "gut feelings."

13 Pert, 26-27.

14 Ratey, 223.

15 Pert, 38.

16 Joseph LeDoux, "The Emotional Brain," presentation at Emotional Intelligence, Education, and the Brain: A Symposium, Chicago, IL, December 5, 1997. See also *The Emotional Brain: The Mysterious Underpinnings of Emotional Life* (New York: Simon and Schuster, 1996).

    Given the typical time lag between findings within the brain research community and education, it will likely be some years into the 21st century before reference to the triune brain is abandoned and new ways of talking about, and implementing, the power of emotion in the bodybrain partnership are developed and put into widespread use.

17 Pert, 133.

18 Antonio Damasio, "Thinking About Emotion," presentation at "Emotional Intelligence, Education, and the Brain: A Symposium," Chicago, IL, December 5, 1997. See also *Descartes' Error: Emotion, Reason, and the Human Brain,* (New York: G. P. Putnam Sons, 1994).

19 Pert, 141-142. Somasensory refers to any bodily sensations or feelings, whether it's the touch of another's hand on our skin or sensations arising from the movement of our own organs as they carry on our bodily processes.

20 Pert, 142.

21 There are many useful definitions of community that can be readily and powerfully applied to the classroom. In *Creating Community Anywhere,* Carolyn Shaffer and Kristin Anundsen define community as "a dynamic whole that emerges when a group of people participate in common practice, depend on one another, make decisions together, identify themselves as part of something larger, and commit over the long term to their own, one another's and the group's well-being." (See *Creating Community Anywhere,* New York: Putnam's Son, 1993), 10.

22 Carla Hannaford, presentation at Summer Institute, Susan Kovalik & Associates, 2000.

23 Ratey, 156.

24 This statement underscores the intertwined nature of movement and the brain. No movement, no need for a brain. Movement is the defining organizer of the brain, sequencing thought as well as physical movement. See Hannaford, Goldberg, Ratey, and Medina.

25 Ratey, 150, 148.

26 This principle is now established science. See Hannaford, Goldberg, Ratey, and Medina. For an extended discussion about how this applies to the classroom, see *Exceeding Expectations: A User's Guide to Implementing Brain Research in the Classroom*, 5th ed., by Susan J. Kovalik and Karen D. Olsen (Federal Way, WA: The Center for Effective Learning, 2010), especially Chapters 2, 12, and 17.

27 The discovery of mirror neurons is rewriting what we know about how the brain learns. Although the research in this field is just getting underway, it is causing a revolution, much as the discovery of DNA did in biology.

28 The tide of neurotransmitters unleashed by aerobic exercise has caught researchers by surprise. From returning a shrunken hippocampus (where new memories are made) to its original size to the increase in student health scores, 35 minutes of daily aerobic exercise, the results are startling. No school can afford to pass up this means of improving student achievement.

LEARNING PRINCIPLE 3 — MULTIPLE INTELLIGENCES

Since the 1980s, our definition of intelligence has changed dramatically. We used to be told that intelligence was a singular, general characteristic set by genetics — people were either across-the-board smart or not so smart. Of course, all of this was determined by a paper-and-pencil test that distilled human capability down to a single number, an intelligence quotient or IQ number. And, clearly, to have an IQ of 120 was far more desirable than 100. Or is it?

NATURE VERSUS NURTURE

The current, broad-based view of intelligence refutes the belief that intelligence, however defined, is immutably set by genetics, that what you were born with is what you will end up with. Although genes do play a significant role, experiences from conception to death also shape intelligence. As science and our own common sense and personal and professional experiences tell us, lots of practice solving real problems and creating products of value does increase capacity to do so. We call this increase in capacity to make connections in order to solve ever more complex problems and create more resourceful and valuable products an increase in intelligence.

For example, the country author, having decided at age five that what she would do with her life was become a teacher, hoped desperately to become a vocal music teacher. Her genetic gifts, however, did not include perfect pitch or even an ear that would allow her to play anything but a fixed-pitch instrument such as a piano. Yet, through her thousands of hours of practice, double and triple what students with innate musical talent spent, she did succeed in significantly increasing her musical intelligence — her problem-solving and product-producing capability in music. However, her product, holding her own in eight-part harmony, was accomplished through compensating measures — using the feel of the vibration in her throat (if it was "off," she knew she had either the wrong note or poor tone; in either case, stop for a bar and then pick up again later). But she also knew she would never be able to rise to the level of excellence that those with inborn musical intelligence could achieve quite easily. Nor could she rise to a level of adequacy to train and direct musical groups. She therefore switched her teaching career to language arts, an area of innate gifts.

The decision to abandon music was deeply disappointing but an important lesson to the country author as a future educator. Even

MARY FROGGINS

And although each intelligence is a distinct entity meeting his research requirements, Garnder acknowledges that ". . . only the blend of intelligences in an individual makes possible the solving of peroblems and the creation of products of significance."[3]

though she couldn't hit the pinnacle of music performance, there wasn't a moment of her musical experiences—singing with community and church groups and as a music minor in college—that she doesn't cherish to this day. Although painful, the lesson she learned is that the purpose of public education ought to be that of assisting students to develop all of one's intelligences. Our goal should be giving students options in life—options which make life rich and deeply satisfying in both work and personal interests.

The country author's story is not uncommon. Parents everywhere have watched their children struggle and triumph, embracing a vocation or hobby challenging to them or pursuing another area that they find easier to develop. In effect, we each have our own experiences and observation of the "nature-nurture" debate as it rages on, becoming more hotly contested with each passing decade. With the discovery of epigenetics,[1] that genes are turned on or off due to the environment, the nature-nurture debate is no longer an argument had by two camps; it's a singular argument about a fully entwined, integrated reality. The environmental effects on one generation can influence the genetic expression in a later generation, and the ongoing environment affects which of our genes will be turned on and which will be turned off throughout our lives, creating a cascading effect influencing who we become year by year.

This area of brain research is riveting and promises profound impact on educational practices.

We believe that it is the responsibility of every teacher to develop curriculum and instructional strategies that will enable every student to develop all his or her intelligences, to become Renaissance citizens, capable of rendering informed decisions in the voting booth, developing rich relationships within family and community, and nurturing a wide range of interests and skills by which to earn an adequate living and pursue a satisfying life richly lived.

THE THEORY OF MULTIPLE INTELLIGENCES

Gardner's definition of intelligence is an infinitely practical way to look at human capacity and behavior across cultures. As he developed his theory of multiple intelligence, he used several criteria:[2]

- Each intelligence had to be relatively independent of the others, with its own timetable for development, peak growth, and the like.

- Each had to operate from a different part of the brain.

- Each had to be valued in at least one culture around the world.

The Multiple Intelligences Defined

According to Gardner, intelligence ". . . entails a set of problem-solving skills, enabling the individual to resolve genuine problems or difficulties that he or she encounters and, when appropriate, to create an effective product; it also entails the potential for finding or creating problems, thereby laying the groundwork for the acquisition of new knowledge."[4]

And, very importantly, an individual's intellectual gifts in one area cannot be inferred from his or her capacities in another.[5] For example, high mathematical ability doesn't necessarily mean the student will also be reading above grade level.

In his first book published in 1983, *Frames of Mind: The Theory of Multiple Intelligences*, Gardner identified seven intelligences. In the 1990s, he added an eighth intelligence, naturalist, and discusses a basis for two others—existential and spiritual.[6]

The brief descriptions of the original seven intelligences and the naturalist intelligence, that begin on the next page, provide curriculum designers and classroom teachers alike with beginning outlines for restructuring curriculum for the classroom. The task is a significant one because most of today's curriculum addresses only two of the multiple intelligences—logical-mathematical and linguistic—yet all are needed to succeed in life.

From core curriculum standards to homework assignments to extra-credit work, the multiple intelligences should be woven into our lesson planning and instructional strategies. We must ensure that our curriculum speaks to all learners, not just those high in linguistic and logical-mathematical intelligences.

Multiple Intelligences Versus Modalities

To grasp the power of Gardner's theory of multiple intelligences, one must make a distinction between how students take in information (through eyes, ears, touch, taste, and body, sometimes referred to as modalities) versus how students process information inside their brains in order to first make meaning of the input and then use it to act upon the world. Remember that these intelligences are sets

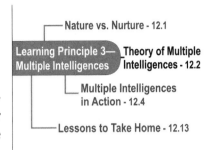

Logical-mathematical

Linguistic

Spatial

Bodily-kinesthetic

Musical

Intrapersonal

Interpersonal

Naturalist

Figure 12A

THE THEORY OF MULTIPLE INTELLIGENCES

The Multiple Intelligences Defined

Multiple Intelligences vs. Modlities

A Reality Check

MARY FROGGINS

Thinking about intelligence as a capability to act upon the real world instead of as a number on an IQ test is an important step toward commonsense and reality.

of problem-solving and product-producing skills and knowledge, not merely gateways through which information passes to reach the brain. Do not equate modalities with Gardner's intelligences.[7]

A Reality Check

As you read this definition of the multiple intelligences, keep in mind real-life examples, such as the occupations of your extended family and friends, the intense interests and capabilities of students you've known over the years. After reading each one, jot down the name of at least three people you know well who typify that problem-solving and/or product-producing capability. You'll find you already know a great deal about these intelligences. Although considered "theoretical" in science, they seem more like common sense in real life.

MULTIPLE INTELLIGENCES IN ACTION

While it's rare that we use only one intelligence at a time, it's useful to describe each one separately. We can then better recognize them in action.

Logical-Mathematical Intelligence

Logical-mathematical intelligence operates primarily in the left hemisphere, front and back of both sides of the brain.

This problem-solving and/or product-producing capability is the home of science and math. The core function of this intelligence is the interaction with the world of objects—ordering and reordering them, assessing their quantity, comprehending numerical symbols, appreciating the meaning of signs referring to numerical operations, and understanding the underlying quantities and operations themselves.[8]

Children high in logical-mathematical intelligence:[9]

- Compute arithmetic problems quickly in their head

- Enjoy using computers

- Ask questions such as, "Where does the universe end?" "What happens after we die?" and "When did time begin?"

- Play chess, checkers, or other strategy games, and win

- Reason things out logically and clearly

- Revise experiments to test out things they don't understand

- Spend time working on logic puzzles such as Rubik's Cube

This intelligence appears early and the most productive work is done by age 40 if not by age 30. The basis for all logical-mathematical forms of intelligence springs from the handling of objects; later these processes become internalized ("done in one's head"). One proceeds from objects to statements, from actions to the relations among actions, from the realm of the sensorimotor to the realm of pure abstraction—ultimately to the heights of logic and science.

The classical description of the development of this intelligence, the home of science and math, is that by Piaget. His work remains an accurate description of the development of logical-mathematical intelligence. However, his work does not describe development of the other intelligences.

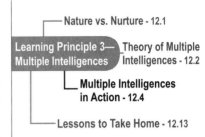

Linguistic Intelligence

Linguistic intelligence operates predominantly in the left hemisphere—temporal and frontal lobes.

Linguistic competence is the most widely and most democratically shared across the human species. As Gardner says, "one could not hope to proceed with any efficacy in the world without considerable command of phonology, syntax, semantics, and pragmatics."[10]

The core operations of language, used with special clarity, include sensitivity to the following: the meaning of words; the order among words, such as using the rules of grammar, and, on carefully selected occasions, choosing to violate them; the sound, rhythm, inflection, and meter of words; and the different functions of language—its potential to excite, convince, stimulate, convey information, or simply to please.

The major uses of linguistic intelligence include[11]

- Rhetoric—the ability to use language to convince others of a course of action

- Mnemonics—a tool to help one remember information

- Explanation—the ability to use oral and written language to teach and learn

- Metalinguistic analysis— the use of language to reflect upon language, to explain its own activities

MULTIPLE INTELLIGENCES
IN ACTION

Logical-Mathematical

Linguistic

Spatial

Bodily-Kinesthetic

Musical

Intrapersonal

Interpersonal

Naturalist

Without question, high linguistic intelligence is over 80 percent of the formula for success in traditional schooling. Without it, schooling is painful and frustrating to students and the failure rate is obscenely high despite their competence in the other intelligences. Current brain research makes clear that there are many ways of knowing, of taking in information about the world. The most powerful of these is not through reading or lecture, but rather, through full sensory input from the real world.

Children strong in linguistic intelligence[12]

- Like to write

- Spin tall tales or tell jokes and stories

- Have a good memory for names, places, dates, or trivia

- Enjoy reading books in their spare time

- Appreciate nonsense rhymes and tongue twisters

- Typically spell words accurately and easily

- Enjoy crossword puzzles and games, such as Scrabble

MARY FROGGINS

We suggest that you ignore the naturalist intelligence during your lesson planning. In our opinion, Gardner's description of the naturalist intelligence is how the brain operates as a whole—as a pattern seeker genetically programmed over thousands of years to make sense of and learn from the natural world. We believe that the new definition of learning as a pattern-seeking and meaning-making activity carried to application and long-term memory is the more valuable notion when developing curriculum and planning instructional strategies.

Spatial Intelligence

The spatial intelligence operates predominantly in the right hemisphere

The core operations of this intelligence depend on the ability to image. It also involves the capacity to perceive the visual world accurately, perform transformations and modifications upon one's initial perceptions, and re-create aspects of one's visual experience, even in the absence of relevant physical stimuli. This intelligence should be arrayed against and considered equal in importance to linguistic intelligence. Loosely put, the mind's link to language is through pictures, not sound. This intelligence is as critical as linguistic intelligence because the two are the principal sources of information storage and solving problems.[13]

Spatial intelligence is a collection of related skills. The images produced in the brain are helpful aids to thinking; some researchers have gone even further, considering visual and spatial imagery a primary source of thought.[14]

For many of the world's famous scientists, their most fundamental insights were derived from spatial models rather than from mathematical lines of reasoning. Einstein once commented: "The words of the language, as they are written and spoken, do not play any role in my mechanisms of thought. The psychical entities which seem to serve as elements in thought are certain signs and more or less clear images which can be voluntarily reproduced or combined. . . . The above mentioned elements are, in my case, of visual and some muscular type."[15] Examples of imaging as a primary source of thought are Darwin and the "tree of life," Freud and the unconscious as submerged like an iceberg, and John Dalton's view of the atom as a tiny solar system.

It's important to note that spatial intelligence should not be equated with the visual sensory modality. Even people who are blind from birth can develop spatial intelligence without direct access to the visual world.

A keenly developed spatial intelligence is not only an invaluable asset in our daily lives but is also essential for understanding the application of what is learned in school.[16] This is particularly true in areas where the elements are abstract and unseen (microscopic in size or invisible physical science areas such as the forces of gravity, electricity, magnets, and so forth).

Children strong in spatial intelligence[17]

- Visualize while reading

- Spend free time engaged in art activities

- Report clear visual images when thinking about something

- Easily read maps, charts, and diagrams

- Draw accurate representations of people or things

- Like it when you show movies, slides, or photos

- Enjoy doing jigsaw puzzles or mazes

- Daydream a lot

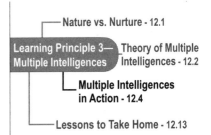

Nature vs. Nurture - 12.1

Learning Principle 3—Multiple Intelligences / Theory of Multiple Intelligences - 12.2

Multiple Intelligences in Action - 12.4

Lessons to Take Home - 12.13

Bodily–Kinesthetic Intelligence

The location where bodily-kinesthetic intelligence operates in the brain is affected by handedness. There is a tendency for left hemisphere dominance in right-handed people and a right hemisphere dominance in left-handed people.

Characteristic of this intelligence is the ability to use one's body in highly differentiated and skilled ways for expressive as well as goal-directed purposes, such as the mime, actor, athlete, and tradesman. This intelligence also brings the capacity to work deftly with objects, both those that involve the fine motor movements of one's bodily motions and the capacity to handle objects skillfully.[18]

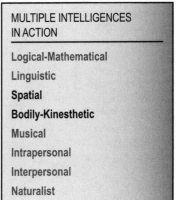

MULTIPLE INTELLIGENCES IN ACTION

Logical-Mathematical

Linguistic

Spatial

Bodily-Kinesthetic

Musical

Intrapersonal

Interpersonal

Naturalist

MARY FROGGINS

Over 100 years ago, for example, Aldous Huxley remarked that "What emerges most strikingly from recent scientific developments is that perception is not a passive reception of material from the outside world; it is an active process of selection and imposing of patterns."[22]

The findings Huxley referred to were well known in fields more scientifically oriented than education then and that are thoroughly established now. Brain researchers of the 1990s accept this as a given. We do not have to look far for confirmation—our own daily experience tells us most convincingly that the brain has this ability and has it to an astounding degree.[23]

Not only is the body an instrument for acting on knowledge, to a degree greater than previously understood, it is also an active partner in learning.

Children strong in bodily-kinesthetic intelligence[19]

- Use body language to communicate thoughts and emotions

- Do well in sports and recreational hobbies requiring physical skill and effort

- Move, twitch, tap, or fidget while sitting in a chair

- Engage in physical activities such as swimming, biking, hiking, or skateboarding

- Need to touch people when they talk to them

- Enjoy scary amusement rides

- Demonstrate skill in a craft like woodworking, sewing, or carving

- Cleverly mimic other people's gestures, mannerisms, or behaviors

- Easily remembers information when given movement cuing systems. For example, the algorithm for long division could be expressed as first you divide (clap-clap), multiply (tap crossed hands twice), subtract (outward slicing movement of both hands twice), and then bring it down (two hands pulling imaginary pipe down as if chinning yourself). (See *I Can Divide and Conquer* video and companion book by Martha Kaufeldt.[20])

Involving the rest of the body in any learning event increases the neural activity of the brain, activates the motor areas of the brain which assist in sequencing thought, increases the positive flow of epinephrine which aids transfer from short-term memory to long-term memory, and releases positive molecules of emotion.

Recent research, reported convincingly by both Elkhonon Goldberg and John Ratey, reveals that movement plays a critical role in learning and life and may not be as separate a function as first suggested by Howard Gardner. In *The Executive Brain: Frontal Lobes and the Civilized Mind*, Goldberg states that various features of cortical representations of objects and of word meanings denoting objects "are stored close to the sensory and motor areas that participated in acquiring information about these objects."[21] Furthermore, it is the motor part of the brain that sequences our thoughts. Ratey, in *A User's Guide to the Brain: Perception, Attention, and the Four Theaters of the*

Brain, states that "movement is crucial to every other brain function, including memory, emotion, language, and learning . . . our 'higher' brain functions have evolved from movement and still depend on it." He goes on to say that "Motor function is as crucial to some forms of cognition as it is to physical movement. It is equally crucial to behavior, because behavior is the acting out of movements prescribed by cognition. If we can better understand movement, we can better understand thoughts, words, and deeds."[24]

Musical Intelligence

Musical intelligence operates primarily in the right hemisphere.

This intelligence is the most separate from the other intelligences and is the earliest to appear. For individuals high in this intelligence, composing and performing at age five, as Mozart did, is not unusual. It makes itself known as early as age three. Core functions include pitch, melody, rhythm, timbre (tone), and pattern.

Students who are unusually high in musical intelligence and relatively low in linguistic intelligence will use their musical intelligence skills to "translate" language into rhythmic patterns. An example of this type of student is the one whose body begins to jive and tap the instant the teacher begins to speak, stopping the second the teacher stops talking, restarting with the next burst of speech—all in rhythm with the teacher's words. Content in rhyme can be readily absorbed by these students while the same information in an uninspiring lecture or in the stilted prose of a science textbook can be completely indigestible. Monotone speakers have particularly deadening effects on highly musical students.[25]

Musically gifted children[26]

- Play a musical instrument and/or sing

- Remember melodies of songs

- Tell you when a musical note is off-key

- Say they need to have music on in order to study

- Collect records or tapes

- Sing songs to themselves

- Keep time rhythmically to music; hum and drum

MULTIPLE INTELLIGENCES IN ACTION

Logical-Mathematical

Linguistic

Spatial

Bodily-Kinesthetic

Musical

Intrapersonal

Interpersonal

Naturalist

Intrapersonal and Interpersonal Intelligences

Both intrapersonal and interpersonal intelligence are far more diverse and culturally dependent than the other intelligences.

Extreme circumstances, such as times of war, subjugation, famine, disaster in general, recession or depression, and life-or-death situations, greatly affect the expression of these intelligences. All of these circumstances make demands for action that most people don't practice. They are one-time or seldom-experienced happenings. Yet the cultural beliefs and premises held by society demand that we respond to these events and express ourself in certain ways, depending upon locale, age, status in the community, etc. In short, these are problem-solving situations requiring problem-solving intelligences. Although not so dramatic, daily living demands the same kinds of problem-solving from us.

 Intrapersonal Intelligence involves the examination and knowledge of one's own feelings, the "sense of self"—the balance struck by every individual and every culture between the prompting of inner feelings and the pressures of others.

The core capacity of intrapersonal intelligences is access to one's own "feeling life"—the range of our emotions, our capacity to instantly discriminate among these feelings and, eventually, to label them, to draw upon them as a means of understanding and guiding our behavior.[27]

At its advanced level, intrapersonal knowledge allows one to detect and to symbolize complex and highly differentiated sets of feelings, e.g., the novelist who can write introspectively about feelings, the patient or therapist who comes to attain a deep knowledge of his own inner world of feelings, the wise elder who draws upon his or her own wealth of inner experiences in order to advise members of the community.

Children strong in intrapersonal intelligence[28]

- Display a sense of independence or a strong will

- React with strong opinions when controversial topics are being discussed

- Seem to live in their own private, inner world

- Like to be alone to pursue some personal interest, hobby, or project

MARY FROGGINS

Both intrapersonal and interpersonal intelligence are far more diverse and culturally dependent than the other intelligences.

- Seem to have a deep sense of self-confidence

- March to the beat of a different drummer in their style of dress, their behavior, or their general attitude

- Motivate themselves to do well on independent study projects

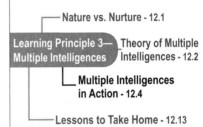

Interpersonal Intelligence involves looking outward toward the behavior, feelings, and motivations of others.

The core capacity of interpersonal intelligence is the ability to notice and make distinctions among other individuals and, in particular, among their moods, temperaments, motivations, and intentions.[29]

In an advanced form, interpersonal knowledge permits a skilled adult to read the intentions and desires of many other individuals — even when those have been hidden. This intelligence also permits us to act upon such knowledge, such as when influencing a group of disparate individuals to behave along desired lines; it's what we call leadership. We see highly developed forms of interpersonal intelligence in political and religious leaders (a Mahatma Gandhi, a John Fitzgerald Kennedy, or a Mother Teresa), in skilled parents and teachers, and in individuals enrolled in the helping professions, be they therapists, counselors, or concerned friends.

Interpersonally gifted children[30]

- Have a lot of friends

- Socialize a great deal at school or around the neighborhood

- Read people's intentions and motives

- Get involved in after-school group activities

- Serve as the "family mediator" when disputes arise

- Enjoy playing group games with other children

- Have a lot of empathy for others

Naturalist Intelligence[31]

The functions of the naturalist intelligence are not specific to a certain part of the brain but rather are dispersed throughout the brain. In fact, the entire brain is a pattern-seeking, allowing people to distinguish among, classify, and use features of the environment.[32]

Howard Gardner suggests that this intelligence develops on its own in most children, ". . . particularly those who have a chance to

MULTIPLE INTELLIGENCES IN ACTION

Logical-Mathematical

Linguistic

Spatial

Bodily-Kinesthetic

Musical

Intrapersonal

Interpersonal

Naturalist

MARY FROGGINS

Our behavior, and that of our fellow human beings, has long been one of life's greater mysteries. Behavior—its building blocks and why specific building blocks are chosen at any one moment in time—must be understood if we are to create schools that foster real learning.

*We act very largely by programs. The word **programs** need not alarm us with visions of robots. It means simply a fixed sequence for accomplishing some **intended objective**. In other words, we act to carry out some purpose, some personal, individual, and usually self-selected purpose—the exact opposite of robot behavior.*

spend time out of doors—in both rural and urban/suburban settings. The real trick is to maintain it, in the face of different pressures in school."[33] The naturalist pays attention to flora and fauna, noticing critical distinctions. Charles Darwin exemplifies the keen observation, curiosity, and awareness of patterns essential for strength in this intelligence. In a farming or hunting culture, persons strong in the naturalist intelligence are highly valued to ensure the group's continued success.

Placed in a culturally diverse environment, the naturalist picks up on characteristic patterns of speech, movement, dress, and the like with the result that he can both recognize group members and choose to conform and fit into the setting. People who move easily from mainstream to minority cultural environments are strong in naturalist intelligence.

Children who are talented naturalists[34]

- Ask many questions about their environment

- Delight in large collections of natural objects, e.g., insect collection

- Enjoy scouting or similar activity allowing them to pursue an interest at their own pace

- Stay intensely involved in an activity, not wanting to stop

- Are sensitive to patterns in the environment such as at the lake, in the woods, on the street, and in the classroom

- See structure and order where others see only noise or random elements

A Note About the Naturalist Intelligence. While it may seem that the naturalist intelligence should be the focus of science study, we suggest that you ignore it during your lesson planning. In our opinion, Gardner's description of the naturalist intelligence is how the brain operates as a whole—as a pattern seeker genetically programmed over thousands of years to make sense of and learn from the natural world. We believe that the new definition of learning as a pattern-seeking and meaning-making activity carried to application and long-term memory is the more valuable notion when developing curriculum and planning instructional strategies.

LESSONS TO TAKE HOME

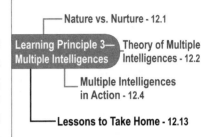

The multiple intelligences identify important ways for students to solve problems and produce products, each of which operates from a different part of the brain. If students are having difficulty learning a concept or skill, provide inquiries which call on the intelligence(s) of their strength. Later, when their understanding is solid and they're practicing how to use concepts or skills in order to wire them into long-term memory, teachers should provide inquiries which call on other intelligences. This wide input and processing not only helps cement long-term memory but also strengthen students' problem-solving and product-producing capabilities in all areas of intelligence.

Also, keep in mind that student demonstrating of what they have learned is a product under Gardner's definition.

Do the activities within each intelligence strike a familiar chord? They should. Each of us is born with all of these intelligences but we tend to develop those valued by our culture (home, school, church, community). It is the goal of the bodybrain-compatible classroom to make sure that all intelligences are developed and used on a daily basis.

LESSONS TO TAKE HOME

END NOTES

1 For fascinating accounts of the interacting of genes and environment, see Ron Kotulak, Richard Restak, MD, *The New Brain: How the Modern Age Is Rewiring Your Mind* (Emmaus, PA: Rodale Inc., 2003), and more recently, a fascinating DVD produced by the BBC, *Ghost in Our Genes*.

2 The criteria used by Howard Gardner to define an area of intelligence helped ground his theory in hard science about the brain. See *Frames of Mind: Theory of Multiple Intelligences*. New York: Basic Books, 1983.

3 Gardner, x.

4 Gardner, 60-61.

5 Gardner, xiii.

6 Since his initial work in the 1980s, Gardner has considered evidence for three additional intelligences: naturalist, spiritual, and existential. See Chapters 4 and 5, *Intelligence Reframed* by Howard Gardner. The naturalist intelligence is considered the strongest candidate so far. However, as you read through this chapter and Chapters 9 and 10 about how to develop bodybrain-compatible curriculum, you will notice that we do not utilize the naturalist intelligence.

There are several reasons:

• Gardner himself states that the naturalist intelligence develops on its own in most children. We believe that well constructed being there experiences, along with teaching the scientific thinking processes, will provide ample practice in observing, classifying, and using features of the environment.

• We believe that Gardner's comment that the "pattern-recognizing talents of artists, poets, social scientists, and natural scientists are all built on the fundamental perceptual skills of naturalist intelligence" is *incorrect*. In our opinion, "pattern-recognition" as described in Chapter 4 *is a general function of the entire brain, not just that of the naturalist intelligence.* This is consistent with the fact that Gardner does not assign the function of naturalist intelligence to a particular region of the brain as he does the first seven intelligences.

• In effect, the naturalist intelligence does not meet Gardner's initial criteria for identifying distinct intelligences.

Gardner's definition of intelligence is an extremely useful alternative to the standard IQ number. See *Frames of Mind*, x.

7 According to Howard Gardner, "Intelligences are not equivalent to sensory systems" (*Frames of Mind*, 68). The theory of multiple intelligences expands and replaces our previous understandings of sensory input, such as the modalities. Such frames of reference were based upon observing from the outside, variations in student learning behavior and then, based on such observations, making assumptions about how students learn.

In contrast, current research into how the human brain learns—the focus of this book—is based on high-tech observations of the inside of the brain as it is operating. These observations about what the brain is actually doing as it thinks and learns then allow us to determine what educational practices will assist the brain to do its job most naturally and thus most powerfully.

This difference is critical because although you may find considerable overlap in recommended instructional strategies for modalities and multiple intelligences, implementation of each of those instructional strategies must differ in subtle but powerful ways because the whys and whats behind what you are trying to achieve are different.

In simple terms, modalities focus on instructional approaches and materials that provide input through different pathways to the brain—kinesthetic, taste, and smell as well as visual and auditory. In contrast, multiple intelligences focus on how the brain processes information once it gets to the brain—how it uses what it learns to solve problems and/or produce products. The difference is between the route through which input arrives versus ways of processing and thinking about what comes in.

8 Gardner, *Frames of Mind*, Chapter 7.

9 Thomas Armstrong, *In Their Own Way* (New York: Tarcher Press, 1987).

10 Gardner, Chapter 5.

11 Gardner, Chapter 5.

12 Armstrong, 20.

13 Gardner, 177.

14 For a teacher-friendly tool for strengthening spatial intelligence, the best resource we have found is Nanci Bell, *Visualizing and Verbalizing for Im-*

proved Language Comprehension and Thinking: A Teacher's Manual (San Luis Obispo, CA: Academy of Reading, 2005).

15 Gardner, 190.

16 Gardner, 190.

17 Armstrong, 18.

18 Gardner, 190.

19 Armstrong, 21.

20 *I Can Divide and Conquer* by Martha Kaufeldt, a 55-minute DVD illustrating how to teach long division, is one of the best illustrations of teaching to the multiple intelligences that we have ever seen. (Federal Way, WA: Susan Kovalik & Associates, 1985). Now available through Books for Educators, www. books4educ.com.

21 Elkhonon Goldberg, *The Executive Brain*, 65-66.

22 Leslie Hart's conceptualization of learning is an extremely important contribution to the field of learning because it is comprehensive enough to cover the wide range of practicalities that teachers, administrators, and parents face on a daily basis—from establishing curriculum to instruction to assessment.

23 Leslie Hart published his first book on the human brain and implications for teaching and learning 35 years ago, *How the Brain Works: A New Understanding of Human Learning, Emotion, and Thinking* (New York, Basic Books, 1975). At the time, Soviet neuroscientists were far ahead of those in the United States.

Hart collected original studies and neuroscience journals from all over the world. His in-home reference library at the time was more extensive and complete than most universities. His synthesis of that early research, and his ability to see practical applications, was astonishing, leading him to an understanding of the brain far beyond his contemporaries and now solidly confirmed by research over the past 20 years.

Human Brain and Human Learning, written in 1987 applies his conception of learning specifically to public education. Last updated in 2001, it's a fascinating book, easily readable by laymen and teachers. See *Human Brain and Human Learning*, 3rd ed. (Black Diamond, WA: Books for Educators, 2002).

24 John Ratey, *A User's Guide to the Brain*, 48.

25 Gardner, Chapter 6.

26 Armstrong, 22.

27 Gardner, Chapter, 10.

28 Armstrong, 24.

29 Gardner, Chapter 10.

30 Armstrong, 23-24.

31 For reasons discussed in End Note 6, we do not use the naturalist intelligence in our curriculum work.

32 E. F. Shores, "Howard Gardner on the Eighth Intelligence: Seeing the Natural World," *Dimensions of Early Childhood* (Summer, 1995), 5-7.

33 Shores, 5-7.

34 Armstrong, 34-35.

NOTES TO MYSELF

PRINCIPLE 4: LEARNING IS A TWO-STEP PROCESS

Leslie Hart, a pioneer in synthesizing and applying brain research to education, defines learning as a two-step process.[1] In his view, and our experiences, students must not only be able to detect and understand patterns but also be able to use them, first with guidance in familiar settings and then in varying situations on one's own until the ability to use the knowledge or skill is readily at hand, almost automatic.

This definition of learning carries us far beyond that assumed by makers of standardized tests. For example, the typical multiple-choice and true/false questions can be answered based on a faint ring of familiarity of one answer over another. "Choice B rings a bell . . ." "Hmm, that statement doesn't sound familiar, so it must be false . . ." The test taker doesn't even have to understand the content.

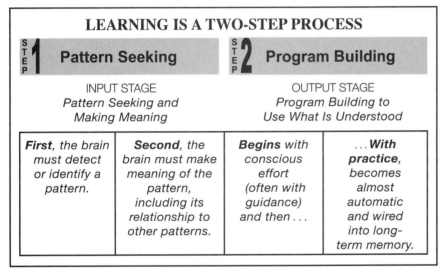

LEARNING IS A TWO-STEP PROCESS

STEP 1 Pattern Seeking		STEP 2 Program Building	
INPUT STAGE *Pattern Seeking and Making Meaning*		OUTPUT STAGE *Program Building to Use What Is Understood*	
***First**, the brain must detect or identify a pattern.*	***Second**, the brain must make meaning of the pattern, including its relationship to other patterns.*	***Begins** with conscious effort (often with guidance) and then . . .*	*. . .**With practice**, becomes almost automatic and wired into long-term memory.*

Figure 13A

Step Two of the learning process—being able to use what is understood and then to apply it until it becomes stored in long-term memory—isn't even considered by test makers.

STEP ONE: PATTERN SEEKING

The most notable characteristic of the human brain is its phenomenal penchant for seeking and detecting patterns. In his book, *Human Brain and Human Learning*,[2] Leslie A. Hart stipulates that ". . . no part of the human brain is naturally logical while it is learning,"[3] i.e., making meaning. (This is distinguished from its ability to use information already learned in a "logical" or sequential way if the situation so requires.) Instead, the brain learns by sifting through massive amounts of input arriving simultaneously from all the senses, processing thousands of bits of information per minute. Obviously, such information is processed in a multipath, multimodal way with the brain attending to changes in the pattern of incoming data.

The simultaneity of its processing makes patterns obvious while processing along one avenue at a time, however speedily, would produce no "aha," no sense of an overall picture whatsoever. Imagine if the brain processed only one set of information at a time, e.g., first vision, then hearing, then bodily-kinesthetic, and so on. Like the three blind men, recognizing an elephant would, at best, be an extremely time consuming and laborious task.

Pattern seeking progresses along a continuum: detection, identification, and understanding.

What Is a Pattern?

Hart defines a pattern as

> "An entity, such as an object, action, procedure, situation, relationship or system, which may be recognized by substantial consistency in the clues it presents to a brain, which is a pattern-detecting apparatus. The more powerful a brain, the more complex, finer, and subtle patterns it can detect. Except for certain species wisdom patterns, each human must learn to recognize the patterns of all matters dealt with, storing the learning in the brain. Pattern recognition tells what is being dealt with, permitting selection of the most appropriate program in brain storage to deal with it. The brain tolerates much variation in patterns (we recognize the letter a in many shapes, sizes, colors, etc.) because it operates on the basis of probability, not on digital or logic principles. Recognition of patterns accounts largely for what is called insight, and facilitates transfer of learning to new situations or needs, which may be called creativity."[4]

As the brain attempts to make sense out of the chaos which surrounds each of us, it constantly searches for patterns that can impose meaning on the input received. Its "aha" moments arise from detection of a recognizable (from the learner's perspective) pattern or patterns. This pattern detection propensity is seen in the operation of each of the senses. The ear registers every sound wave within its perceivable frequency but attends only to those that provide a meaningful pattern; for example, sounds of traffic or workshop chatter are ignored

MARY FROGGINS

Over 100 years ago, for example, Aldous Huxley remarked that "What emerges most strikingly from recent scientific developments is that perception is not a passive reception of material from the outside world; it is an active process of selection and imposing of patterns.[5]

The findings Huxley referred to were well known in fields more scientifically oriented than education then and that are thoroughly established now. Brain researchers of the 1990s accept this as a given.[6] We do not have to look far for confirmation—our own daily experience tells us most convincingly that the brain has this ability and has it to an astounding degree.

and only a friends's voice is tuned in or noted as a pattern to attend to. Similarly, the eye recognizes a chair. Be it a three-legged milking stool, a church pew, or the more common no-frills chair at the kitchen table, the eye does so by looking for the pattern or collection of attributes necessary for something to be a chair when one wants to sit down.

From the time we are born until we die, the brain takes in these patterns as they present themselves, sorting and categorizing in an attempt to make sense out of our complex world. Learning takes place when the brain sorts out patterns using past experiences to make sense out of new input the brain receives.

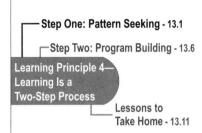

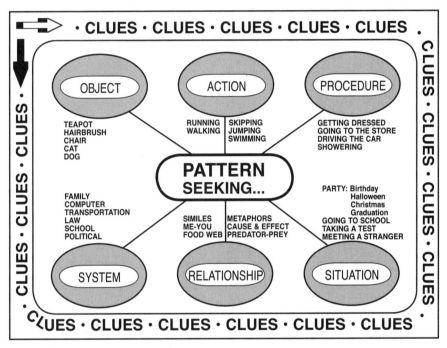

Figure 13B

Examples. This pattern-detecting aspect of the brain can be clearly seen in the brain's mastery of one of its biggest accomplishments: learning the mother language. Watch mothers just home from the hospital with their newborns (or even listen to them talk to their child in utero!). Mothers know how to teach language. They do not "dumb down" their language to the infant to single syllable communications. Instead, mothers discuss the everyday happenings of life and share their hopes and dreams for their little one—"When you grow up, you'll go to Stanford and become an astronaut. You'd like that very much, I think. Very, very exciting occupation." "Yikes, there are so many choices at this grocery store. Which brand was it that we tried last week that was so good?" "Come, it's time to toss in a load of laundry; we'll do the whites first with hot water." Why do mothers do this? Because it works. Because every noun and verb in the English dictionary (and in our curriculum) represents a pattern. Each has at-

STEP ONE: PATTERN SEEKING

What Is a Pattern?

Amazing Flexibility

**Perception: Pattern
or Hodgepodge**

tributes that distinguish one word from another. The more experience with the attributes, the finer the patterns that can be perceived; thus, choosing among words such as *pensive* and *melancholy* is not a random choice but a decisive match with someone's emotions at the moment.

Such a barrage of sounds coming at the child would at first seem a hopeless environment in which to master language. But an environment similar to the one previously mentioned—rich, random, even chaotic—gives large amounts of input to the child, and thus provides his or her mind with the opportunity to search for patterns. As educators, we have been carefully and logically taught that such an environment would make the task of learning a language impossible. Consequently, we teach English as a second language logically and carefully, "This is a pen. What is this? This is a _____." Unfortunately, the human brain does not learn well from such logical, tidy, greatly restricted input because it's so antagonistic to the learning methods the brain has perfected over the ages.

Natural Complexity Versus Piecemeal and Oversimplified.

In short, the mind is genetically designed to learn from the natural complexities of the natural world. To the extent that schools oversimplify, or make logical, or restrict the world's natural complexity is the extent to which schools inhibit the natural workings of the brain and restrict students' ability to learn. In contrast, meaningful input engages all of the senses. Logical, sequential curricula are highly brain antagonistic. Comments Hart, "Perhaps there is no idea about human learning harder to accept for people familiar with classrooms and schools than this: That the ideal of neat, orderly, closely-planned, sequentially logical teaching will, in practice with young students, guarantee severe learning failure for most."[7] A common mistake of the public schools is stripping down the input to a small amount of content, all analyzed and dissected into small bits, so that the "right" answer seems inescapable. This does *not* work. Patterns are the building blocks of meaning and should be the heart of curriculum development.

Stripping a learning situation of its richness also robs the child's brain of the possibility of perceiving patterns and thus making sense of what's in front of him or her. Ironically, we do this consistently with students who need special help. If they are slow, conventional wisdom has dictated that the task be broken into smaller and smaller pieces. We've now achieved pieces that are so small and so "easy"—only one item to focus on at a time—that there is no longer any pattern to perceive. Consequently, Chapter 1 students with their finely-chopped, oversimplified diet say, "I don't get it," which confirms to us that they are "slow." However, most Chapter 1 students are adept learners from away-from-school input. They come to us having learned their mother tongue and a wide range of skills for coping with life. Consider the

MARY FROGGINS

Step One—The brain makes meaning through pattern seeking. As it does so, it is not logical or sequential. **Step One of learning** *is the extraction, from confusion, of meaningful patterns.*[9]

Step Two—Most information we use is embedded in programs, a planned sequence to accomplish a purpose or goal; information not embedded in programs is generally unretrievable and thus unusable. **Step Two of learning** *is the acquisition of a mental program.*[9]

immigrant child who is the translator for the entire family, the urban child with street savvy, the migrant child with flexibility and resourcefulness to figure out each new setting from town to town.

Amazing Flexibility

The amazing flexibility of the brain in its pattern seeking is apparent in its ability to recognize the pattern of the letter *a*. We recognize it amid an amazing range of fonts, sizes, shapes, and positions.

Figure 13C

This speed and flexibility can occur because the brain naturally works on a probabilistic basis. The brain does not add up, for example, all the parts of a cat until all parts are perceived and accounted for: four legs, a tail, fur, meows, and purrs. Rather, the mind "jumps to the conclusion" that the pattern "cat" applies when only one or a few characteristics have been noted. While this jumping to conclusions sometimes gets us in trouble, it's crucial to rapid completion of myriad actions minute by minute. The rapid reader, for example, does not see every letter before deciding what the word is. Context clues or the mere outline of the word are used, in probabilistic fashion, to jump to conclusions.

In the example of our infant learning its mother tongue, language pours around the child for hours and hours a day. The more input, the more readily the child learns. The first patterns perceived are those that are most meaningful—the child's name and then the name of mom and dad. Patterns are at first quite gross, i.e., "Dadda" means any man in trousers. Over time, with continued rich input and immediate feedback, the patterns become more and more refined until, finally, the educated adult ends up with a vocabulary of 10,000+ words with subtle shades of meaning and the ability to use them with considerable precision.

The entire structure of language is based on pattern. For example, plurals mostly end in *s* except for mice, moose, and fish. Past tense ends with *ed.* Words ending in *ing* are a real thrill for most children. When they first grasp the *ing* pattern, everything is jumping, leaping, hitting, running, and so forth for several days until another pattern of language gets discovered. Every noun and verb in our language reflects a pattern.

STEP ONE: PATTERN SEEKING

What Is a Pattern?

Amazing Flexibility

Perception: Pattern
or Hodgepodge

Perception: Pattern or Hodgepodge

Pattern seeking is the brain's way of striving to extract meaning from the thousands of bits of input pouring into the brain each minute through the 20 senses. And, very importantly, what's one learner's pattern is another learner's hodgepodge. This is to say that we cannot predict what any one particular child will perceive as a pattern because so much depends upon prior knowledge, the existing neural networking of the brain used to process the input, and the context in which the learning takes place.

However, if the input is rich and varied, all learners can arrive at an understanding of the pattern to be learned.

STEP TWO: DEVELOPING PROGRAMS TO USE WHAT WE UNDERSTAND

According to Leslie Hart, the key to understanding behavior is "the realization that we act very largely by programs . . . a fixed sequence for accomplishing some intended objective." In other words, to carry on activities, one must constantly select a program from among those stored in the brain and put it to use.[10]

What Is a Program?

Hart defines a program as "A sequence of steps or actions, intended to achieve some GOAL, which once built is stored in the brain and 'run off' repeatedly whenever needed to achieve the same goal is perceived by the person. A program may be short, for example giving a nod to indicate 'yes,' or long, as in playing a piece on the piano which requires thousands of steps. A long program usually involves a series of shorter subprograms, and many parallel variations that permit choice to meet conditions of use. Many such programs are needed, for instance to open different kinds of doors by pushing, pulling, turning, thumbing a button or lever, and so on. Language requires many thousands of programs, to utter each word, type it, write it in longhand, print it, and so forth. Frequently used programs acquire an 'automatic' quality: They can be used, once selected, without thinking, as when one puts on a shirt. Typically, a program is CONSCIOUSLY selected, then run off at a subconscious level. In general, humans operate by selecting and implementing programs one after another throughout waking hours."[11]

MARY FROGGINS

Our behavior, and that of our fellow human beings, has long been one of life's greater mysteries. Behavior—its building blocks and why specific building blocks are chosen at any one moment in time—must be understood if we are to create schools that foster real learning.[12]

*The key to understanding human behavior is the realization that we act very largely by programs. The word **programs** need not alarm us with visions of robots. It means simply a fixed sequence for accomplishing some **intended objective**. In other words, we act to carry out some purpose, some personal, individual, and usually self-selected purpose—the exact opposite of robot behavior.*[13]

Examples. To understand the power of Hart's statements, consider some everyday examples. Simple ones are such things as a procedure for putting on one's shoes. There are the "right-foot-first" people and the "good heavens, no—the left first" folks. Same with putting on a coat. For high good humor, watch someone in a restaurant offering to help another with their coat. Of course, the assistant offers the coat in the manner that he or she would put it on—from the left, high up near the shoulder—while the recipient turns to receive the coat low from the right.

Or, how about the shower? Your favored hand grabs the soap and that soap knows just what to do. Zip! You're done with the shower. But, if for some temporary reason that hand can't get wet, the soap no longer remembers what to do. The result is much fumbling about, a shower that takes much longer, and the feeling of being not quite as clean and refreshed as usual. You can almost hear your mother's voice asking, "Did you wash behind your ears?"

For another example, think how many of us have driven miles with absolutely no recall of the journey. A little scary! Or, after being reassigned to a new school, we find ourselves one morning in the parking lot of our former school. How did that happen! Clearly, the wrong program was inadvertently selected; once selected, the brain ran the program through with no conscious thought from the owner.

The Program Cycle

The second step of learning—developing programs for using what is understood—has three stages:[14]

- Evaluate the situation or need (detect and identify the pattern or patterns). For example, is it a birthday, graduation, holiday, costume, or office party? (Each demands certain considerations, such appropriate dress, gift, contribution to the potluck, and so forth.) Ah, it's a birthday party.

- In response to the incoming patterns, select the most appropriate program from those stored. For example, because it's a birthday party you prepare to RSVP, buy a present, wear party clothes, and eat a skimpy breakfast and lunch because you know there will be cake and ice cream.

- Implement the program. For example, you execute your plans by going to the party and following the anticipated protocols, thereby having a great time.

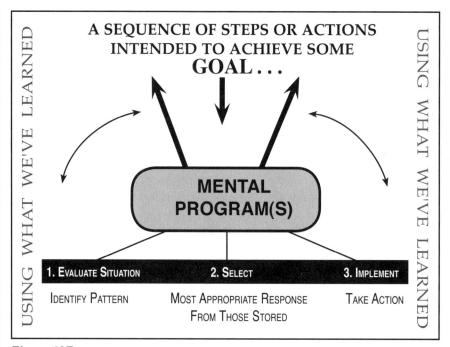

Figure 13D

MARY FROGGINS

We select the most appropriate program from those stored in the brain to deal with what is happening at the time. For example, seeing stairs ahead, I select a going-up-stairs program. Having accidentally jostled somebody, I choose an offering-apology program. Facing an arithmetical problem, I tap my division program. Meeting a neighbor, I select a greeting program, complete with smile, nod, and suitable words.[17]

Misbehavior in the classroom is best looked at as a failure of programs rather than as a cold-blooded effort to annoy the teacher. For example, too many programs for the wrong behavior or not enough programs for appropriate behavior or failure to recognize the clues which tell the student what programs or behaviors are appropriate under the circumstances.[18]

Remember, the learning process engages two steps where the first is detecting pattern (Step One—Pattern Seeking). Once a situation has been analyzed, and if action is required, the brain scans its repertoire of stored programs (Step Two—Program Building), selecting the one that is most appropriate or calling forth two or more and using them in fresh combinations. This step is carried out in three stages:[15]

EVALUATE   +   SELECT   =   IMPLEMENT

Program Cycle on a Continuum. The range of behaviors possible by this program cycle is enormous.

Toward the positive end of the continuum, such capacity to "use old programs in fresh combinations" underlies what we call creativity.[16]

On the negative end, this process is seen in the case of the student who repeatedly misbehaves. Wanting to attract the teacher's attention, this student reaches into his or her mental bag of programs and, as unconsciously as the driver arriving at the wrong parking lot, automatically pulls out a behavior that will attract attention. Unfortunately, the behavior also makes the teacher furious. In such students' mental bag of programs, there are too many of the "wrong" behaviors or programs and too few of the "right" ones, i.e., ones that get the attention of the teacher but without the anger.

Equally somber is the child-grown-adult who has no program for using multiplication for real-world applications such as computing mortgage payments or figuring the real cost of an item he or she purchased on the Visa credit card. Unpleasant consequences flow from lack of appropriate mental programs.

Successful implementation of a mental program is its own reward, accompanied by feelings of accomplishment and increased satisfaction. Aborting a mental program that doesn't work is emotionally unsettling because it leaves us unsure of what to do next and decreases our sense of self-confidence.[19] When orchestrating your curriculum, provide the time and experiences that allow youngsters to master new information and add it to prior knowledge in a meaningful way, thereby creating new mental programs.

The Acquisition of USEFUL Programs

Hart, in fact, defines learning as "the acquisition of useful programs."[20] Learning that does not result in acquisition of a mental program, such as getting an A on a paper-and-pencil test, is not learning from Hart's perspective because it doesn't stick. Hart points out that information that does not become part of a program is usually unretrievable—dumped from short-term memory and lost. For example, recall your sophomore college days and the traditional Western civilization class. The characteristics of this stunning experience: yearlong, 99.9 percent lecture, and an enormously fat textbook. For the midterm and final exams, you used the ubiquitous blue book. Weeks later when the blue book was graded and returned, you glanced inside. To your total shock, there were paragraphs of stuff you didn't even recognize—never heard of before! A classic example of information that never became part of a program and, thus, is unretrievable and often unrecognizable, even a bare three weeks later. In other words, most information that we use is embedded in programs; the corollary is: Information that is not used is also not retrievable and, if truth be told, was probably never "learned" in the first place. Thus, "covering information" is a colossal waste of time for both students and teachers.

The implications for the classroom of the 21st century are obvious—students must master concepts and skills with depth of understanding and use what they understand. We in turn need to present less content and give students time to "use" the information again and again in varying settings until the information is recallable in a usable form, i.e., a behavior, a program.

It should be noted that programs and subskills are not identical and have little in common. A program, while it can be enormously complex, such as driving a car, is a sequence for accomplishing some end—a goal, objective, or outcome—an end with meaning to the learner. Subskills, such as the blend *ch* or short *i* are not a sequence

STEP TWO: DEVELOPING
PROGRAMS TO USE WHAT
WE UNDERSTAND

What Is a Program?

The Program Cycle

Acquisition of Useful Programs

The Power of Programs

MARY FROGGINS

No aspect of being human appears more dominant than this incessant accumulation of programs. The process, of course, is most rapid in the earlier years, then gradually tapers off. But since we live in a world that changes constantly, we are under far greater pressure than our forebears to continue to learn, to continue acquiring new programs. The man of 75 who is given a DVD recorder to honor that birthday must master some new programs to operate his new machine. A few centuries ago, the programs acquired by age 25 would pretty well see one through a full life; today, much of what is learned by age 25 will become obsolete.[22]

Failure to keep on learning can prove restrictive, costly, or embarrassing.

for accomplishing some end; they are experienced as isolated, fragmented pieces. In contrast, the program to be attained is the act of reading—an insight young students can easily miss.

To reinforce the difference between pattern seeking (making meaning of input) and program building (using what is learned), consider diapering a baby. Everyone recognizes the patterns diaper and baby; however, as Diane Keaton makes clear in the movie *Baby Boom,* not everyone can diaper a moving baby. The same is true with returning a rental car. Everyone knows what the words car, return, rental, and airport mean. But not everyone has a mental program of the steps for returning a rental car to an airport.

Because this discussion of building programs and wiring knowledge and skills into long-term memory is so critical to what we as teachers do in the classroom, we are providing here part of Hart's description of program building from his book *Human Brain and Human Learning.*

The Power of Programs

According to Leslie Hart, the implications of the program concept of behavior—evaluate, select, implement—are stupendous, bringing not only fresh insights into human behavior but also generating some major guidelines for improving learning achievement.

Hart summarizes as follows:[21]

1. We live by programs, switching on one after another, selecting from those that have been acquired and stored in the brain.

2. As humans, we are far more dependent on programs acquired by the tens of thousands after birth, in contrast to animals that rely more on programs genetically transmitted.

3. A program is a fixed sequence for accomplishing some end—a goal, objective, or outcome. Our human nature makes the working of a program pleasurable; the concept of some after-the-event "reward" is neither necessary or valid. However, feedback is essential to establish that the program did work more or less as intended.

4. We can use only those programs that have already been built and stored. What programs another person has, or many people have, has no bearing. If a person does not possess a program, efforts to force its use are absurd.

5. We routinely use a three-step cycle: evaluate the situation (involving pattern detection and recognition), select the

program that seems most appropriate from our store; and implement it.

6. The abortion of a program—upon its failure to work—calls for recycling. When a high proportion of self-selected programs work well, confidence rises; when too many programs are aborted, confidence is reduced and the learner may become far less able to self-select programs.

7. Although laboriously built, fully acquired programs have an automatic quality that can easily lead one to forget that other individuals may not have acquired these programs.

8. Learning can be defined as the acquisition of useful programs.

9. Learning progress can be properly evaluated only by observing undirected behavior.[23] Questioning and testing dealing primarily with information can reveal little. It shows only poorly what individuals can do.

10. Effective transfer of learning depends on using established programs in new applications and combinations. (Skill in putting together new combinations may equal "creativity.") The learner who can adapt established programs to new tasks, by seeing similarities of patterns involved, learns much more rapidly than one who cannot.

11. In general, if we regard human learning and behavior in terms of continually asking, "What program is being used?" sharp new insights can be gained, and many confusions avoided.

LESSONS TO TAKE HOME

For educators, viewing behavior as a function of the program implementation cycle significantly expands our ability to observe and analyze student behavior during the learning process. Key observations include the following:

1. Unless the learner can reasonably and accurately evaluate the need or problem at hand (that is, detect and identify the patterns involved), the cycle goes astray at the outset. The student simply does not know what to do.

A familiar example is the student trying to cope with an arithmetic problem couched in words. Unable to detect the pertinent pattern, the student flounders, wondering whether to add, or divide, or give up entirely. Another example is spelling of longer words. Lacking any sense of the

MARY FROGGINS

The definition of learning as a Two-Step Learning Process is a powerful tool for lesson planning, formative assessment, making in-the-moment changes based on formative assessment.

Teach this definition to students and have them use it on a regular basis during their Learning Club debriefings.

structure or pattern of the word, the student tries to simply remember the order of the letters—perhaps producing some weird versions.[24]

2. People can access and use only those programs they already possess. However much one may be coerced or urged, or motivated or rewarded, there is no way to perform the program unless it has already been stored. He or she does not know how to do it. No program, no ability to perform the needed action.

There is no way to force a person to ride a bicycle, or play Chopin on the piano, or write a scientific paper, if those programs have not previously been acquired. That many other people can do these things has no bearing. Yet in almost any classroom, at any level, this principle is ignored. On the playground, one may hear a child being called "clumsy" or "poorly coordinated" when the real difficulty is that the child has not yet learned certain programs. In homes, parents scold children; in businesses, bosses scold employees—all in the same futile way for the same futile reason. If the program has not been acquired, the solution is to acquire it, not in criticizing, labeling, or giving a poor mark, practices that prove devastating to learners.

3. A student cannot implement a program unless given the chance to do so.

A test question might ask, "How can you verify the correct spelling of a word?" The answer intended is, "Look it up in a dictionary or on Google." A student who gives that answer, we must note, is not using that program. Rather, he or she is using a program for answering a question on a test. So commonly are tests used in instruction that this all-important difference may be overlooked; students may pass tests yet often be unable to carry out the programs themselves—a complaint loudly uttered today by both parents and next year's teacher. Similarly, if students are always directed to use certain programs, there is no way to know whether they can detect the pattern, have a program to select, and can implement it. Rather, they are implementing programs for following directions. Such "learning" may prove fictitious.

END NOTES

1   Leslie A. Hart, *Human Brain and Human Learning*, 3rd ed. (Black Diamond, WA: Books for Educators, 2002), Chapters 7–10. This definition forces us to rethink every aspect of education — curriculum content, instructional strategies, time allocation, tools and materials, and assessment. For an extended discussion of how this new brain-based definition of learning impacts the classroom, see *Exceeding Expectations: A User's Guide to Implementing Brain Research in the Classroom*, 5th ed., by Susan J. Kovalik and Karen D. Olsen (Federal Way, WA: The Center for Effective Learning, 2010), especially Chapters 4, 13–14, 16–17, and 19. Also see *What Brain Research Can Teach About Cutting School Budgets* by Karen D. Olsen (Thousand Oaks, CA: Corwin, 2010), especially Chapters 2–10.

2   To grasp the significance of Hart's conceptualization and definition of learning as a two-part process, consider for a moment what is required of a student taking a typical standardized test with its multiple-choice and true/false items. With both kinds of test items, the right answer is present. The student has only to detect the answer (pattern) that is most familiar (a process usually accompanied by a small niggling in the back of the brain that says, "Hey, we've heard of that one before!") "Familiar" doesn't represent understanding of the concept inherent in the test question; ability to apply in a real-life setting is clearly light-years away. Thus, in essence, the multibillion dollar testing juggernaut assesses only the first half of the first stage of learning. To push this realization further, consider the Friday quiz, also typically weighted heavily toward multiple-choice and true/false items. Often 80 percent is accepted as indication of mastery or merely turned into a letter grade, A–F, and then the whole class moves on to the next topic.

If America is disappointed in the student outcomes of its public schools, it must examine what definition of "learning" is serving as the basis for the design and implementation of its curriculum and instructional practices. If Hart's two-part definition of learning were adopted, outcomes would — and do — soar because it forces profound and radical change at the very core of the business of teaching-learning. See Hart, 166.

3   Hart, 100–101, 103.

4   Hart, 349.

5   Hart, 108.

6   Recent brain researchers have accepted *pattern seeking* as a descriptor of how the brain learns, including Goldberg, Ratey, Hawkins, and Medina to mention but a few. We have based the discussion on Hart's view of learning because his is a complete model of learning and he puts it squarely in the context of America's public schools. Thus, readers don't have to make the leap from theory to practice on their own. We strongly recommend that you take the time to read Hart's book.

7   Hart, 101.

8   Hart, 127.

9   Hart, 139, 151, 153, 159.

10 Hart, 143.

11 Hart, 350.

12 Hart, 152–153, 168-170.

13 Hart, 141.

14 Hart, 145.

15 Hart, 145, 165-168

16 Hart, 151.

17 Hart, 144.

18 Hart, 193.

19 Hart, 167. Self-esteem or self-concept programs have long had a questionable base, primarily a misguided approach aimed at helping students feel good about themselves as a result of others' telling them so rather than through helping them gain competence and build programs that work. Current brain research tells a different story about the brain's producing and receiving its own opiate-like molecules as a response to mental programs that work, to a sense of competence in handling the world. See Candace Pert, Ph.D., *Molecules of Emotion*; Stanley I. Greenspan, M.D. with Beryl Lieff Benderly, *The Growth of the Mind and the Endangered Origins of Intelligence* (New York: Addison-Wesley Publishing Company, 1997), 104; and Robert Sylwester, "The Neurobiology of Self-Esteem and Aggression" in *Educational Leadership*, 54, no. 5 (February, 1997), 75–78.

20 Hart, 139, 151-153, 159.

21 Hart, 152-153.

22 Hart, 143.

23 Hart, 167.

24 James Doran, director of Algonquin Reading Camp, Rhinelander, Wisconsin, once demonstrated to

Leslie Hart a simple, quick technique for giving students a sense of pattern that produced startling gains in their competency in spelling and reading. Examples such as this were the proof of the pudding for Hart . . . pattern seeking is the way the brain learns. Period. No exceptions, no matter what the subject area is.

For truly surprising gains in reading, spelling, and speech, see the LiPS program: Lindamood Phoneme Sequencing (formerly called Auditory Discrimination in Depth [ADD]) and the Visual-izing and Verbalizing for Improved Thinking and Comprehension programs by Lindamood-Bell. For information, contact the Lindamood-Bell Learning Processes center, San Luis Obispo, California, 800-233-1819 or visit www.lindamood-bell.com. This program has been churning out mindboggling results for over 30 years. And, you guessed it, they help students identify patterns, and learn to process those patterns, until new programs are created and wired into the brain.

CHAPTER 14

CREATING A BODYBRAIN-COMPATIBLE LEARNING ENVIRONMENT

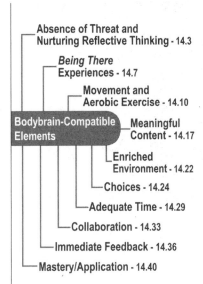

The term *brain-compatible* was coined by Leslie A. Hart in 1983 in his book *Human Brain and Human Learning*. Hart comments that

> ". . . today we have the knowledge to design brain-fitting, *brain-compatible* environments, instructional strategies, and curriculum. The 'compatible' concept may startle us, simply because we are not used to it in education. All around us are hand-compatible tools and machines and keyboards designed to fit the hand. We are not apt to think of them in that light, because it does not occur to us that anyone would bring out some device to be used by human hands without being sure that the nature of hands was considered. A keyboard machine or musical instrument that called for eight fingers on each hand would draw instant ridicule. Yet we force millions of children into schools that have never seriously studied the nature and functioning of the human brain, and which, not surprisingly, prove actively brain-antagonistic. We know less than we might and will; but we already know ample enough to bring about instructional environments that, being brain compatible, will produce huge gains in learning."[1]

When one thinks about it, the human brain is enormously powerful and inventive. If it weren't, our species would not have survived. The concept of a brain-compatible learning environment simply suggests that we should create schooling environments that would allow the brain to work as it naturally — and thus most powerfully — works rather than asking it to adapt itself to a new, foreign mode of operation — one that is awkward and less effective. We would like to suggest to you that, although print is omnipresent in our lives in America, it's a fairly recent invention for humans. Thus, what the human mind has evolved to succeed at is not reading books and utilizing computers, but rather mastering the physical world. We argue in this book that schools should begin with where the human mind is prepared to begin — the real world — and utilize print as a follow-up, not a lead-in to learning.

How to do this? Where to begin? We start with the 10 bodybrain-compatible elements. These 10 elements help translate brain research into practical, everyday approaches needed to create a world class science education program. They make EFT (Effective First Teaching) a reachable goal.

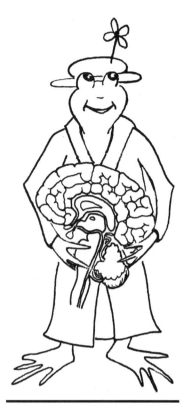

MARY FROGGINS

The concept of a bodybrain-compatible learning environment simply suggests that we should create schooling environments that would allow the brain to work as it naturally—and thus most powerfully—works rather than asking it to adapt itself to a new, foreign mode of operation—one that is awkward and less effective.

TEN ELEMENTS OF A BODYBRAIN-COMPATIBLE ENVIRONMENT

These element—practical, everyday means—are the 10 most needed to create a world-class science program.

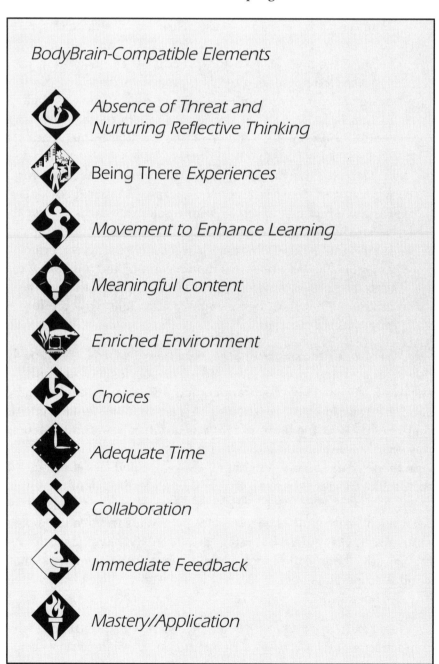

Figure 14A

ABSENCE OF THREAT AND NURTURING REFLECTIVE THINKING

BODYBRAIN-COMPATIBLE ELEMENT 1

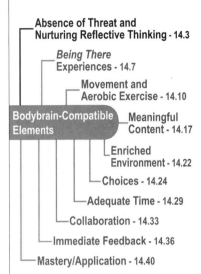

Absence of Threat and
Nurturing Reflective Thinking - 14.3

Being There
Experiences - 14.7

Movement and
Aerobic Exercise - 14.10

Bodybrain-Compatible
Elements

Meaningful
Content - 14.17

Enriched
Environment - 14.22

Choices - 14.24

Adequate Time - 14.29

Collaboration - 14.33

Immediate Feedback - 14.36

Mastery/Application - 14.40

Given the primacy of emotions to drive attention and thus memory, problem-solving, and virtually every other aspect of learning and performance,[2] the number one job of a teacher is creating and maintaining an environment free from threat. Once this is in place, that environment must also actively nurture reflective thinking. These two qualities form the heart and soul of a bodybrain-compatible learning environment and are at the very core of EFT and the *HET* model. They are also the beginning point of implementation, and the ongoing touchstone, of effective teaching. Once created, they cannot be ignored but must receive consistent, ongoing, daily attention from teacher and students.

Creating Absence of Threat

When creating absence of threat, consider two important truisms:

- Like beauty, what constitutes threat is in the eye of the beholder. What is threatening to one person may not be considered threatening to another. However, that does not minimize the sense of perceived threat held by that person. Its effects on learning are as profound as the effect of threat all may agree is the real and imminent.

- Absence of threat does not mean absence of consequences. Misbehavior and failure to complete work have consequences in the real world and so should they in the classroom. What matters is fairness, consequences appropriate to the nature of the infraction, and emotional consistency of those who apply the consequences.

Curriculum That Contributes to a Sense of Threat. Curricular aspects that have a strong bodybrain–antagonistic effect include the following:

- Frustrating because content is not understandable—the material is not age appropriate and/or is composed of factoids

- Difficult to understand if no perceivable relevance to their life; humiliating when they can't get it; source of acting out

- Frustrating when content is too easy

ABSENCE OF THREAT
AND NURTURING
REFLECTIVE THINKING

Creating Absence of Threat

Nurturing Reflective Thinking

Implications for Curriculum
and Instruction

MARY FROGGINS

For some traditionalists, a little bit of threat is often considered a good thing— "keeps them on their toes" and "shows them who's in charge." However, research into the effects of stress on the brain—which is extensive—paints a very different picture. Among other things, chronic stress hurts our ability to learn: declarative memory, executive function, and problem solving. It also disconnects neural networks, stops the hippocampus (where new memories are formed) from birthing new neurons, even kills hippocampal cells, and pushes people into depression. And the list goes on.[5]

Academic learning is all but impossible in an atmosphere with threat. But absence of threat is only the beginning of the emotional continuum. In-depth learning begins to occur when the learning environment nurtures reflective thinking.

Conditions Contributing to a Sense of Threat. The following conditions contribute to a sense of threat and exert a strong bodybrain antagonistic effect on learning:

- Lack of a sense of belonging

- Lack of personal relationship between teacher and students

- Poor leadership—students uncertain about what's happening and why or what will happen next

- Restricting body movement in the classroom (limited to recess, lunch, and P.E.)

- Adherence to rigid timelines, inadequate time to complete tasks

- Threat of bad grades (potential negative consequences from teacher, parents, and fellow students)

An environment with absence of threat is fundamental to learning and a prerequisite for reflective thinking.

Nurturing Reflective Thinking

The ability—and the inclination—to think reflectively is an invaluable habit of mind. It lowers stress, improves learning and decision making, and enhances performance. In learning situations, reflective thinking allows students to move from "So what?" to "How can I use this now and in the future?" Without such automatic questioning, learning will be on the surface in the short run and will probably fail to trigger the brain's decision to store learning in long-term memory.

While reflective thinking may seem a vague or elusive term,[3] each of us can recall times when we were so immersed in something that we lost track of time and external distractions stayed at bay. Mihaly Csikszentmihalyi provides a wonderful description of the state of mind that is home to reflective thinking, a state he calls "flow experience."[4] This state of mind is attained in exceptional moments when we find ourself totally and completely immersed in to the degree that outside distractions are not able to penetrate. This metaphor of flow is one that we have experienced and can reflect upon as some of the best times of our lives. It is also a state of mind ideal for learning because engagement is extremely high and learning seems effortless.

Reflective Thinking as an Act of Discipline. Reflective thinking doesn't just happen automatically. It is an act of either conscious discipline or habit of mind. We must first slow down,[6] clear away distractions, focus our thoughts on what we're learning and doing and why, and use self-talk to guide our thinking when puzzled or stuck.

To be reflective is a choice, a decision that can be made only by the learner. No teacher can hammer thoughtfulness into a student; it must come from within. The Latin base for the word *educate* means "to lead forth." As part of leading forth, we must create conditions that nurture reflective thinking. Most importantly, we must model it and then provide ample opportunities for students to develop and practice it.

Implications for Curriculum and Instruction

To implement the bodybrain-compatible element of absence of threat and reflective thinking, we recommend the following:[7]

CURRICULUM DEVELOPMENT

- Know your students. Make sure that your curriculum is age appropriate and thus understandable to them. Nothing rips apart a student's sense of confidence faster than knowing that he or she doesn't understand what is going on when others do.

- Develop, and begin with, inquiries (activities) that help students bring forward any prior experiences related to the key point.

INSTRUCTIONAL STRATEGIES

- Use a daily agenda and written procedures to ensure students know what to expect within a time frame.

- Provide adequate time to reach understanding and complete tasks.

- Provide a good mix of collaborative time and intrapersonal time, of stimulation and reflection.

- Provide immediate feedback in order to keep self-doubt and frustration at a minimum.

- Ensure that the physical environment is healthful, aesthetically pleasing, and uncluttered.

- Be readily available to refocus, reenergize, and redirect students; during student work time, keep circulating through the classroom taking advantage of the teachable moment and building a personal relationship with each student.

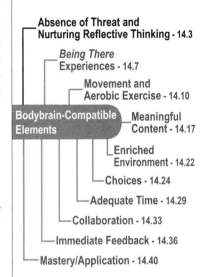

Absence of Threat and Nurturing Reflective Thinking - 14.3

Bodybrain-Compatible Elements

Being There Experiences - 14.7

Movement and Aerobic Exercise - 14.10

Meaningful Content - 14.17

Enriched Environment - 14.22

Choices - 14.24

Adequate Time - 14.29

Collaboration - 14.33

Immediate Feedback - 14.36

Mastery/Application - 14.40

ABSENCE OF THREAT AND NURTURING REFLECTIVE THINKING

Creating Absence of Threat

Nurturing Reflective Thinking

Implications for Curriculum and Instruction

MARY FROGGINS

Stress in all its forms, including threat (real or perceived), almost always makes us retreat to more familiar territory, coping strategies, and habits of mind. For example, when under stress, we tend to revert to old eating habits and styles of interacting with others—thus regaining the same 10 pounds and starting up the same old frictions with other. In the classroom, this translates into reverting to old behaviors that are often more annoying to others than supportive of our own learning and less effective problem-solving or product-producing strategies.

- Balance time for collaborative learning with personal time for applying skills and knowledge to individual interests, for exploring related ideas, and for reflecting on what one is learning and how it could be used now and in the future (vocations and hobbies).

- During collaborative work,

  – Build in time for students to jot down their own thoughts before joining brainstorming or discussion.

  – Teach group leaders to insist on wait time when questions are posed to the group.

  – Use collaborative strategies such as think-pair-share and three-before-me.

- Create classroom procedures for instituting daily periods for intrapersonal time. They are an important part of classroom leadership.

- Provide time for and model reflective thinking for your students. Orchestrate conditions that encourage reflective thinking. Share how you use the voice inside your head to lead your reflective thinking.

- Teach students how to redirect themselves when things get in the way of their learning, for example, when any of the four psychological needs identified by William Glasser are not in place (belonging, fun, power, and freedom).[8]

- Teach students simple techniques, such as Freeze Frame,[9] for bringing themselves to a reflective state of mind.

- Provide a range of individual performance formats such as individual study projects, inquiries for personal choice, and journal writing.

- Create a daily journal entry assignment: How does or could this concept or skill apply to your personal life?

- Create an "Australia," a quiet place equipped with comfortable seating, books, ear phones with quiet music (60-beats per minute music), and a huggable stuffed animal. Allow students who are very angry or otherwise emotionally upset to use the area for 10 to 15 minutes until they can get their emotions under control.

BEING THERE *EXPERIENCES*
BODYBRAIN-COMPATIBLE ELEMENT 2

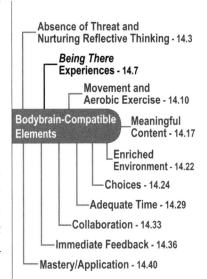

Just as the field of biology was revolutionized by the discovery of DNA, the discovery of mirror neurons has equally ground-shaking implications for the field of brain research. And for education. Fortunately, each of us has experienced the power of mirror neurons in our own lives. We know that we can learn something more accurately, more comprehensively, and more quickly if someone shows us how, lets us try, gives us feedback, and demonstrates again. We know this. Humans have known for centuries. Its truth has worked its way into our traditions, such as the medieval guilds and current apprenticeship and mentoring programs, and into our language. "A picture is worth a thousand words." "Do what I say, not what I do." (We know it's futile, but we say it anyway!).

It is time to set aside those traditional tools for the classroom that brain research does not support—such as textbooks, workbooks, and worksheets—and focus our policies and resources on those tools that significantly enhance learning. Number one is the emotional environment as described earlier in BodyBrain-Compatible Elements; the second most important is providing *being there* experiences at real-world locations, locations that anchor curriculum by illustrating for students how the concepts and skills appear in real life and how they are used by the people who work at and visit the location.

Why Being There *Experiences?*

As discussed in Chapter 9, *being there* experiences elicit all 20 senses, activate our mirror neurons, and pique our curiosity and thus positive emotions, which in turn drive attention and memory. A stronger set of strategies to enhance learning simply doesn't exist.

Why Not? So perhaps the question should be, "Why not *being there* experiences?" Inconvenience, not enough chaperones, cost of buses, liability concerns? These are all conquerable administrative issues. And although pesky and inconvenient—and they are just that, inconveniences, not insurmountable barriers—they are insignificant compared to the benefits to be reaped.

Being there experiences are your most powerful strategy for moving students through the Two-Step Learning Process.

Science and Being There *Experiences—The Great Equalizers.* The greatest academic differences among students occur in reading, especially among second-language learners. As Elizabeth Cohen points out, every child in class can rank each classmate in

BEING THERE EXPERIENCES

Why *Being There* Experiences?

Where?

The When and How of *Being There* Experiences

Implications for Curriculum and Instruction

reading achievement and even place themselves in that ranking with amazing accuracy.[11] Unfortunately, within three years, or less, students in the bottom third of the ranking become convinced that they are stupid.

In contrast, in science the differences among students are the least. *Being there* experiences further level the playing field because after 30 minutes on-site, all students share a common experience, a common vocabulary, and, eventually, mastery of the same concepts from the curriculum illustrated at the site. Any weaknesses in reading can easily be circumvented through direct experience and sharing of information within the Learning Club. From this, all students develop confidence in their ability to learn.

Schools with large numbers of disadvantaged students, second-language learners, and/or special education students have the most to gain from basing their curriculum in *being there* experiences.

Where?

Being there locations should be chosen with three criteria in mind:

1. What locations would best illustrate the selected concepts and skills? This is a chicken or the egg exercise. Whether you start with state standards in mind or begin with a location that promises to be engaging and accessible, you must jump back and forth from the chicken to the egg (curriculum content and *being there* location) and back again multiple times. Only then can you create the best possible meld of content and *being there* study visits.

2. Of those locations, which would be the most engaging for my students? Don't assume that frequently visited locations, such as a grocery store, would not intrigue students. We have taken teachers on behind-the-scenes visits to grocery stores at which they routinely shop, and they have been electrified. Right under their noses for years and yet full of surprises!

3. Of those locations, which could be visited frequently? Begin your survey of possible locations starting with the school itself. Then work outward through the neighborhood. Include neighbors' backyards and hobbies. Then check out each business in the area. Expand your perimeter until you find several good candidates.

Clearly, the above questions may produce conflicting priorities. To solve this, consider rating each potential location on a five-point

MARY FROGGINS

The greatest academic differences among students occur in reading, especially among second-language learners.

In contrast, in science the differences among students are the least. Being there experiences further level the playing field.

Schools with large numbers of disadvantaged students and/or second-language learners have the most to gain from basing their curriculum in being there experiences.

rating scale on each of the above questions. This should pop one of the choices up to the top of your list.

The When and How of Being There Experiences

The timing of *being there* visits is critical. Traditionally, field trips occur at the end of study and is often treated as a reward. However, mirror neurons can't wait. If you goal is to teach effectively the first time, the first *being there* visit must occur at the beginning of study.

Provide just enough information to frame the visit and whet their curiosity. Then go! For tips on planning a *being there* study trip, see Appendix A.

Also make your best judgment about when return visits (or visits to a similar location(s) which illustrates the same concepts and skills with similar but different applications) would be most beneficial.

The first visit allows students to use their mirror neurons to grasp the patterns of the concepts and skills and to make meaning of them. This greatly enhances and speeds up Step One of the Learning Process.

A return visit after considerable study allows them to check their understandings for accuracy and comprehensiveness and to again use their mirror neurons to sharpen their understanding of how to apply concepts and skills in real-world ways. Again, mirror neurons provide for rapid acquisition of ability to use and apply. In *Star Trek* terms, this is mind-meld time; mirror neurons allow students to absorb not only an understanding of what something is but also the hierarchy of action to use it and the emotions of people who are doing it. Mind meld worked for Spock; mirror neurons work similarly for our brains.

Implications for Curriculum and Instruction

To implement the bodybrain-compatible element of *being there* experiences, we recommend the following:

Curriculum Development

- Expect to massage your state and district standards. Slice and recombine as needed so that your curriculum content fits together in the same integrated way that students will experience it at the *being there* location.

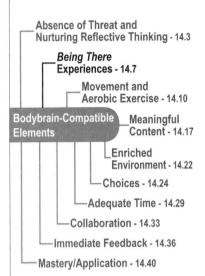

Absence of Threat and Nurturing Reflective Thinking - 14.3

Being There Experiences - 14.7

Movement and Aerobic Exercise - 14.10

Bodybrain-Compatible Elements

Meaningful Content - 14.17

Enriched Environment - 14.22

Choices - 14.24

Adequate Time - 14.29

Collaboration - 14.33

Immediate Feedback - 14.36

Mastery/Application - 14.40

BEING THERE EXPERIENCES

Why *Being There* Experiences?

Where?

The When and How of *Being There* Experiences

Implications for Curriculum and Instruction

MARY FROGGINS

So perhaps the question should be, "Why not being there experiences?" Inconvenience, not enough chaperones, cost of buses, liability concerns? These are all conquerable administrative issues. And although pesky, individually and as a group, the these inconveniencies—and they are just that, inconveniences, not insurmountable barriers—are insignificant compared to the benefits to be reaped.

- If necessary, restate a standard or benchmark to make it as conceptual as possible. Although state standards have improved nationwide, many are still not as conceptual as they should be.

- At each new location your students visit, include an exploration of how previously studied concepts and skills apply to the new location. Encourage students to make this a habit of mind. The more they understand about a location, the easier it is to learn new concepts about it. This greatly increases efficiency of learning and students' power to master their world.

Instructional Strategies

- Plan your *being there* study trips with care. Methodically work your way through the three questions on the previous page.

- Follow the suggestions in Appendix A step by step. Add your own recommendations as you go. Insist that volunteers follow each step to the letter. Remember, administrative permission to use *being there* study trips will likely hinge on how well you plan and execute them.

- Adopt the goal of Effective First Teaching (EFT) and know that your best strategy for reaching that goal is using *being there* study trips to maximize students' opportunities to fully use their mirror neurons throughout the learning process.

MOVEMENT AND AEROBIC EXERCISE TO ENHANCE LEARNING
BODYBRAIN-COMPATIBLE ELEMENT 3

The Western world's view of the brain is that it is rational, logical, ruler of all; the body in this scheme has been primarily viewed as merely the vehicle that carries the brain from one cerebral task to another. Today, it's clear that there is no hierarchy, no separation between the body and the brain. What the Greeks knew 2,500 years ago is being confirmed by today's high-tech brain research—if you want the best performance from your brain, tune the body and brain together.

Movement

Movement is fundamental to who we are. Only an organism that moves from place to place even requires a brain.[12] This is not a casual link! The brain and body are an inseparable partnership. As John Ratey points out, "What the brain communicates to the body depends largely on what messages the body is sending to the brain. Together they collaborate for the good of the whole organism."[13] In classroom life, this means that the body and brain are always talking and working together. When one member of the bodybrain learning partnership is shut down, told to sit still and not move, the functioning of the other partner is deeply affected.

As we think about the traditions of the educational system we inherited, we can't help but marvel at how far off the mark some of its features are. Children sitting quietly in rows, not moving, not talking. What a recipe for failure to learn!

This suggests that the pendulum swings in school reform over the past century may have failed not because they were inherently flawed but because throughout those reforms the bodybrain partnership remained divided and thus ineffective at learning.

Almost Half of the Entire Brain Is Devoted to Organizing Action. And the newest, most powerful parts of the brain at that. This is another powerful message for teachers. The frontal cortex learns, routinizes, and processes motor and mental functions in parallel. Movement, then, becomes inextricably tied to cognition.

This feature of the physiology of the brain underscores the importance of defining learning as a two-step process: understanding and then using what is understood. It turns out that the brain expects to use what it understands and is wired in anticipation of doing so.

Movement Is Crucial to Every Brain Function. Although Olympic athletes have discovered the impressive power of the brain to improve the performance of its partner, the body, we must acknowledge the reciprocal power of the body on brain function. According to Ratey, "our physical movements can directly influence our ability to learn, think, and remember. Evidence is mounting that each person's capacity to master new and remember old information is improved by biological changes in the brain brought on by new activity."[14]

What does this all mean for the classroom teacher? Nothing short of a revolutionary shift in our view of our students as learners. What this means is that the bodybrain partnership perceives, processes, and stores concepts and skills by their usability and usefulness in long-term memory. If it is perceived as not useable (who cares?), not useful (irrelevant), then, it's not worth learning. We must reframe what we teach and why we teach it. Learning not for the sake of learning but for the sake of using what we learn—for our own lives and as contributing citizens.

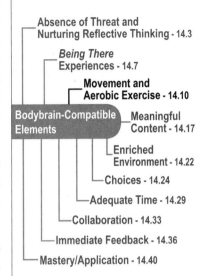

Absence of Threat and Nurturing Reflective Thinking - 14.3

Being There Experiences - 14.7

Movement and Aerobic Exercise - 14.10

Bodybrain-Compatible Elements

Meaningful Content - 14.17

Enriched Environment - 14.22

Choices - 14.24

Adequate Time - 14.29

Collaboration - 14.33

Immediate Feedback - 14.36

Mastery/Application - 14.40

MOVEMENT

Almost Half of the Entire Brain is Devoted to Movement

Movement Is Crucial to Every Brain Function

The Power of Mimicry

Implications for Curriculum and Instruction

MARY FROGGINS

Ya gotta love this brain research stuff! In summary, the relationship between movement and cognition is startling and the implications for classroom teachers are clear:

- *Movement is fundamental to the very existence of a brain. Only an organism that moves from place to place requires a brain.[17]*

- *The entire front half of the brain—the newest in evolutionary terms—is devoted to organizing action, both physical and mental.[18] Higher brain functions have evolved from movement and still depend on it.*

- *Movement is crucial to every brain function including planning and executing plans, memory, emotion, language, and learning.[19]*

- *The ability to mimic, one of young human's most powerful avenues for learning, is movement based.*

- *Emotional states are easily reset by movement.*

The Power of Mimicry. Startling research is emerging that suggests the presence of "mirror neurons," a subset of movement-related neurons in premotor cortex area[15] that buzz away when we watch someone do something that interests us. Whether these neurons merely assist us to understand or to mirror gestures or actions is still uncertain. Some researchers such as Ramachandran believe that mirror neurons play a bigger role than is generally appreciated. Ramachandran believes that not only are they the missing link between gesture and language but that they also help explain human learning, ingenuity, and culture in general. "Language, imitative learning, and mind reading, seemingly unrelated human developments, may all be shown to be linked through these intriguing nerve cells."[16]

Movement is the quickest and most reliable way to add fun to the moment. Movement resets our emotional state. It provides opportunities for wiggly students to let off steam, tired students to get reenergized. When movement is planned as an extension or application of the concepts or skills being learned, additional parts of the brain wake up and content gets encoded in additional areas of the brain.

Movement in this context means using the bodybrain partnership fully and joyously to learn the concepts and skills of the curriculum—science, social studies, art, language arts, science, and technology. Movement for sports, the traditional view of P.E., is not included in this discussion.

Implications for Curriculum and Instruction. To implement the bodybrain-compatible element of movement, we recommend the following:

Curriculum

- Add to your key points an example of how the concept is used so the movement inherent in using the concept becomes part of the brain's encoding. Do the same with skill key points unless the use of the skill is obvious. Whenever possible, point out applications of the key point that affect students now at home, school, their favorite mall, etc., not just down the road later in life.

- Develop bodymaps and movements to mimic that act out the key attributes of the patterns within the concept or skill you are teaching. Include these in your direct instruction and in inquiries. Involve students in developing them.

- When writing inquiries for linguistic intelligence, consider adding mnemonics through music and rhythm, such as rap, dance, drama, and other bodily-kinesthetic actions.

- When developing immersion experiences, include role-playing of the actions of people working and conducting commerce at your being there locations. Go for richness; focus on the most important attributes of the patterns of the concepts/skills in the key point.

- Use movement as an extension or application of content rather than as a separate activity.

- Invite students to help you plan movement sequences that will help the class master concepts and skills.

- Teach students the skills for reading and using body language effectively. For example, miming, role-playing, acting, public speaking, and dancing.

- The curriculum addresses movement both as a content itself (for example, teaching students of the importance of movement in learning and positive emotional states) and as a means of enhancing academic learning (e.g., using the body to explore through the 20 senses and using the body to role-play, react, and so forth).

- Design inquiries that ask students to act out the sequence of steps or processes inherent in the key point.

Instructional strategies

- Design inquiries that ask students, in Learning Clubs or in pairs, to create movements as mnemonics for applying and remembering the concept or skill of a skill point.

- Add music and singing to your movement sequences. Melody, rhythm, rhyme, and words add fun and increase retention.

- Use movement throughout the day to

  - Reset emotions (to energize or slow the pace as needed)

  - Pique interest by illustrating how things are used

  - Use the body to do memorable simulations (such as make the shapes of the letter of the alphabet, mimic animal movements, perform plays, skits, and hand signs)

- During direct instruction, checking for understanding, and groupwork, include as many forms of the dramatic arts as you can; for example, role-play, miming, simulations, planned and impromptu skits, impersonations (of people and machines), and so forth.

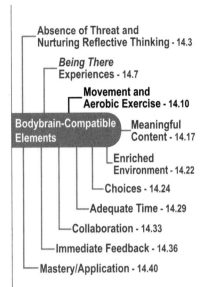

Absence of Threat and Nurturing Reflective Thinking - 14.3
Being There Experiences - 14.7
Movement and Aerobic Exercise - 14.10
Bodybrain-Compatible Elements
Meaningful Content - 14.17
Enriched Environment - 14.22
Choices - 14.24
Adequate Time - 14.29
Collaboration - 14.33
Immediate Feedback - 14.36
Mastery/Application - 14.40

MOVEMENT

Almost Half of the Entire Brain is Devoted to Movement

Movement Is Crucial to Every Brain Function

The Power of Mimicry

Implications for Curriculum and Instruction

MARY FROGGINS

The popular press has extolled and sold the virtues of physical fitness as a means reducing stress and increasing overall health and well-being. But the story now emerging from brain research is amazing. As Carla Hannaford is fond of saying, "The body grows the brain."[24] Indeed, animals that don't move, don't have a brain. And, those like the sea squirt that move early in its life cycle, later reabsorb their brain when they permanently affix themselves to a stationary object.

- Think movement, think action, think doing something worthwhile while introducing key points.

Aerobic Exercise

All work and no play may make Jack a boring guy to be around, but a sedentary lifestyle with no aerobic exercise—induced by work or play—will result in achievement levels far below the intellectual potential a student was born with.

Those who believe that young brains walk through the classroom door equally ready to learn—or even learn at all—are sadly mistaken. Genetics, prior experiences, and nutrition are but a part of the ingredients needed for effective and efficient learning. Far more important are the brain chemicals produced by the body that prepare the brain to learn.

Preparing the Brain to Learn. Aerobic exercise kick-starts brain chemicals essential for forming new memories and wiring learning into long-term memory. High aerobic exercise (heart rate at 70 percent or higher) for 35 minutes daily produces the following benefits:[21]

- Kick-starts a leap in the growth of stem cells in the hippocampus (where new memories are formed)

- Produces significant increases in the chemicals the brain needs to spark attention and the physiological changes called learning (dendrite sprouting and connecting)

- Vastly improves most mental health conditions; particularly relevant for schools are depression, ADD, anxiety, and addiction.[21]

Here are a few examples of the changes such a daily aerobics program can kick start in the brain:[22]

In the hippocampus[23] —

- Stimulates regenesis, the growth of new stem cells

- Spurs new stem cells to develop into new nerve cells

- Can cause a shrunken hippocampus (due to inactivity or aging) to return to normal size

These changes are crucial to learning because the hippocampus is where new memories are formed.

Production of chemicals to spark attention, learning, and long-term memory —

- Elevates BDNF (brain-derived neurotrophic factor), a protein that builds, protects, and maintains neuron circuitry, giving neurons the tools they need to learn—to process, associate, put in context, and remember.[24]

  BDNF is especially important in the formation of long-term memories.

- Rate of learning is directly correlated with levels of BDNF. Levels rise as the amount of exercise increases.[25]

In summary, BDNF gives the synapses the tools they need not only to take in information but also to process it, associate it, put it in context (with prior experiences and other elements in the current situation), and remember it.

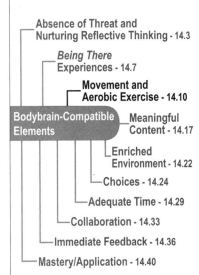

Vastly improves most mental health conditions, particularly depression, anxiety, ADD, and addiction by stimulating the production of serotonin, norepinephrine, and dopamine and balancing them for optimum performance of the brain.[26]

- Serotonin helps keep brain activity under control by influencing mood, impulsivity, anger, and aggressiveness.
  [Note: Prozac is a serotonin substitute.]

- Norepinephrine amplifies brain signals that influence attention, perception, motivation, and arousal.

- Dopamine is thought of as the learning, reward (satisfaction), attention, and movement neurotransmitter.
  [Note: Ritalin is used to increase dopamine levels.]

According to John Ratey, "Voluntary exercise has a profound impact on cognitive abilities and mental health. It is simply one of the best treatments we have to most psychiatric problems."[27]

The amount of movement matters — The amount of exercise has a profound effect on the number of new stem cells that are formed.

The kind of movement matters — The more complex the movements, the more complex the synaptic connections. Aerobic exercise should also include new learning—acquisition of new physical skills and/or new mental skills and knowledge used for problem solving.

Impact on Academic Achievement. Studies by the California Department of Education have consistently shown that students with higher fitness scores also have higher test scores.[28]

- In 2002, fit kids scored twice as well on academic tests as their unfit peers.[29] Those fifth-, seventh-, and ninth-grade students passing all six portions of the fitness test significantly out-

AEROBIC EXERCISE

Preparing the Brain to Learn

Impact on Academic Achievement

Implications for Curriculum and Instruction

MARY FROGGINS

Make no mistake about it. America's couch-potato sloth and poor eating habits create a dismal teaching scenario.

ranked their unfit peers. In reading, scores doubled (27th percentile to the 54th percentile);[30] in math, scores jumped from the 35th to the 68th percentile.[30] Even when socioeconomic status was factored in, the trend remained. And, among low-income students, fitter students scored better than unfit students.[31] In 2004, the similar story.

- Six areas of fitness were tested—aerobic capacity, percentage of body fat, abdominal strength and endurance, trunk strength and flexibility, upper body strength, and overall flexibility.[32] When researchers at the University of Illinois near Naperville replicated the CDE study, they found that two areas of the test were particularly important in relation to academic performance: increased aerobic fitness had a strong, positive relationship and increased body mass had a strong, negative influence.[33] Researchers discovered that an EEG (electroencephalogram) showed more activity in fit kids' brains, indicating that more neurons were being recruited for the assigned tasks. Hillman also discovered that even a single, acute bout of exercise had a positive impact on learning. The formula goes something like this: aerobic exercise = faster cognitive processing speed = better attention (greater attentional control resulting in more accurate responses) = better learning.[34]

In summary, physical activity has a positive influence on attention, concentration, memory, and classroom behavior. Clearly, fitness should not be looked upon as extracurricular but rather as a vital component in students' academic success.[35]

Despite such research, the increase in minutes for reading and math in response to No Child Left Behind, has pulled the nation in the opposite direction. Many districts have cut or eliminated their P.E. programs. Some districts have even eliminated morning recess. Illinois, because of PE4Life, is now the only state that requires daily P.E.

While many classroom teachers may dread the thought of becoming an aerobics instructor, we can no longer afford to ignore the extensive impact aerobic exercise has on the learning brain. For more information, see *Spark: The Revolutionary New Science of Exercise and the Brain* by John Ratey.

Make no mistake about it. America's couch-potato sloth and poor eating habits create a dismal teaching scenario. Marion Diamond first sounded a dire warning in the 1980s, "Use it or lose it"; we didn't listen. John Ratey's 2008 message is delivered in even stronger words, "... inactivity is killing our brains—physically shriveling them."[36] To ignore this information any longer is unacceptable. To do so puts teachers at a disadvantage that cannot be overcome and knowingly fails children — particularly those children most dependent upon public education.

Implications for Curriculum and Instruction. To implement the bodybrain-compatible element of aerobic exercise, we recommend the following:

Curriculum development

- Develop or adapt aerobics curriculum for every classroom, every grade level. The Naperville School District curriculum is a good place to start.[37]

- Where possible, include activities that are logical outgrowths of other subjects, such as history/social studies (games/physical exercise children of the historical period being studied) or high action science studies at *being there* locations (such as a hike around the pond to count certain tree species before starting water sample analyses), and so forth.

Instructional strategies

- Ensure that each classroom teacher gets adequate training for conduct his or her own 35-minute daily aerobic exercise program.

- Ensure that each classroom teacher gets several heart monitors and other equipment essential to implementing the aerobics program.

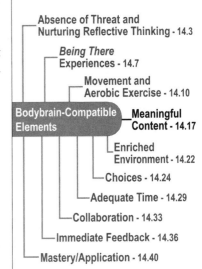

Absence of Threat and Nurturing Reflective Thinking - 14.3

Being There Experiences - 14.7

Movement and Aerobic Exercise - 14.10

Bodybrain-Compatible Elements

Meaningful Content - 14.17

Enriched Environment - 14.22

Choices - 14.24

Adequate Time - 14.29

Collaboration - 14.33

Immediate Feedback - 14.36

Mastery/Application - 14.40

MEANINGFUL CONTENT
BODYBRAIN-COMPATIBLE ELEMENT 4

No one — student or teacher — gets up in the morning and says, "Oh, boy, I hope this day is boring!" Quite the opposite; children and adults dread boredom. For the brain, it is the straight-line equivalent of a heart monitor showing no heartbeat . . . death by multiple paper cuts. So what makes content meaningful? Who says so?

Some Universal Truths

Who says so? The learner of course, not the teacher or the state standards.

What is meaningful? Brain research provides some important clues. Intrinsically meaningful to the brain are things that are useful, novel, embedded in the activities of a group important to the learner.

MEANINGFUL CONTENT

Some Universal Truths

Words Alone Are Weak Conveyors of Meaning

The Power of Meaningful Content

Implications for Curriculum and Instruction

MARY FROGGINS

Because it is the movement centers of the brain that sequence thinking, it is essential that movement— doing—be part of learning from beginning to end, from the conception of curriculum content to instruction to assessing outcomes. Said more strongly, restriction of movement and all forms of passivity significantly impede learning. So, whether such active learning is a personal preference or not, we owe it to our students to make learning in our classroom the active, joyful process that it naturally is.

Useful. The brain never takes a vacation from its role in ensuring survival. Thus, anything the brain views as useful will be attended to. Tips for ensuring learning is useful include

- Real-life situations with high and varied sensory input

- Content that relates to an existing interest, hobby, or favorite activities

- Content with which the learner has prior experience, especially with something outside of school (If the association is positive, the learner will continue searching for meaning.)

- Content that relates to the learner's future aspirations

Novel. In its ever-vigilant survival scan of the environment, anything novel catches the brain's immediate attention. However, novel must be quickly followed by a decision that the novel thing is useful or important to the learner's social setting. Tips for planning novel (to the learner) situations that pique curiosity include

- *Being there* locations, even an unusual aspect at a familiar location such as a behind-the-scenes tour of a grocery store

- Role-playing scenarios that engage every member of the team

- Problem-solving and/or product-producing situations in which no one knows the answer or how to go about making the product so that all are needed to accomplish the task

Social. Tips for planning learning opportunities within a social context include

- Embedded in social activities important to the learner

- Activities and knowledge that respected Learning Club members do and/or find fascinating

- Concepts and/or skills that help the learner meet Glasser's four fundamental needs:

  - Belonging (want to learn what others in the club do)

  - To love and be loved (learning the personal and social skills necessary to be successful in collaborative environments; the deep sense of personal satisfaction and connection to others that comes from contributing to the community through political and/or social action projects)

  - Power (knowledge and skills to become a competent person)

  - Fun (the teacher's classroom leadership style makes learning enjoyable and joyous)

Words Alone Are Weak Conveyors of Meaning

Words fail to convey much meaning except as the listener already has experience and extracted patterns that give meaning to the words. For example, consider these two statements. A stock broker: "If you sell a security to establish a loss, you just wait 30 days to buy it back or it will be viewed as a wash sale but the waiting period doesn't apply to gains." Or a musician: "Since the B-flat clarinet is a transposing instrument, the note you play from the written music will actually sound a full tone lower." These are perfectly understandable statements if we bring prior experience to bear. Without prior experience, the words are meaningless.[38]

Limitations of Words. We must accept that words convey only limited meaning and that if our students lack relevant prior experience, we must rely on input from the real setting. Whether in speech or in print, understanding words demands bringing information to the situation.[39] Even in social conversation, a comment or question off the subject usually produces a "Huh?" response until the new topic is settled on and the relevant prior experience is brought into focus.

In a bodybrain-compatible learning environment, learning occurs like this:

> **Brain-Compatible Learning:**
>
> *BEING THERE EXPERIENCE* ☛ CONCEPT ☛ VOCABULARY ☛ APPLICATION TO REAL WORLD

In contrast, conventional schooling starts with language and definitions *about* things and attempts to move to concept development. The fading ink illustrates the drop-off in learning.

> **Old Notions About Learning:**
>
> VOCABULARY ☛ ? CONCEPT ☛ ? ☛ ? ☛ APPLICATION

The power of real-world examples to enable learners to generalize and transfer knowledge and skills can't be overestimated. For example, the idea of "3/4" becomes clear only when it is recognized and used in multiple contexts such as those in the graphic on the next page.

One trip to the mall or a visit to a vet's office (or medical lab), with a pizza lunch on the way, can put all of these math patterns into a single perspective for students. Mastery follows automatically.

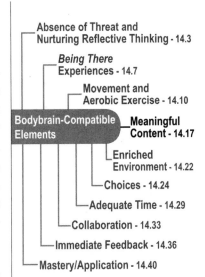

Absence of Threat and Nurturing Reflective Thinking - 14.3

Being There Experiences - 14.7

Movement and Aerobic Exercise - 14.10

Bodybrain-Compatible Elements

Meaningful Content - 14.17

Enriched Environment - 14.22

Choices - 14.24

Adequate Time - 14.29

Collaboration - 14.33

Immediate Feedback - 14.36

Mastery/Application - 14.40

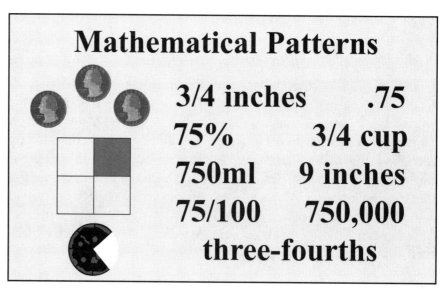

Figure 14B

MARY FROGGINS

Having students sit quietly in rows is a worst-case scenario for the brain. What it needs is active participation from its partner, the body. In contrast, being there experiences are tailored made for the body-brain partnership. There is action, emotion, and plenty of raw material for cognitive processes.

Frank Smith, in Insult to Intelligence: The Bureaucratic Invasion of Our Classrooms, makes the point that when meaning is reached, learning occurs automatically and simultaneously.[40] The learner is always asking, What does this situation or information mean to me? How can I use it? How does it affect me now and in my future? "Making sense of the everyday world in relation to ourselves, our needs (physical, emotional, mental), and motivations (interests and need for fun in our lives) is our greatest concern and motivator."[41]

The Power of Meaningful Content

Meaningful content, or lack of, also plays an institutional role.

Overcoming Inequities. Brain research and our common sense tell us that the more you know about something, the more meaning you can extract. Given the disparity of experiences that students bring to the classroom, the playing field is anything but level. Only massive sensory input through *being there* experiences simultaneously provide the needed catch up experiences for those with no prior relevant experience plus challenge for those that have been there, done that.

Luckily for readers of this book, the subject area in which the gaps among students can most readily be overcome is science, a subject that begs for *being there* experiences, immersion, and hands-on of the real thing. Within minutes, enough sensory input can be provided that students can all be on equal footing.

Powering Up Second-Language Acquisition. Everything that's just been said about words and making meaning and overcoming inequities is doubly true for second-language acquisition students.

Implications for Curriculum and Instruction

To implement the bodybrain-compatible element of meaningful content, we recommend the following.

Curriculum Development

- State curriculum as concepts and base them in community locations, situations, and events.

- Ensure that curriculum is age appropriate—comprehensible to the student given his or her stage of brain development.

- When planning your curriculum and daily lessons, find out what prior experiences students have had. What concepts and skills do they already understand and can apply? Don't assume that students have the necessary conceptual building blocks from prior experience to understand what your curriculum is about. Investing the time to get to know each student pays big dividends.

- Be alert to misconceptions. To correct them, provide massive amounts of sensory input.

Instructional Strategies

- Make the classroom a complete immersion experience for the being there location your curriculum is based on.

- Invite guest speakers that will present their experiences using *hands-on of the real thing*. Insist that students include examples of their concepts/skills from their experiences.

- Deliberately use collaboration as a way of increasing input and practice using concepts and skills.

- Use analytical tools that help students key in on important attributes of a concept or skill. For example, T-charts that compare what something is and what it is not, Venn diagrams that compare similarities and differences between two items, and organizers that help students identify prior related experience (KWU charts that identify what we now **think we know, want to know**, and, afterwards, what we now **understand**). For young children, dot-to-dot puzzles are useful to help them reveal visual attributes of things such as a frog or butterfly.

- When under the pressure of ever higher expectations, be realistic. Don't assume that because a concept is assigned to

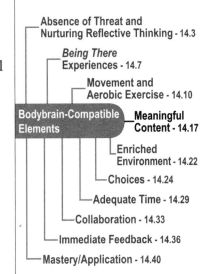

Absence of Threat and Nurturing Reflective Thinking - 14.3

Being There Experiences - 14.7

Movement and Aerobic Exercise - 14.10

Bodybrain-Compatible Elements

Meaningful Content - 14.17

Enriched Environment - 14.22

Choices - 14.24

Adequate Time - 14.29

Collaboration - 14.33

Immediate Feedback - 14.36

Mastery/Application - 14.40

MEANINGFUL CONTENT

Some Universal Truths

Words Alone Are Weak Conveyors of Meaning

The Power of Meaningful Content

Implications for Curriculum and Instruction

MARY FROGGINS

As 80 percent of reading comprehension is based on prior knowledge, one can only take from a book what one brings to the book. Books can expand our knowledge but cannot create it from scratch. According to Frank Smith, "Much of today's school failure results from academic expectations for which students' brains were not prepared—but which were bulldozed into them anyway. Deficits in everything from grammar to geography may be caused by teaching that bypasses the kind of instruction that could help children conceptually come to grips with the subject at hand."[42]

your grade level, it can be made understandable to students at your students. If something in your state standards, such as atoms at first grade, solar system at second, the chemical processes of photosynthesis for sixth graders, is age inappropriate, leave those concepts for the end of the year, all the while being aware that there will never be enough time to do everything. We call this process "selective abandonment." For more information about age appropriateness, see Chapter 7.

ENRICHED ENVIRONMENT
BODYBRAIN-COMPATIBLE ELEMENT 5

Given the choice of spending a day in a five-star hotel or in an old, ramshackle, chaotic house on the corner of the busiest street in the city, which would you choose? Or a day at Disney World or Epcot versus the nearby strip mall? In which environments would you smile the most, in which would time pleasantly zip by? In which would you be most likely to form long-lasting pictures of what you experienced? Clearly, we'd choose the places that were planned using the best available science about what environments best support the visitor in becoming engaged with his or her surroundings.

Enriched Does NOT Mean Cluttered or Overly Stimulating

There is a massive amount of research about the physical and emotional/mental impact of color, space, architectural design, traffic flow, and more—information that can reveal how to engage people in the environment and message it's intended to convey. All of this affects openness to learning and ability to stay engaged. We are talking here of issues that have a powerful effect on the bodybrain partnership. An enriched environment takes planning intention, and discipline.

Enriched Does Mean Sensory Rich

The brain can't learn new things or make connections among previously learned concepts and skills without new input that forces us to reshuffle the deck. Nothing does this better than rich sensory input, with a problem to be solved and/or a product to be made

Make sure that every element you introduce into the classroom—especially the immersion wall—directly supports learning the key points for the current topic.

Enriched Environment Defined. An enriched environment is a learning environment that focuses sensory input on the concept or skill to be learned. Maximizing sensory input is a fundamental goal when developing curriculum and planning instructional strategies for a number of reasons. First, input through the senses is the brain's only way to bring in information from the outside world; there are no short cuts. Second, large amounts of sensory input enable students to grasp the concepts and information accurately and completely, thereby eliminating misunderstandings. Third, large amounts of sensory input is what causes physiological changes in the brain, resulting in the phenomena of learning.

Immersion Walls. The immersion wall replicates the *being there* location in the classroom as fully as possible. For example, if the *being there* site is the local landfill or transfer station, the wall becomes a 3-D representation of the community's handling of garbage—what's underground and above the ground. A CD plays the sounds of slowly dripping water to represent healthy downstream water environments. At least 50 books, other printed materials, multimedia resources, and Internet sources about recycling and garbage fill the room. Models and pictures of recycling and landfill construction are available for close analysis and exploration. Part of the immersion wall depicts the journey garbage takes from our back door to the landfill—one including recycling, one straight to the landfill. The classroom social/political action project includes recycling the cafeteria waste.

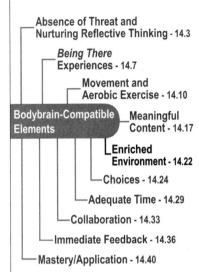

Implications for Curriculum and Instruction

To implement the bodybrain-compatible element of enriched environment, we recommend the following.

Curriculum Development

- Knowing there is a fine line between an enriched environment and a cluttered environment, make sure you have finished writing your key points and inquiries before you begin gathering resources to create an enriched environment. Once you know exactly what you want your students to understand and how you will have them use what they understand, be selective. Remove input about other topics from the room. Then, for each key point and inquiry, plan your input in descending order: first *being there,* then immersion, then hands-on of the real thing, and so on. If possible, eliminate hands on of representational items in favor of the above three kinds of input. Include secondhand and symbolic input last.

ENRICHED ENVIRONMENT

Enriched Does NOT Mean Cluttered or Overly Stimulating

Enriched Does Mean Sensory Rich

Implications for Curriculum and Instruction

MARY FROGGINS

In Hart's view of learning, input is a key factor. "Input is critically important in any kind of learning situation, whoever the learner and whatever is to be learned. The process of learning is the extraction, from confusion, of meaningful patterns. Input is the raw material of that confusion, what is perceived through the senses by the individual that bears on that particular pattern in any way."[43]

The subject area in which the gaps among students is the greatest and takes the most time and work to bridge is language arts. Why? Because it trades primarily in second-hand input and symbolic input.

- Provide an area of the room for movement that will enhance learning the key points and wiring those skills and knowledge into long-term memory.

Instructional Strategies

- Include resource people, preferably from the *being there* locations upon which your curriculum is based. Work with them in advance so they understand what students have done prior to their coming and what new input would be most valuable.

- Request that your expert guest speakers bring as many hands on and immersion items as possible. Work with them in advance to create scenarios for role-playing, problem solving, and groupwork assignments. Have them emphasize *how they use* the knowledge and skills.

- Make the classroom a complete immersion experience reflecting the being there location upon which your curriculum is based.

- Select materials and other resources appropriate to the lesson. Provide contrasting points of view so that the attributes of issues become clear through their comparison with each other, such as that of the polluter and of the family whose child developed cancer, land use through the eyes of the cattleman and the farmer.

- Realize that what you find acceptable or endearing may have very opposite effects on some students due to their different strengths. Base your classroom decor (color, furniture, flow, and so on) on how the brain responds to those elements.

CHOICES
BODYBRAIN-COMPATIBLE ELEMENT 6

As every parent quickly learns, offering a two-year old a choice of A or B—do what I've asked or go to time-out—significantly defuses a potential power struggle and improves the child's attitude toward the task chosen. The same is true in the classroom. Giving students a choice of inquiry A, B, or C often makes the difference between sloppy work performed with indifference or a project given one's personal best. Yet despite our own experience and common sense, in schools we too often succumb to the law of bureaucracies: Mind-numbing insistence on assembly-line sameness. We foolishly perpetuate the same input—textbook and lectures—believing that they will produce the same learning outcomes, that "same" equals equity and fairness.

Offering Choices

Offering choices is a frontal assault against the bureaucratic mentality of sameness and control and a huge emotional boost for the bodybrain partnership. Although some may believe that offering choices is a left over flower-power idea from the 1960s or antithetical to adhering to state standards, let us assure you that the learning benefits of providing choices is based in hard science. And, as for state standards, the choices of which we speak are not in the area of what concepts and skills should be taught but in how you go about teaching them.

Why Offer Choices? Offering students choice strengthens their commitment to learn because

- Having choices allows students to design their own path between too hard (leading to failure) and too easy (leading to boredom). It also allows them to alternate between intelligences of strength and those they are working to strengthen. This increases the likelihood of students' success in learning skills and knowledge and wiring them into long-term memory.

- The higher the level of interest, the higher the level of motivation and commitment to learn, and thus the higher the level of neurotransmitters generated to assist the learning process.

- The power to choose gives students a measure of power and control over their own learning, prerequisites for emotional stability[44] and becoming a lifelong learner.

- Having choices makes learning easier. As Frank Smith points out, thinking is made easy and effective when two fundamental requirements are met:

  —We understand what we are thinking about; and

  —The brain itself is in charge, in control of its own affairs, going about its own business.[45]

Innate Inequity. In reality, nothing could be more unfair than giving two very different brains the same input and expecting the outcome to be the same. If we want the same learning outcomes from different brains, we must provide different input to each—whatever each brain needs to arrive at the standard end point. And given the huge differences in prior experiences, intelligence strengths, person-

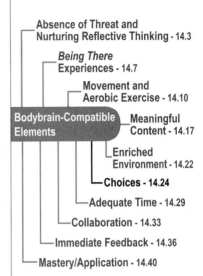

Absence of Threat and Nurturing Reflective Thinking - 14.3

Being There Experiences - 14.7

Movement and Aerobic Exercise - 14.10

Bodybrain-Compatible Elements

Meaningful Content - 14.17

Enriched Environment - 14.22

Choices - 14.24

Adequate Time - 14.29

Collaboration - 14.33

Immediate Feedback - 14.36

Mastery/Application - 14.40

CHOICES

Offering Choices

Implications for Curriculum and Instruction

MARY FROGGINS

According to Hart, "How much is learned by rote is a direct function of time and effort. But when the learning is meaningful we learn much faster and without effort."[46]

ality preferences, and brain processes, reliance on the textbook and lecture are ineffective.

The choices to be offered should also vary greatly due to age, ability to stay focused on the task, and experience with making and sticking with decisions.

Choices Need Not Be Complicated

For the young learner, for example, choice can be as simple as chalk versus crayon or paint and the number of options need to be limited to two or three. Although learning to speak and write standard English is not an item of choice for an educated person, the content of essays could and should capitalize on student interests. Also, students who have never been to the ocean need more time exploring tidepools and more time discussing what they find than students who frequently visit the ocean. First timers would also benefit from construction projects creating an immersion experience of the tidepools while the frequent visitor might be ready to move to secondhand resources at the library.

The truth is that offering choices is essential if one's goal is mastery and application of concepts and skills, not to mention creating lifelong learners who possess a passion for learning.

Implications for Curriculum and Instruction

The multiple intelligences are a way of thinking, not a subject, not a modality.

To implement the bodybrain-compatible element of choices, we recommend the following.

Curriculum Development

- Teach the theory of multiple intelligences to your students. Help them distinguish between the intelligences as ways of thinking to solve problems and/or produce products versus a subject content of the same name, such as music or language arts. For example, writing lyrics for a song is not necessarily using one's musical intelligence; it's likely just another linguistic activity. But figuring out how to use music composition skills as a study technique (to go from Ds to As in college) is a way of using musical intelligence to solve problems and produce products.[47] Also, doing arithmetic, carrying out the mechanics of a long division problem, is not the same as thinking mathematically to solve a problem in your environment, as in the popular TV show *Numb3rs*.

- Develop inquiries which offer real choice rather than more of the same; this is particularly important for the practice and mastery of skills (reading, writing, speaking, and mathematics). Do so by building on the multiple intelligences and using everyday situations. Also make sure there are inquiries for Learning Club work and for individual exploration as well as for whole class assignment.

- Develop a sufficient number of inquiries to allow for real choice. For example, being assigned one's choice of three out of seven rather than three out of four is real choice. However, it takes time to increase students' capacity to handle choice. Start small and build upward as quickly as you can.

- Invite students, from third grade and up, to develop their own inquiries from which you as teacher select the best. (The most important criteria is whether they are a real application of the concepts and skills identified in the key points. Activities for the sake of activities is a huge waste of time.) Learning to pose our own questions is more important to lifelong learning than being able to answer someone else's questions. Encourage students to apply the concepts and knowledge of your curriculum to areas of their personal interest.

- Develop at least 5–7 inquiries for every key point.

  - Make sure that you build in choice based on the multiple intelligences and Bloom's taxonomy.

  - Make them action-oriented requiring students to apply concepts and skills in ways they can see meaningful outcomes and products. (See the Inquiry Building chart on page 4.3.)

  - Design some for whole class work, some for collaborative choice, and some for individual choice.

- Teach students that there are usually multiple ways to go about solving problems. Provide several examples and then let them devise others. Once you determine that the child has a pattern that they prefer—and that unfailingly produces correct answers—stop teaching other ways or patterns, even if they are the traditional ones.[48] Accept their method or pattern if it consistently gives them correct answers. For example, there are at least 16 algorithms for multiplication. Let students use the one that works best for them.

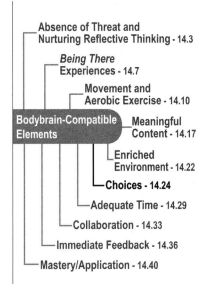

Absence of Threat and Nurturing Reflective Thinking - 14.3
Being There Experiences - 14.7
Movement and Aerobic Exercise - 14.10
Bodybrain-Compatible Elements
Meaningful Content - 14.17
Enriched Environment - 14.22
Choices - 14.24
Adequate Time - 14.29
Collaboration - 14.33
Immediate Feedback - 14.36
Mastery/Application - 14.40

CHOICES

Offering Choices

Implications for Curriculum and Instruction

MARY FROGGINS

Providing students with real-life context for learning is especially critical if students have no prior experience (or no successful experience) with the concept or skill to be learned.

Instructional Strategies

- Provide choice through activities, all of which you deem equally effective to help students learn the agreed upon curriculum for your school. Do so whenever possible. Be open to thoughtful proposals from students; always ask them how their proposal will ensure that they learn concepts X and skill Y (those in the key points) that is part of your curriculum. Help them monitor their progress. Learning to "know when you know" and "know when you don't know" is essential to becoming a successful lifelong learner.

- Have students identify their strongest intelligences and those they would like to strengthen. Have them set goals and strategies for developing their intelligences on a weekly basis.

- Prepare resource people to talk about how they use the multiple intelligence most critical to their area of expertise. Prep them for such questions from students as "When did you first know you had this capability?" "How did you build it when you were a student?" "What other occupations could you have chosen using this intelligence?" Explore these same issues with people at your being there locations.

- During the process of creating meaning of concepts and skills, invite students to select inquiries that rely on intelligences in which the student is strong; during practice applying what is understood, encourage students to select inquiries requiring intelligences that they wish to strengthen.

- When teaching a concept or skill, always illustrate several ways it can be used in their environment (home, school) and give several examples of what it is not. Such attributes assist pattern seeking and meaning making by clarifying the pattern and making it more specific. Also, the fuller their sense of the pattern, the more likely they are to recognize it in their prior experiences.

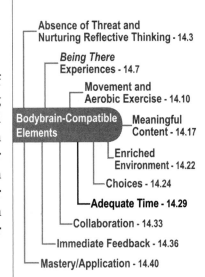

ADEQUATE TIME
BODYBRAIN-COMPATIBLE ELEMENT 7

Lack of time is our society's number one cause of anxiety and stress. It starts early when infants must wake according to the family work and school schedules instead of their own internal time clock. In school, our rigid schedules ensure that most children will fail to finish the assigned task. Or, and equally nightmarish for children, after speeding through the assignment, there is too much time with nothing engaging to do; boredom sets in. The baby-bear experience of time being just right is exceedingly rare. Few children learn good time-management skills because time is not under their control nor are most of the elements important to the task.

Learning Takes Time

Those who liken the brain to a computer fail to appreciate the true biological nature of the brain. While it may take nanoseconds to switch from 0 to 1 and back again, the gist of learning in computers, *learning requires physiological growth* of neurons, dendrites, axons, and time for mylination to occur. Such growth takes time. And lots of sensory and emotional input as well.

Wish as we may, wish as we might, there are no short cuts. Brain research demands teaching concepts and skills well once (effective first teaching), guided practice as students apply what they understand in varying circumstances (not just rote memorization), and then using that learning until the physiological process is hard-wired into long-term memory.

Teaching the concept and skill of long division in a single, uninterrupted day is a perfect example of adequate time in action. (See the DVD *I Can Divide and Conquer: A Concept in a Day* by Martha Kaufeldt.) Division Day has been replicated in schools and districts across the country over the past 15 years. The results are always the same—mastery for all students that day and a program wired into long-term memory that doesn't slip away over time. And, yes, we did say all students.

Factors That Affect Time. Because every brain is different, so is each student's approach to detecting patterns and making meaning. So, too, is the amount of time needed.

Factors that directly affect the amount of time students need to detect patterns and construct their own meaning are

ADEQUATE TIME

Learning Takes Time

Implications for Curriculum and Instruction

MARY FROGGINS

The Divide and Conquer *day has been replicated dozens of times across the country. Using the same brain principles and planning format, schools have also had great success with Multiplication Week, Mission Addition (half week), Fraction Day, Contraction Day, Apostrophe Half Day, and so on.*

- The wiring of the learner's brain

- Prior experience

- Level of personal interest in the topic

- Whether the concept or skill is studied in context they can relate to

- Whether the kind and amount of input allows the learner to use his or her intelligence of strength

Like It or Not. Regardless of why a student may need more time, the critical point is that we must provide it. To close the grade book on a student because he or she didn't master something in the allotted time is discrimination of the worst kind. The implicit message is that if you aren't like everyone else, you will be cut off and abandoned. In such an environment the focus is not on mastery but on the inhumane, lock-step demands of bureaucracy.

In a bodybrain-compatible classroom, the grade book is held open until the end of the year. Demonstration of mastery the last day of school is as good as mastery the first day the key point is studied—provided, of course, that provision is made to support students in achievement such mastery over time).

Implications for Curriculum and Instruction

To implement the bodybrain-compatible element of adequate time, we recommend the following.

Curriculum Development

- Reduce the number of things to be learned by teasing out the underlying concepts and presenting them in meaningful chunks. Once students understand the concept, additional related knowledge can be learned much more easily. As Frank Smith says, "Understanding takes care of learning." Learning then becomes nearly effortless and automatic.[49]

- Use your *being there* locations to naturally integrate content and skills. Thus, a one-hour writing assignment about their favorite ecosystem equals two hours of learning because language arts and science are both used simultaneously. This helps free time for practicing basic skills, such as writing, math, speaking, and so forth, without ever losing focus on the study of ecosystems. Similarly, if the focus were on math, you could explore the math possibilities at your current being there plus revisit earlier sites while maintaining focus on math.

- Encourage students who need more practice to use spare time during the school day and at home to complete inquiries. Invite them to develop their own inquiries to practice with.

- To help you cut back some of the overwhelming amount of curriculum content, use the principle of selective abandonment. Put at the end of your curriculum those things you believe are least important for students to understand and be able to apply. Chief among these are factoids that won't affect their lives now or in the future. Then, if you run out of time—and who doesn't!—you will have given students the gift of what will most serve them later in life.

- When writing inquiries, keep in mind the time frames in which you will have students use them, e.g., all morning or all afternoon, for an hour before the schoolwide assembly, the 30 minutes before the bus arrives for your being there experience, and so forth. If the inquiry requires more time than the schedule permits, even after using maximum flexibility, think through natural breaking points in advance.

- Teach students useful ways to organize their work and related materials. Help them find a balance between efficiently organized for tasks and their personality preferences, e.g., example judging versus perceiving.[50] An optimum balance here will do much to reduce threat and enhance reflective thinking now and for the rest of their lives.

- Embrace the concept that less is more. Make it your number one goal for the year. Teach conceptually through to long-term memory rather than "covering" all the chapters of a textbook.

Instructional Strategies

- Develop, with student input, written procedures for what to do when they finish their assignment early. Include "looking back" questions—questions that help them evaluate whether the information has been fully wired into their long-term memory, introspections about how they might use such information in the future, and other questions that help students realize that their learning is for them, not for the teacher or the grade point or other external audiences or purposes.

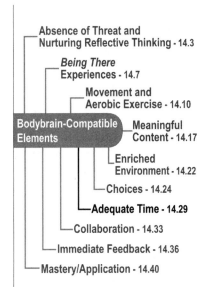

Absence of Threat and Nurturing Reflective Thinking - 14.3
Being There Experiences - 14.7
Movement and Aerobic Exercise - 14.10
Bodybrain-Compatible Elements
Meaningful Content - 14.17
Enriched Environment - 14.22
Choices - 14.24
Adequate Time - 14.29
Collaboration - 14.33
Immediate Feedback - 14.36
Mastery/Application - 14.40

ADEQUATE TIME

Learning Takes Time

Implications for Curriculum and Instruction

MARY FROGGINS

It was Albert Einstein who said that man invented the concept of time and has spent the rest of his life being controlled by it!
It seems all the more true today when technology has literally added 20 percent to our work week, mainly because we take on larger and larger undertakings due to the fabled promise of assistance from our technological helpers—computers, fax machines, cellular telephones, and instantaneous worldwide communication.

- Create an agenda every day and use it throughout the day to organize your time and your students' time.

- Teach students time management skills through modeling, mini-lessons during teachable moments, and through reflective thinking questions before, during, and after collaborative work and individual assignments, especially those lasting over multiple days. Give students genuine control over relevant elements of their work so that they can realistically practice effective time management.

- Model good time management practices and talk out loud as you think your way out of time crunch dilemmas and your stress reactions to them.

- Just as there's a silent period before vocalization when learning another language, so there's a quiet period when students are learning a new concept or skill. Don't rush through such silences or periods of delayed responses. Allow students intrapersonal time to

  - Observe and sift through what they already know and how this new concept or skill relates to what they already understand (the patterns and the interrelationships among the patterns) and can do (the programs for using what they understand).

  - Explore the patterns involved and to arrive at their own understandings—about how things work, what makes things tick, why they might be important to them.

  - Explore, through sketching or diagramming, graphing, or mindmapping, the patterns they see and how they interrelate with other patterns.

  - Try out what they understand, to correct or add to what they understand with nonjudgmental, supportive peers.

  Only then ask for personal performances that will be evaluated or critiqued by an audience. New understandings are not sifted into the brain as separate things; they are integrated into prior understandings or patterns.

- Take time to plan for and effectively teach a concept or skill the first time. Effective first teaching is a huge timesaver but you must invest time up front.

- Deep understanding comes from identifying attributes of things and their uses and coming to understanding interrelationships among them. Such mental work requires rewiring and new wiring—physiological tasks of the brain that require time and massive sensory input.

- Teach students to manage their time and to recognize plateau points in their work—natural breaking points at which a pause would be productive rather than disruptive.

- Make time for reflecting on what was accomplished—individually and as a group.

- Provide adequate wait time; let students benefit from self-talk or dialogue with Learning Club members before you accept an answer to your question. Make answering a question an adventure in reflective thinking rather than a competition to be first.

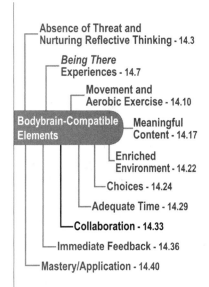

Bodybrain-Compatible Elements

- Absence of Threat and Nurturing Reflective Thinking - 14.3
- *Being There* Experiences - 14.7
- Movement and Aerobic Exercise - 14.10
- Meaningful Content - 14.17
- Enriched Environment - 14.22
- Choices - 14.24
- Adequate Time - 14.29
- **Collaboration - 14.33**
- Immediate Feedback - 14.36
- Mastery/Application - 14.40

COLLABORATION
BODYBRAIN-COMPATIBLE ELEMENT 8

Almost all learning occurs in a social context. At birth we are genetically wired to connect with others[51] and to learn through imitating[52]—be it learning to speak, the rules and strategies of a playground game or etiquette at a community BBQ. We are social animals. Collaborating isn't something we do; it's who we are and the context in which we live. Over the millennium, collaboration has often meant the difference between life and death. Collaboration, with few exceptions, has always increased the likelihood of success. However, like most social skills, collaborating—with family, friends, and in the workplace—must be learned, through modeling and practice. Done poorly, it's a lifelong source of emotional upset. Done well, it's the key to satisfaction and success throughout one's life. Learning how and when to collaborate is essential to our emotional health, our capacity to learn, and our performance levels throughout life.

Solid Research Base

Research provides a very compelling endorsement of the power of collaboration to increase learning, improve the quality of products, and make the work or learning environment more pleasant and productive. The research over the past 50 years is conclusive.[53]

Also, from a brain perspective, collaboration helps provide great quantities of input to the brain. Active learning processes result in active brains. Collaboration is important not just for the social growth and development of students; it's a vital way of enhancing academic learning.

Full understanding of what is being learned and the ability to apply it with—creative problem solving and flexible use of what is learned—depend upon ample opportunity to manipulate information

COLLABORATION

Solid Research Base

A Balancing Act

Implications for Curriculum and Instruction

in our heads, to test it, expand it, connect it with prior learnings. Collaborating with others allows us to examine our own thinking while expanding our knowledge base. One teacher facing a classroom of thirty brains, each with very different ways of learning, is insufficient to the task. Collaboration—students teaching each other and providing a sounding board for each other—is an essential classroom structure in a bodybrain-compatible learning environment. It effectively increases the number of teachers available to support learning.

A Balancing Act

As powerful as collaboration is, it's a strategy among many and must be counter balanced by time for reflective thinking, the introspection time during which we learn to use the voice in the back of our head to guide ourselves through intrapersonal work—learning, problem solving, producing products, and creating and nurturing relationships that enrich our life.

Implications for Curriculum and Instruction

To implement the bodybrain-compatible element of collaboration, we recommend the following.

Curriculum Development

- The content for good collaboration should be

  - A challenge that no one group member working alone can do. Thus, genuine inclusion of all is a must rather than a sociological nicety.[54]

  - Reflective of real life, engaging as many senses as possible.

- The content of inquiries assigned for collaborative work should include social and personal skills as well as curriculum content.

- In a bodybrain-compatible environment, collaborative groups are called Learning Clubs.[55] The goal of collaborative tasks should always be increased achievement and higher quality products. Collaboration is a means to an end (learning), not an end in itself. Never use collaboration as a social event. If you want to have a party or allow chatting to fill in an odd moment or two, have the party or allow chatting in pairs. Collaboration should be viewed by students as genuine work, serious study. The value of the work should be obvious to all during collaborative work.

MARY FROGGINS

Each brain is wired differently due to genetics, environment, and prior experiences. Consequently, every student goes about using what they understand differently. This is particularly important when teaching basic skills. Unless our goal is blind uniformity of both process and outcome, there is no justifiable reason for insisting on only one way, one algorithm (a mathematical term for pattern) for multiplication when there are more than 16 that do the job just as well. Likewise for long division, addition, and on and on. Also, remedial readers use reading skills much more fully if they get to choose the content—car magazines or fashion magazines, spy novels or Ranger Rick, sports magazines or romance novels.

- Change the composition of the Learning Clubs monthly or at least every six weeks. Getting to know others well accelerates learning, prevents cliques, and increases opportunities to practice applying the Lifelong Guidelines and LIFESKILLS.[56] Changing group members gives an opportunity for a fresh start for students who get off on the wrong foot with their first Learning Club group. Learning how to get to know others, and be comfortable doing so, is a critical personal and social skill.

- In addition to the ongoing class family group, create skill and interest groups:

  - Skill groups—short-term, ad hoc groups for studying specific skills or concepts among which students shift from group to group as mastery is attained

  - Interest groups—opportunities to share or work on a topic of special interest

- Make sure that the curriculum content for collaborative work is specifically designed for collaboration. An appropriate task for collaborative work is one that the brightest student can't do alone; every member of the group is needed to be successful. Otherwise, collaborative work negatively reinforces low social status for middle and lower achieving students and the brightest students end up doing all the work.[57]

- Have students review the content of the Lifelong Guidelines/LIFESKILLS they will most need to be successful at their task and make decisions about how they will apply it to their work.

- Teach students to look for patterns. Model it in your questioning strategies and when leading approaches to solving problems and producing products.

- Teach them the patterns in thinking and behavior in the multiple intelligences, personality preferences, and their own habits of mind.

Instructional Strategies

- The two primary purposes of collaboration are to

  1. Enhance achievement by increasing input to the bodybrain learning partnership and increasing emotional engagement and opportunities to apply what is learned.

  2. Equalize social status in the classroom.

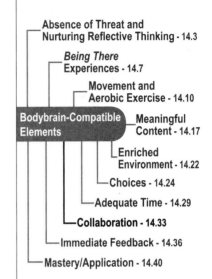

Absence of Threat and Nurturing Reflective Thinking - 14.3

Being There Experiences - 14.7

Movement and Aerobic Exercise - 14.10

Bodybrain-Compatible Elements

Meaningful Content - 14.17

Enriched Environment - 14.22

Choices - 14.24

Adequate Time - 14.29

Collaboration - 14.33

Immediate Feedback - 14.36

Mastery/Application - 14.40

COLLABORATION

Solid Research Base

A Balancing Act

Implications for Curriculum and Instruction

MARY FROGGINS

Each of us can recall a time when we were deeply immersed in something and then were interrupted. Not only do we immediately feel irritated—a sense of loss—but when we can again return to the task, the enjoyment is gone. Worse, it takes some time before we are able to figure out where we were in our thinking process. Inadequate time causes tremendous stress and kills motivation for all of us.

The more important completion of a task is to us, the greater the stress, anxiety, and frustration—all elements that add up to perceived threat. Consequently, many students unconsciously withdraw their commitment to completion with high standards as a way of protecting themselves against high levels of emotional upheaval. In effect, our rigid schedules train students to not care, to be surface thinkers and mediocre performers.

- Use collaboration with the intention of dramatically increasing opportunities for the bodybrain partnership to play an active rather than passive role in learning.

- Reflective thinking: After they are finished with each collaborative task, have students analyze how well they utilized the Lifelong Guidelines/LIFESKILLS, how they felt about the process of working together, how they could have improved both process and product, and, very importantly, what they learned about their personal and social skills for working together. How will they put that knowledge into action during the next collaborative work session.

IMMEDIATE FEEDBACK
BODYBRAIN-COMPATIBLE ELEMENT 9

Immediate feedback is a necessary element in the learning environment—both for pattern seeking (making accurate meaning) and for program building (correctly using what we understand). In all learning environments except the school, it is present in abundance. Consider, for example, when children first begin to talk. Each time they say something incorrectly, we immediately give them the correct word, usage, and pronunciation. Imagine letting all their mistakes pile up during the week and correcting them on Friday!

The more immediate, intrinsic, and unambiguous the feedback, the faster and more accurate the learning. For example, when learning to ride a bike, if you don't get the balance right, you hit the ground. Ambiguous? Not! In contrast, taking an essay test that will be graded and returned next week (and that is fast as essay exams go!) or doing all the odd number problems for math homework and getting a response from the teacher, hours or days after the task is done, violates all the important rules for learning. By then, the brain either has learned it wrong or didn't learn it at all.

Few worksheets provide feedback that is self-correcting or intrinsic. As a consequence, children feel rudderless, confused, powerless, dependent on someone else, and either anxious or bored. Hardly the characteristics of a bodybrain-compatible learning environment. Without immediate feedback, learning is seriously impeded and students are left to tug at their teacher's shirtsleeve to ask, "Teacher, teacher, is this right?"

Why Immediate Feedback Is Important

The most difficult thing for a brain to do is unlearn something. We're all familiar with this one. Is it *maintainence or maintanence* or *maintenance*? And every time we have to spell the word, all three choices pop up with competing intensity? Why? Because each time they simultaneously come to mind as options, the wiring of the three is equally reinforced. Or how about the < and > signs? Is the number off the pointed end the smaller? Or does it depend on the order in which you say them? Or hang it, I don't know! And you have trouble learning it because the confusion is wired in just as strongly as the right answer each time you try to recall which of the options is the correct one.

The number one purpose of immediate feedback is to prevent such mental sputtering. Give feedback to students before they begin to practice something incorrectly or incompletely. Immediate feedback helps ensure that students come to a full and accurate understanding of a skill or concept—that they discover the critical attributes and understand how they fit together. This is especially important when students begin to integrate new experiences with prior learnings. For example, the videotape *A Private Universe*[58] provides an astounding example of how childhood experiences with heat (the closer you get, the hotter it becomes) overrides lecture and textbook. As the interviews with graduating Harvard students illustrate, even course work in advanced planetary motion can fail to dispel the assumption put together in childhood—that summers are hot because the earth gets closer to the sun.

Accept the challenge of effective first teaching, ensuring that students learn something correctly and thoroughly the first time.

The Best Kinds of Immediate Feedback

The best feedback is that built into the learning situation and materials—inherent, immediate, consistent. For example, learning to play a saxophone, use a hand lens or microscope, match yesterday's colors for painting in oils or water color, and so on. In each case, learners knows immediately if they have successfully performed the action. No one needs to tell them.

The most hazardous kind of feedback for learners to rely on is teacher feedback. Why? Because it is external not internal, and therefore can't be replicated by the learner, and because it's rarely immediate due to the demands on the teacher by other learners. Grading papers overnight, even by the end of the day, does little to help a learner develop accurate programs. To be useful, feedback must come at the time the learner is engaged in using the knowledge or skill. This axiom is especially urgent when learning new material.

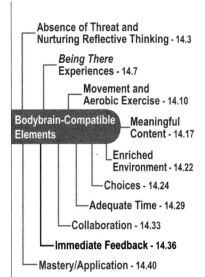

Bodybrain-Compatible Elements

- Absence of Threat and Nurturing Reflective Thinking - 14.3
- *Being There* Experiences - 14.7
- Movement and Aerobic Exercise - 14.10
- Meaningful Content - 14.17
- Enriched Environment - 14.22
- Choices - 14.24
- Adequate Time - 14.29
- Collaboration - 14.33
- **Immediate Feedback - 14.36**
- Mastery/Application - 14.40

IMMEDIATE FEEDBACK

Why Immediate Feedback Is Important

The Best Kinds of Immediate Feedback

Immediate Feedback and Motivation

Implications for Curriculum and Instruction

This discussion brings up some interesting observations about homework. From a brain research point of view, it's clearly a mistake to assign a page of division problems if students have not yet mastered division because it is likely that they will get as much practice doing the task incorrectly as they will doing it right. This only serves to deepen the confusion and makes reteaching more difficult the next day. On the other hand, if students have already mastered division, why should we burden them with a page of busywork? In our opinion, homework should consist primarily of students applying concepts and skills to real-life situations around the home and neighborhood through meaningful projects.

Immediate Feedback and Motivation

Immediate feedback that tells us if we're on track or not is one of the greatest sources of motivation. Lingering on with a task that we suspect we're doing "all wrong" and therefore will have to do over again, all the while feeling stupid, is a recipe for giving up and not wanting to try again.

Another motivation downer is having to rely on external sources for our feedback, especially a control figure such as one's classroom teacher. The older students get, the more they, like we adults, begin to resent being dependent on someone else and feeling powerless.

Inadequate feedback produces highly charged negative emotions. It is critical that teachers master this late phase in the learning process; otherwise, all earlier efforts are in vain. In contrast, feedback that tells us we have succeeded at a learning task produces a burst of neurotransmitters, producing a "chemical high" that's readily observable in the spark in a child's eye as the "aha" registers. As Frank Smith points out, learning does not require coercion or irrelevant reward. Learning—driven by immediate feedback—is its own reward.[59]

Implications for Curriculum and Instruction

To implement the bodybrain-compatible element of immediate feedback, we recommend the following.

Curriculum Development

- Design action-oriented inquiries whose tasks provide clear feedback as the students carry out the inquiry.

- Inquiries that require reflective thinking and that model asking questions that the voice in the back of one's head can ask in the future.

MARY FROGGINS

Few worksheets provide feedback that is self-correcting or intrinsic. As a consequence, children feel rudderless, confused, powerless, dependent on someone else, and either anxious or bored. Hardly the characteristics of a bodybrain-compatible learning environment. Without immediate feedback, learning is seriously impeded and students are left to tug at their teacher's shirtsleeve to ask, "Teacher, teacher, is this right?"

- Rubrics that enable students to provide feedback to themselves.

Instructional Strategies

- Teach students to identify what they will need before they begin a learning task, e.g., the LIFESKILLS needed, prerequisite skills and knowledge, and how to assess if they are being successful at coming to an accurate understanding of and ways to apply concepts and skills, and time needed. Model or teach them to use self-talk to help them when they feel confused, bogged down, or discouraged.

- Increase the number of "teachers" by organizing students into Learning Clubs, eliminating ability grouping (in which students are equally unable to help each other), creating multi-age classrooms (at least three grade levels is ideal), and arranging for cross-age tutoring.

- Commit yourself to being an effective first teacher. Limit your direct instruction to 16 minutes or less, then follow up with guided practice inquiries. Circulate among the students to give them immediate feedback individually and as a group.

- Teach them to use simple, self-constructed or teacher-made rubrics by which they can assess their progress. Often just asking a self-assessment question helps guide learning.

- Develop a repertoire of ways you can provide students with immediate feedback and use them often:
  - Brief talk-with-your-neighbor breaks during presentations to reflect on a question or check for understanding about something just presented
  - Walkabouts—opportunities to observe/listen/ask questions as students work collaboratively
  - Journal writing assignments asking students to reflect on what they've just learned and how they might use it in their lives now and in the future
  - Self-check procedures of many kinds, such as rubrics, answer sheets, self-developed criteria
  - Tasks to be completed while the visiting resource person is still available to provide expert feedback.

- Develop a repertoire of ways classmates can provide each other with immediate feedback and use them often:

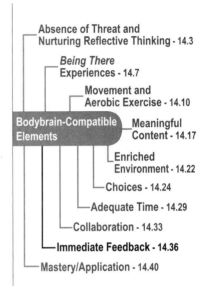

Bodybrain-Compatible Elements

- Absence of Threat and Nurturing Reflective Thinking - 14.3
- Being There Experiences - 14.7
- Movement and Aerobic Exercise - 14.10
- Meaningful Content - 14.17
- Enriched Environment - 14.22
- Choices - 14.24
- Adequate Time - 14.29
- Collaboration - 14.33
- Immediate Feedback - 14.36
- Mastery/Application - 14.40

IMMEDIATE FEEDBACK

Why Immediate Feedback Is Important

The Best Kinds of Immediate Feedback

Immediate Feedback and Motivation

Implications for Curriculum and Instruction

MARY FROGGINS

Immediate feedback that tells us if we're on track or not is one of the greatest sources of motivation. Lingering on with a task that we suspect we're doing "all wrong" and therefore will have to do over again, all the while feeling stupid, is a recipe for giving up and not wanting to try again.

- Rubrics for Learning Club members and study partners to check each other's work immediately (thereby eliminating overnight grading by teachers)

- Think-pair-share, reflective thinking (before and after an activity), and other similar cooperative learning strategies[60]

- Peer review and assessment; cross-age buddies.

• Develop opportunities for immediate feedback outside the classroom and use them frequently through

- Developing legitimate audiences who hold real-world expectations for work by students

- Using inquiries during being there study trips that require students to compare notes and check for accuracy

• Develop long-term projects such as the Yearlong Research Project, social/political action projects, service projects, Kids Vote America, and so forth.

MASTERY/APPLICATION
BODYBRAIN-COMPATIBLE ELEMENT 10

Commitment to mastery—by teacher and students—is a habit of mind that drives us to expect that we go beneath the surface to really understand something, to press on to learn how to apply it in meaningful ways in real-world situations, and to practice using what we understand until we are certain that it becomes wired into long-term memory.

Teacher Tools for Ensuring Mastery

To ensure mastery, the teacher must know exactly what he or she wants students to learn and why. Key teacher tools are these two questions:

These two questions guide your curriculum development efforts. The first question gets you to the substance of your key points. The second guides you in developing inquiries, activities that give students practice in using what they understand in meaningful ways.

These questions parallel the new, brain-based definition of learning as shown in the following graphic.

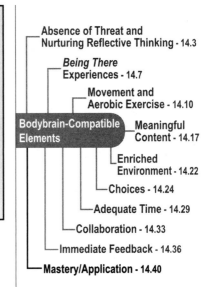

> **LEARNING IS A TWO-STEP PROCESS**
>
> *Step One — Pattern Seeking* **(Input Stage)**
>
> - Identify patterns
> - Make meaning of the pattern/reach understanding
>
> *Step Two — Program Building* **(Output Stage)**
>
> - Ability to use what is understood with support
> - With practice, ability to use what is understood becomes automatic and wired into long-term memory

Figure 14C

Student Tools for Ensuring Mastery

Students need the above tools as well. Teach them this information. Invite them into a partnership with you. In the classroom, as in politics, united we stand, divided we fall. Give them the gift of a lifetime—an invitation to sit in the driver's seat of their own learning processes. Once they know what mastery looks like, they can apply it to every aspect of their lives, not just when sitting in the classroom.

Unfinished homework and poor student work in the classroom is most often due to lack of understanding or misunderstanding between adult and student about the criteria for judging performance. Students should have access to the same formative and summative assessment tools their teachers use. See Chapter 8: Assessment.

Mastery and Emotions

The emotional side of mastery is the foundation of positive self-concept, of seeing oneself as a competent person, capable of handling whatever life puts in front of us. Such positive, learning-enhancing emotions are the lifeblood of the lifelong learner. They make the classroom sizzle with excitement and love of learning and invite the bodybrain partnership to use what we understand, putting to use what we know and can do in ways we value.

Just as successful implementation of a mental program is its own reward, accompanied by feelings of accomplishment and increased satisfaction, having to abort a mental program that doesn't work is emotionally unsettling because it leaves us unsure of what to do next and decreases our sense of self confidence.[61] In other words, the brain has its own built in means of evaluating whether we've achieved mastery. The brain knows the difference between scoring 100 percent on a quiz versus being capable of performing something needed and valued in the real world.

Bodybrain-Compatible Elements

- Absence of Threat and Nurturing Reflective Thinking - 14.3
- *Being There* Experiences - 14.7
- Movement and Aerobic Exercise - 14.10
- Meaningful Content - 14.17
- Enriched Environment - 14.22
- Choices - 14.24
- Adequate Time - 14.29
- Collaboration - 14.33
- Immediate Feedback - 14.36
- **Mastery/Application - 14.40**

MASTERY/APPLICATION

Teacher Tools for Ensuring Mastery

Student Tools for Ensuring Mastery

Mastery and Emotions

Implications for Curriculum and Instruction

MARY FROGGINS

Commitment to mastery—by teacher and students—is a habit of mind that drives us to expect that we go beneath the surface to really understand something, to press on to learn how to apply it in meaningful ways in real-world situations.

Revisit the analysis you did of one of your most vivid learning experiences in Chapter 1. Having now read this chapter, what would you add to that analysis? Which intuitions have been validated, which have been given physical form and a vocabulary with which to talk about them?

What's next? What's your plan for the future?

Implications for Curriculum and Instruction

To implement the bodybrain-compatible element of mastery, we recommend the following.

Curriculum Development

- Make sure that the curriculum you present to students is in fact "getable" or understandable by children their age. If not, mastery is not possible. (If in doubt, see *Thinking and Learning: Matching Developmental Stages With Curriculum and Instruction* by Larry Lowery.)

- Embed the curriculum in experiences, preferably locations where people work and conduct commerce or where Mother Nature can be studied. Make these experiences action-oriented rather than look and hear events. Seeing concepts and skills used in the workplace makes recognition of patterns and their attributes much easier for students. It also increases motivation to learn and master.

- Encourage students to write their own inquiries applying what they understand to problems and situations important to them. Make sure they state what actions would convince them they have mastered the knowledge or skill in the inquiry.

Instructional Strategies

- Model how to use the different intelligences to assess a product or a problem-solving process.

- Help students develop a sense of "knowing when they know" and "knowing when they don't know." If a little knowledge is a dangerous thing, a person with a little knowledge who perceives it to be a lot is a detriment to himself and to others. For example, the online investors who lose their retirement nest egg because they failed to recognize what they didn't know about investing. Or meetings with people who hog the agenda yet have no grasp of the extent of their ignorance on the topic (but nonetheless were adamant in their opinions)—a nightmare in a democratic society when citizens gather together to solve a problem!

- Provide time for students to reflect in their journals about how they can tell if they know enough about a topic to make decisions responsibly and when they need to gather more information.

- Provide models of quality products so students can see what mastery looks like.

- Involve students in designing portfolios that demonstrate mastery.

- Front load initial instruction with a wide variety of sensory input—*being there,* immersion, and hands-on-of-the-real thing. Stop frequently to provide students opportunities to experience and share observations; check frequently for accuracy and completeness of understanding.

- Have students use visual organizers for note-taking rather than the standard outline format. For example, KWU charts (what students _k_now before you start, what they _w_ant to know, and later what they _u_nderstand by the end of study), mindmaps to show multiple relationships, Venn diagrams to compare attributes, and so forth. Have students compare their notes within their Learning Club, checking for accuracy and completeness, and resolving any differences in pattern-seeking before you move on. If more than one group has the same difference in understanding, bring the issue to the whole class. Tease out what previous learnings are interfering with correct understanding of the current concept or skill and then reteach by giving correct information about both prior and current concepts and skills. Then, recheck for understanding.

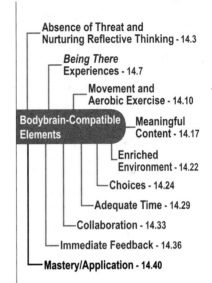

MASTERY/APPLICATION

Teacher Tools for
Ensuring Mastery

Student Tools for
Ensuring Mastery

Mastery and Emotions

Implications for Curriculum
and Instruction

END NOTES

1   The third edition of Leslie A. Hart's *Human Brain and Human Learning* is now available (Black Diamond, WA: Books for Educators, 2002), 44.

2   Robert Sylvester, PhD, has synthesized a good deal of research into a very useful and memorable phrase: "Emotion drives attention, attention drives learning/memory/problem-solving/just about everything else." From "The Role of the Arts in Brian Development and Maintenance," 6. Available at http://www.ode.state.or.us/teachlearn/subjects/arts/resources/rolesbraindevelopment.pdf. See also *A Celebration of Neurons: An Educator's Guide to the Human Brian* (Alexandria, VA: ASCD, 1995), especially Chapter 4.

3   There are many terms for an established, on-going performance review process. "Metacognition" is used by Costa and Garmston in their peer coaching model. "Thinking about thinking" is used by Caine and Caine. Jeanne Gibbs uses the phrase "processing the process." Following through on brain research findings, we use the term "reflective thinking."

    Warnings against the unexamined life are as old as Socrates: "The unexamined life is not worth living." Because there are so many personal and social skills that need to be honed for successful groupwork, we recommend that the you make reflective thinking a regular part of your classroom life—before, during, and after groupwork on a daily basis.

4   Mihaly Csikszentmihalyi provides a useful definition for assessing engagement for learning and several necessary ingredients: See *Flow: The Psychology of Optimal Experience* (New York: Harper Row, 1990), 74–75.

5   Stress research has been extensive and still continues. For readable introductions to the material, see John Ratey's *A User's Guide to the Brain: Perception, Attention, and the Four Theaters of the Brain* (New York: Pantheon Books, 2001) and John Medina's *Brain Rules: 12 Principles for Surviving and Thriving at Work, Home, and School* (Seattle, WA: Pear Press, 2008).

6   Part of slowing down is allowing the brain and heart to come into coherence. See Doc Childre and Howard Martin with Donna Beech, *The HeartMath Solution* (San Francisco: HarperCollins, 2000). This fascinating book opens new windows on the relationship between brain and heart, a connection not considered important by neuroscience until very recently.

7   For a more in-depth exploration of the implication of brain research on curriculum and instruction for each of the bodybrain-compatible elements, see *Exceeding Expectations: A User's Guide to Implementing Brain Research in the Classroom*, 5th ed., by Susan J. Kovalik and Karen D. Olsen (Federal Way, WA: The Center for Effective Learning, 2010).

8   We are mistaken if we believe that discipline, dropouts, and drugs are what is wrong with today's schools. They are merely symptoms of a much larger underlying problem: far too many capable students make little or no effort to learn. In the landmark book *Control Theory in the Classroom* by William Glasser, MD (New York: Harper & Row Publishers, Inc., 1986), a new and powerful explanation of how we behave explains why this problem exists and how we can begin to solve it through learning teams. See also Diane Gossen, *It's All About We: Rethinking Restitution* (Saskatoon, SK: Chelsom Consultant. Ltd., 2004).

9   See Doc Childre, *Freeze Frame: A Scientifically Proven Technique for Clear Decision Making and Improved Health* (Boulder Creek, CA: Planetary Publications, 1998). The well-known HeartMath Freeze Frame technique shows how to manage thoughts and emotions in the moment by applying five simple steps which enhance performance and creativity.

10 The authors believe that the most profound principle to be drawn from recent brain research is this two-step definition of learning. It appears frequently in this book because it should frame every aspect of the classroom from curriculum design to lesson planning to assessment of student and teacher performance.

11 Elizabeth Cohen, *Designing Groupwork: Strategies for the Heterogeneous Classroom*, 2nd ed. (New York: Teachers College Press, 1994).

12 This inseparable brain-body partnership is now accepted science. For more information, see Carla Hannaford, *Smart Moves: Why Learning Is Not All in Your Head* (Alexander, NC: Great Oceans, 1995), Candace Pert, *Molecules of Emotion: Why We Feel the Way We Feel* (New York: Scribner, 1997). Also see John Ratey and John Medina.

13 Ratey, 148–150.

14 See Elkhonon Goldberg. *The Executive Brain: Frontal Lobes and the Civilized Mind* (Oxford: University Press, 2001).

15 Alison Motluk, *New Scientist Magazine*, January 27, 2001, 188.

16 For further reading, see "Mirror Neurons and Imitation Learning As the Driving Force Behind 'the Great Leap Forward' in Human Evolution" by V. S. Ramachandran at www.edge.org/documents/archives/edge69.html; Victorio Gallese and Alvin Goodman, "Mirror Neurons and the Simulation Theory of Mind-Reading," *Trends in Cognitive Sciences*, Vol. 2 (1998), 493; and Giacomo Rizzolatti and Michael Arbib, "Language Within Our Grasp," *Trends in Neurosciences*, Vol. 21 (1998), 188.

17 Carla Hannaford, presentation, Summer Institute sponsored by Susan Kovalik & Associates, 2000.

18 Hannaford, *Smart Moves*.

19 Ratey, 148, 150, 156.

20 Carla Hannaford, *Playing in the Unified Field in the Unified Field: Raising and Become Conscious, Creative Human Beings* (Salt Lake City, UT: Great River Books, 2010), 158.

21 Perhaps the best-known fitness versus sports program is that pioneered by the Naperville School District near Chicago, IL. Called PE4Life, it has fostered considerable research. Outcomes are impressive. For more information about the schools behind the thumbnail sketches here, see the websites for Woodland Elementary School, Kansas City, Missouri; Titusville Public Schools, PA; and Naperville, respectively. Other useful sources of individual school test scores are GreatSchools.net or trulia.com. Also see the discussion of this fitness-learning revolution in *Spark: The Revolutionary New Science of Exercise and the Brain* by John J. Ratey, MD with Eric Hagerman (New York: Little, Brown and Company, 2008). This is a pivotal book for educators wanting to improve student achievement despite declining budgets. Every staff member should have his or her own copy and the school library should have several copies that parents can access.

Note that this time and pace—35 minutes daily—is the minimum necessary to spark the brain responses described here; time for dressing, showering, getting organized, cooling down, etc., is NOT included in this 35 minutes. Also, complexity and challenge matter. Complexity refers to activities that challenge the body-brain partnership such as novel (to the learner) movements or music with an unusual beat, and, most important of all, immediate post-exercise cerebral challenge, such as reading in a subject area that is a stretch for the learner, crossword puzzles, problem solving of any kind, novel experiences, etc. In schools, an optimum scenario would be aerobics just prior to a student's most difficult subject.

These effects of aerobic exercise, based on numerous studies over the past decade, have been widely reported and are also generally accepted science. For a user-friendly summary, see "The Effects of Exercise on the Brain," www.serendip.brynmawr,edu/bb/neuro/neuro05/web2/mmcgovern.html.

22 See *Spark: The Revolutionary New Science of Exercise and the Brain* by John Ratey with Eric Hagerrman (New York: Little, Brown and Company, 2008.)

23 This area of research is well-established. For one of many surveys, see "The Effects of Exercise on the Brain" by M. K. McGovern, serendip.brynmawr,edu/bb/neuro/neuro05/web2/mmcgovern.html.

24 Numerous studies have explored the role of BDNF in learning; they overlap and confirm. For more information, see Carl W. Cotman, *Activity Dependent Plasticity in the Aging Brain*, University of California Irvine, 2004. For a brief, user-friendly overview, also see M. K. McGovern.

25 It is important to note that there is a point beyond which increased aerobic exercise does not continue to increase BDNF. However, few push their exercise regimen beyond this point. And certainly 35 minutes daily comes nowhere close to reaching this plateau.

26 See M. K. McGovern, a reader-friendly summary (serendip.brynmawr.edu/bb/neuro/neuro05/web2/mmcgovernhtml).

27 Ratey, 7.

28 According to Jim Grissom, although "the overall health benefits of organized physical activity are probably much more important than possible academic benefits . . . when policy makers need to make difficult decisions about where to spend

public funds and administrators need to make decisions about where to focus resources in a climate of academic accountability, a proven relationship between physical fitness and academic achievement could be used as an argument to support, retain, and perhaps even improve physical education programs." "Physical Fitness and Academic Achievement," *Journal of Exercise PhysiologyOnline (JEPonline)*, 8, no. 1, (February 2005), 12.

29 See the summary, "California Physical Fitness Test: A Study of the Relationship Between Physical Fitness and Academic Achievement in California Using 2004 Test Results" by Jim Grissom (California State Department of Education, 2004). For a more academic discussion, see "Physical Fitness and Academic Achievement," *Journal of Exercise PhysiologyOnline (JEPonline)*, Vol 8, Number 1, February 2005.

30 Grissom, *JEPonline.* Stanford Achievement Test/9 mean curve equivalent increases were from 42 to 60 in reading (roughly a 33 percentile increase) in reading and a 37 to 52 MCE increase (24 percentile increase) in math. See page 16.

31 Grissom, CDE study, 5–6.

32 The CDE physical fitness test, called the Fitnessgram, was developed by the Cooper Institute for Aerobics Research in Dallas, Texas. Included in the CDE study were 371,198 fifth graders, 366,278 seventh graders, and 298,910 ninth graders.

33 Castelli, Darla, C. H. Hillman, S. M. Buck, and H. E. Erwin, "Physical Fitness and Academic Achievement in Third- and Fifth-Grade Students, Journal of Sport & Exercise Psychology, 29, 2007, 239-252.

34 See C. H. Hillman, M. B. Pontiflex, L. B. Raine, D. M. Castelli, E. E. Hall, and A. F. Kramer, "The Effect of Acute Treadmill Walking on Cognitive Control and Academic Achievement in Preadolescent Children," *Neuroscience* 159 (2009), 1044--1064. In preadolescents, a single acute bout of moderately-intense aerobic exercise improves cognitive performance in reading, increases response accuracy (improved cognitive control). According to the researchers, acute exercise might serve as a cost-effective means for improving specific aspects of academic achievement and enhancing cognitive control during preadolescence (1059–1060).

Hillman also found that in adults, single bouts of exercise may increase attentional resource allocation and improve cognitive processing speed

(from a 2003 study, Hillman, "Effect of Acute Treamill Walking, 2009, 1046). In schools, what's good for the goose is also good for the gander. Staff, and parent volunteers, should explore the benefits of becoming fit and consider becoming role models.

35 Conversation, July 13, 2009, with Jim Grissom, PhD, Research and Evaluation Consultant, Standards & Assessment Division, California Department of Education.

36 Ratey, 4. See also the work of enrichment theory pioneer Marion Diamond and Janet Hopson, *Magic Trees of the Mind: How to Nurture Your Child's Intelligence, Creativity, and Healthy Emotions From Birth Through Adolescence* (New York: Penquin, 1998). The lethal nature of inactivity has been known for more than 20 years. "Use it or lose it" is a solid brain research fact.

37 The originators and most progressive trainers of the Naperville Schools aerobic exercise program model is the Naperville staff. See End Note 21.

38 Leslie A. Hart, *Human Brain and Human Learning,* 3rd ed. (Black Diamond, WA: Books for Educators, 2002).

39 Hart, 135.

40 Frank Smith, *Insult to Intelligence: The Bureaucratic Invasion of Our Classrooms* (New York: Arbor House, 1986).

41 Smith, 62.

42 Smith, 62.

43 Leslie Hart, *Human Brain and Human Learning,* 223.

44 William Glasser, *Control Theory.* (Harper Row, New York, 1986), 23.

45 Smith, *Insult to Intelligence,* 27.

46 Hart, 67.

47 Co-author Karen Olsen interviewed a young man who had given up on college due to low grades and frustration. After touring with a band for several years, he returned to college. Determined to succeed, and armed with information about Gardner's multiple intelligences, he began to figure out ways to use his considerable musical talent as study aids. For classes with a lot of details and definitions, he would first choose a letter or word representing each element and then compose a short melody using those letters or words. Before long, he was composing and singing his way to high grades — consistently As and B+s.

48 The authors believe that our reading and math reforms have failed over the years because we have continued to insist that there is only one way to teach all students instead of finding a best way for individual students. For example, children that learn to read at age four and who can read and spell years ahead of their grade level, have discovered their own patterns for decoding and spelling. It's a disservice to inflict the standard phonics lessons on them. Doing so usually slows down their reading speed and often also diminishes their enjoyment of reading without providing any benefits. The more unconscious their system of pattern seeking, the more space they have in their conscious mental processing to deal with comprehension. On the other hand, students who haven't detected patterns for decoding that work do need the standard phonics lessons. Pattern identification and understanding is as unique as each child's brain. And, it is far more powerful than our brief lessons can ever be. So, observe your students' pattern-seeking processes and outcomes carefully. Complement them rather than force them.

49 Smith, 74.

50 David Keirsey, *Please Understand Me II: Temperament and Character Intelligence* (Del Mar, CA: Prometheus Nemesis Book Company, 1998).

51 See YMCA of the USA, Dartmouth Medical School, and Institute for American Values, *Hardwired to Connect: A New Scientific Case for Authoritative Communities* (New York: Institute for American Values, 2003), and the work of Sigurd Zielke.

52 "Mirror Neurons and Imitation Learning as the Driving Force behind 'the Great Leap Forward' in Human Evolution" by V. S. Ramachandran at www.edge.org/documents/archives/edge69.html.

53 There are many collections of data about the power of collaboration to improve learning and performance. *The Handbook of Research on Improving Student Achievement, Second Edition*, cites over two dozen studies beginning in 1985 (Gordon Cawelti, Editor, Arlington, Virginia: Educational Research Service, 1999), 159). Robert J. Marzano, in *Classroom Instruction That Works: Research-Based Strategies for Increasing Student Achievement*, summarizes nine synthesis studies on collaboration, from 1987–1996 (Alexandria, VA: ASCD, 2001), 86–87. An author who makes important connections to curriculum development for collaborative work is Elizabeth Cohen; see *Designing Groupwork: Strategies for the Heterogeneous Classroom* (New York: Teachers College Press, 1994).

54 This sage advice comes from Elizabeth Cohen. She provides the best guidance for developing curriculum for collaborative tasks that we have found to date. See *Designing Groupwork: Strategies for the Heterogeneous Classroom, Second Edition* (New York: Teachers College Press, 1994), Chapter 5.

55 Learning Clubs is a term used by Frank Smith who describes the glue of social clubs in real life. For example, when we join a golf club, our sense of belonging propels us to learn what others in our club know — golf, the style of dress of the members, stock market, etc. See Smith, *Insult to Intelligence*.

56 The Lifelong Guidelines and LIFESKILLS are the agreed upon behaviors that sharp classroom culture. See *Exceeding Expectations*, Kovalik and Olsen, Chapters 8 and 9.

57 Elizabeth Cohen, *Designing Groupwork: Strategies for the Heterogeneous Classroom.* (New York: Teachers' College Press, 1994).

58 *A Private Universe* is a fascinating video illustrating the power of concepts generated by full sensory input as a child to override adult learning limited to lecture and reading. Harvard graduates are interviewed in their caps and gowns. The question, "What makes for the seasons?" is answered the same by liberal arts students and those with science backgrounds, even including a student who had taken a course in advanced planetary motion — the earth gets closer to the sun in the summer (thus hotter) and farther away in the winter (thus colder).

59 Frank Smith, *Insult to Intelligence*, 32.

60 See *Cooperative Learning* by Spencer Kagan (San Clemente, CA: Kagan, 1994) and Kagan's Smart Cards.

61 Leslie Hart, *Human Brain and Human Learning*, 160–161.

NOTES TO MYSELF

GETTING THE MOST OUT OF YOUR BEING THERE STUDY TRIPS[1]

Being there study trips are a powerful way to introduce curriculum because they provide full sensory input to the brain, create an emotional experience, and provide real-world application of concepts and skills. Through a combination of exploration (individual and group) and mediation[2] (guided tour with interpretation). They also level the playing field, giving students with no prior experience an opportunity to catch up with more advantaged peers. Study trips are a key strategy in applying brain research to the classroom; therefore, they are not to be used as rewards, nor should students be left behind as a punishment.

To ensure that your *being there* visitation is more than a motivational tool or fun fling, you need detailed planning and a range of instructional strategies not called for when relying on textbooks and worksheets.

PREPLANNING

A successful study trip to a *being there* location starts before you leave the classroom. Make sure you have completed the curriculum planning work outlined in Chapters 2–4 before you begin planning the study trip. As you plan your study trip, keep in mind these two questions as you proceed:

- What do people (workers and visitors) need to know and be able to do at this location in order to work at/use this site effectively?

- What are the most important concepts and skills from my curriculum standards that describe what people need to know and be able to do at this site?

Although logistics and paperwork may not make the heart sing, they do help ensure that your study trip goes off without a hitch. Complete the following several weeks before the study trip.

On-Site

- Once the site has been chosen, get permission from your principal and district office. Inform the students and parents well in advance.

- Visit the study trip location to finalize what you want your on-site resource person (tour guide, docent, store manager, etc.) to show/explain to your students. Give him or her a copy of the Lifelong Guidelines and LIFESKILLS and your concept and key points (conceptual, significant knowledge, and skill).

- As you tour the site together, be clear what you want him or her her to focus on with your students. Often tour guides have their own agenda and want guests to see or tour parts of the site that are not applicable to your concept/ key points. Don't go there! Insist that he or she stick to your concept/key points. You are not asking for the usual tour. Leave other content for later trips.

- Share your on-site inquiries with the on-site resource person and ask for ways to improve them. Get feedback on their accuracy, appropriateness, and centrality to what employees and visitors should know and be able to do. Send the final version of the inquiries to the guide before you arrive with students. If possible, also share your follow-up inquiries, especially the social/political action inquiries.

- Ask the guide if it is possible to break the students into smaller groups. One with the guide, the other with you (or another guide) for exploration. (It is almost impossible to hear and stay on task when standing in the midst of a pack of 25-plus students.)

At the School

- Fill out the necessary paperwork to request a bus.

- Find out about procedures for bus drop-off, parking, and pick-up.

- Meet with the person in charge of students' medication (school nurse or school secretary). Know clearly who gets what, when, and how to dispense them on the trip. Do not delegate this job; keep this responsibility yourself.

- Organize materials and emergency plans.

- Assemble your clipboard and have it ready to pick up as you board the bus. Information, in addition to what you give students and chaperones for their clipboards, should include:

  – Class list and emergency numbers for school and parents

  – Student allergies

  – Schedule for site and contact person's phone number

  – Bus garage phone number

  – Notes about the site from your pre-visit

  – Blank paper for questions and notes

- Prepare content and logistics for a parent/chaperone training.

TRAINING CHAPERONES

Hopefully this is not the first training you have done for your parents because it's best to begin training them on how to help out in your classroom and go on study trips beginning the first week of school. Offer the training several times on different days and times, such as after school, evenings, or even a Saturday morning.

If you cannot get enough parents, recruit qualified candidates wherever you can find them, college students, grandparents, neighbors, friends, classroom aides from other classrooms, and so forth.

Agenda

There are a number of things that your chaperones need to know thoroughly so they be confident enough about their responsbilities that they can perform them without your presence and support if necessary. Include the following topics:

- Confidentiality — After the trip, do not talk about students, parents, or other chaperones or what you may have heard them say.

- Role — They are here to coach students, to ask questions rather than give answers. Tell them they can answer questions only with a question. For example:

  - What do you think?

  - How could you find the answer to that question?

  - What do you see or notice that is different or the same?

  - What do you hear, smell?

  - What is that like?

  - Why do you ask that?

  - Does anyone know the answer to that?

  - Good question. Let's write that down and we will ask the tour guide or the teacher.

- Expectations — Chaperones should expect students and other adults to behave in accordance with the Lifelong Guidelines and LIFESKILLS. Remind them that this study trip is not a reward but a serious and central piece to the curriculum of the classroom. (This might be a good time to share some brain research information with them.)

  Give parents a copy of any additional behavior guidelines and procedures for this particular study trip

- Life Lingo — Describe how to use Life Lingo to guide and support students

- Curriculum — Explain what students will be studying. Give them copies of the concept/key points. Also give them copies of all assignments — a blank form and sample completed form — so that the parents have the answers in advance and feel confident about the content students are to learn.

- Procedures — Go over the procedures for the study trip. Remember, most parents have only experienced field trips for fun; they need to develop a new mental program for what an *HET being there* study trip is. Typical procedures for all chaperones include:

1. Arrive 30 minutes before the trip for last minute instruction, to review procedures for the trip, and to learn about any last-minute changes.

2. Keep ALL of your students with you at all times. If one has to go to the bathroom, everyone goes totgether, including you, the chaperone!

3. Don't purchase anything for the students, including food, trinkets, or souvenirs.

4. Don't bring any children or students not enrolled in the class.

5. Work with your assigned group only; do not join up with another group so the adults can chat. Students have been placed in small groups for a reason—the opportunity to communicate with you.

6. Don't smoke, eat, or drink (even coffee.) You may have a student snack when the students have theirs (if one is provided).

7. Sit with your student group on the bus.

8. Bring the fanny pack/backpack and materials provided by the teacher (see list that follows). Don't hesitate to contact the teacher in person or via the cell phone (in your pack) if you need to. If students are not using the Lifelong Guidelines/LIFESKILLS or you have an emergency, let the teacher know ASAP.

9. Be on time. Know the time you are to meet with tour guides and the time and sites for each rendezvous during the tour and for departure.

10. Have fun! Enjoy the opportunity to spend some time with your son or daughter and his or her Learning Club friends.

Equipment for Chaperones

Equip your chaperones with the tools and supplies they might need. These items help make their responsibilities concrete and give them confidence that they can handle the job. Ask a local store or other business to provide fanny pack/backpacks for the chaperones. This is an opportunity for local businesses to offer support in a tangible way. Get one for each chaperone (about six).

Include the following items in the packs:

- Cell phone (borrow from teachers, parents, friends, whoever you can find, so that every chaperone has one). Be sure you tape the number of your cell phone onto each chaperone's cell phone.

- Facial tissue

- Bandages

- Rubber/latex gloves

- Extra pens/pencils

- Camera (optional)

- A clipboard with the same contents as that on the students' clipboards plus the following:

  - Procedures and responsibilities for chaperones

  - Names of students in his or her group

  - Times his or her group is to meet with the tour guide, for departure time and other details

  - Filled-in version of student worksheets

PREPARING YOUR STUDENTS

Prepare your students for the *being there* location they are about to visit. Tell them where they will be going and explain why you have chosen this site and how it relates to the curriculum. This does not mean that all the content must be taught before they go; that is an old picture of "field trips" conducted at the end of a unit of study.

Content for the Study Trip

- Explaining what they are going to see and how it fits in with what they will be studying — the theme on the wall

- Brainstorming the questions they want to ask of those who work at and use the location

- Completing the K and W columns of a KWU chart (know, want to know, and understand)

Procedures for the Study Trip

- Engaging students in a discussion of the Lifelong Guidelines and LIFESKILLS they will need to use

- Inviting them to help you write procedures for all to follow

- Creating a bus trip assignment that students will do when going to and returning from the site. Relate these to what students will be studying on-site; explain it thoroughly so they know what to do without having to ask a lot of questions once on the bus

- Asking them to predict what they think they might see at such a *being there* location; keep these responses so that students can test these assumptions when they return

Equipment for Students

Each student should have a clipboard that includes the following items:

- Pencil attached with a string

- Lifelong Guidelines/LIFESKILLS laminated and taped to clipboard (backside)

- Procedures for the bus and when at the *being there* location

- Assignments for the bus (to and from) and on-site

- Blank paper for recording questions and illustrations

- Names of the chaperones

THE DAY BEFORE THE STUDY TRIP

The day before the study trip, double-check your arrangements:

- Review your procedures.

- Generate questions. Discuss information-gathering techniques, such as brain-storming A to Z, sketches, journals.

- Call the site to confirm the visit time and your expectations for the tour.

- Call the bus garage to confirm when the bus will arrive at school for departure and when it will return to the school after the study trip.

- Call the chaperones to confirm their assignment and the time they are to arrive. Remind them how important it is that they are on time.

- Form student groups (about 4–5 students per parent/adult chaperone). Unless there is an overriding reason for not doing so, keep students in their Learning Clubs.

- Assign a chaperone to each group. Invite student input; some students do and some do not want their parent as a chaperone for their group.
  [Note: Do NOT assign yourself as a chaperone for a group; you need to be the leader of the total group. Your job is to ensure that each group functions well to maximize learning and to be available to handle an illness, accident, or difficulty a student or chaperone might have.]

- If you do not have an active parent group to act as chaperones on a study trip, consider asking local businesses if they would allow their employees to volunteer. You could also ask grandparents, senior citizens, or even the teacher aides from other classrooms. Remember, you need one chaperone per Learning Club.

30 MINUTES BEFORE THE STUDY TRIP

Just before getting on the bus, meet with parents and with students to review expectations and duties. Give each student and adult a name tag to wear (use tags with a cord; put emergency info on the back of each).

With Chaperones

Review the important points with parents. This serves both as a reminder and as a confidence booster. Review the following:

- Standard procedures

- Student assignments (on the bus and at the site)

- How to use target talk for the Lifelong Guidelines and LIFESKILLS

- Any questions about the trip or curriculum content

- The contents of the chaperone backpack

Have chaperones come to the classroom (stand at the back of the room) during your final review with students.

With Students

Before leaving for the bus:

- Introduce the chaperones.

- Review the site procedures (use chart) which should include the following:

  - Use the Lifelong Guidelines and LIFESKILLS.

  - Focus on the LIFESKILL of Curiosity.

  - Stay with your group and follow the directions of your group's chaperone.

  - Represent yourself and your school in a positive way.

- Generate questions to pursue.

- Hand out the study trip clipboard.

- Answer any questions about what's to be studied.

- Make a final count of the total number of students going on the trip. Have each chaperone count—and remember!—the number of students in his or her group. Have each chaperone say out loud to the class how many students are in his or her group; as they do so, add the numbers on the board to make sure they equal the count for the total class.

For Yourself

Don't forget your clipboard as you board the bus! And make sure you count the students as they board.

THE BUS TRIP

Don't allow bus time to deteriorate into a bus driver's nightmare. Once students lose their focus, it's harder to refocus them when you arrive at the *being there* site.

Setting up expectations for travel to and from the *being there* site is critical.

Getting on the Bus

Start off on the right foot.

- Introduce the bus driver by name and tell students about the Lifelong Guidelines and LIFESKILLS the bus driver will be using to drive them safely to the *being there* location.

- Introduce the chaperones to the bus driver.

- Review the bus procedures (use chart).

  – Sit with someone from your Learning Club (if uneven numbers, sit with your group's chaperone). Sit as near to your chaperone as possible.

  – Stay in your seat.

  – Talk quietly with your seat mate.

  – Use the Lifelong Guideline of Active Listening and the LIFESKILL of Responsibility at all times.

  – Complete the bus assignment with your seat partner.

- Review the bus assignment and answer questions about how to complete it.

- Count students (and chaperones!) twice—once using a total student count and again by having each chaperone count the students in his or her group.

On the Way to the Site

Give students an assignment(s) that will last the length of the drive. This forces students to direct their attention to the world outside the bus and bridges your pre-departure orientation and the visitation. Make sure that the assignment relates to the site to be visited.

Here are some examples for bus time activities while traveling to the site:

- Reading through the field guide and developing at least three questions to ask the guide (the field guide must be developed in advance).

- A from-the-bus window scavenger hunt for items that students think can also be found at the site.

- A variation of an acrostic (a series of lines or verses in which the first, last, or other particular letters when taken in order spell out a word, phrase, etc.) For example:

L — lake, laundromat, ladies' restroom

A — aquatic center, airport, arena, airplane

N — nursery, neighborhood

D — dog, donut shop

F — factory, fence

I — ice, inlet, iron, ice cream parlor

L — light, leaf

L — lawn, lip

- List and tally items for an acrostic based on the name of the *being there* location.

- List and tally names for an acrostic based on commercial signs or a key concept to be studied at the *being there* location.

- List and tally names for an acrostic based on a category of items chosen by students (the acrostic must be based on the name of a concept to be studied at the *being there* location).

On the Way Back From the Site

Make sure you have everyone—students and adults! Count students (and chaperones!) twice—once using a total student count and again by asking each chaperone to give a count of the students in his or her group. Then, don't lose momentum. Provide an assignment(s) that lasts the duration of the return bus drive. This time, have them look for examples of something they learned at the *being there* site. Examples include:

- With your seatmate, (who is also a member of your Learning Club), review your notes in your field guide. Complete writing down your findings. Compare notes with your partner. Add any information that he she gathered that you did not. If you have any blank spaces, discuss with someone sitting across the aisle from you to add to your notes. Complete all items in the study guide.

- With your partner, list the Lifelong Guidelines and LIFESKILLS your bus driver used on this trip. Write an acknowledgment thanking him or her for supporting your study trip. Be specific. Give your note to the bus driver as you get off the bus. Also tell him or her thank you in person.

- With your partner, write a thank-you note to your chaperone. Be sure to mention specifically what you most appreciated about his or her support during the *being there* visit.

- As you exit the bus, check for belongings.

RESPONSIBILITIES ON-SITE

- Organize the groups. Make sure each chaperone has collected his or her students and they are ready to begin. Check that chaperones and students have their clipboards with them. Make sure each chaperone has his or her backpack.

- Touch base with each group at least once during the trip. Check on the chaperone and provide needed assistance and support. Offer expertise.

- Check on target kids.

- Keep the tour guide on target (time and content).

- Point out Lifelong Guidelines/LIFESKILLS as they occur.

- Provide a time for snacks, drinks, and bathroom breaks.

- Report any accidents to the manager at the site and, on your return, to your principal.

- Follow time schedule.

TEACHER RESPONSIBIITIES AFTER THE STUDY TRIP

To make sure that you squeeze every ounce of value from your study trip, don't pass up an opportunity to have students review in their minds what they experienced.

On Re-Entering the Classroom

This is a chance to demonstrate the LIFESKILLS of Organization and Initiative for your students.

- As students reenter the classroom, have them remove their papers from the study trip clipboards and put them on their desks. Then, have them sharpen the clipboard pencils and put the clipboards back in the box ready for the next study trip.

- Brainstorm things about the tour guide that you most appreciated learning. If possible, include chaperones in this activity. Have students write personal thank-you notes to the guide(s), chaperones, and/or bus drivers.

While the experience is still fresh in their minds (students and chaperones), debrief the *being there* experience.

- What did they learn? What most impressed/surprised them? What did they learn that they can use this week in the classroom? Outside of school? What did they learn about the concept being studied?

- How did the procedures work? Should any changes be made before the next *being there* study trip?

- What were the highlights, surprises, disappointments? If we were to do the same study trip again, what changes would we make? And so forth. Preface the discussion with the request that people (students and chaperones) use the Lifelong Guideline of Truthfulness and the LIFESKILLS, including Caring.

- Complete the U column of the KWU chart.

Follow-Up Strategies

To carry the momentum of student enthusiasm from the *being there* experience back into the classroom, choose your most engaging instructional strategies:

- Bring in resource people to further explain what they do at the *being there* site and why it is important. Before their arrival, have students prepare a prioritized list of what they want the resource person to address and the questions they want to pursue.

- Base your direct instruction on examples from the common experience of the study trip.

- Involve students in role-playing activities so they can explore why the concepts and skills of your curriculum are important and how and when they might use them.

- Engage students in both structured and unstructured discussion.

- Structure Discovery Processes that will carry them deeper into the concepts.

- Invite students to select and pursue their own independent study which extends and deepens the concepts and skills of the curriculum.

- Revisit the site.

- Recreate the *being there* experience in the classroom, especially on the immersion wall. Involve students in the design and construction. Include photos, pamplets, models, maps, sketches, and so forth. Aim for a 3-D, high sensory product.

END NOTES

1 These recommendations for planning and conducting a study trip are adapted from the work of Linda Jordan and Sue Pearson, masters of Highly Effective Teaching (Susan Kovalik & Associates). As most teachers already know, students may or may not come away from a study trip having learned what the teacher intended. Mediation—structuring what students focus on, process, and practice using—is essential.

2 This information is provided in the book titled *Exceeding Expectations: A User's Guide to Implementing Brain Research in the Classroom,* 5th ed., by Susan J. Kovalik and Karen D. Olsen (Black Diamond, WA: Books for Educators, 2005), Appendix C.

LESSON PLANNING TEMPLATE

The following lesson plan template is used by the *HET* (Highly Effective Teaching) team of associates when coaching and when teaching students as part of the Model Teaching Week training.

A sample is provided so you can view what powerful lesson planning tools these can be. Adapt the format to your personal organizational style.

Lesson Planning Template

Topic: _____   Organizing Concept: _____

Date: _____   *Being There* location: _____

Conceptual Key Point:	**Lifelong Guidelines/LIFESKILLS Focus:**
Standards Addressed:	**Creating a Sense of Belonging Activity:**
Inquiries: • • •	**Town Hall:** • • •
Significant Knowledge Key Point:	**Quote of the Day/Week:**
Standards Addressed:	**Reading Selection:**
Inquiries: • •	**Journal Topic:** **Reflection Question:**

Skill Key Point:	Movement:
	•
	•
	•
	Collaboration:
	•
	•
Standards Addressed:	
	Music:
	•
Inquiries:	Graphic Organizers:
•	•
	•
	•
	•
•	
	Extended Learning Opportunities:

Celebration of Learning (Assessment):

Social/Political Action Focus:

Reference Resources Used:

Lessons for Which I Will Give Direct Instruction:

Lessons Using the Discovery Process or Other Exploratory Processes:

Example of Lesson Planning Template for Fifth Grade

Topic: __Balancing the System__   Organizing Concept: __Systems__

Date: __September 12, 2009__   *Being There* location: __Huntington Reservoir__

Conceptual Key Point:
A system is a collection of things and processes (and often people) that interact to perform some function. Most systems, living and nonliving, are made up of smaller parts that, when put together, can do things the parts couldn't do by themselves. Our day-to-day living depends on the successful operation of countless systems. (RATIONALE: *Understanding how these systems operate leads to a better understanding of the world around us.*)

Standards Addressed:
Indiana Social Studies: 3.1.2, 3–5.6.1
Indiana Social Studies: 3–5.3.5

Inquiries:
• Analyze the system you brought from home. Using the System to Parts chart, distinguish the parts of the system and record their functions. Share your system and your chart with your Learning Club. (LM, L)
• In your Learning Club, create a Catch Phrase for key concept of your Conceptual Key Point. Your Catch Phrase should include a Bodymap. Develop or find a picture that would be a visual representation of the Catch Phrase. Record your phrase into your Systems Journal. In the Town Hall meeting, share your Catch Phrase, Bodymap, and Picture. (L, S, BK)

Significant Knowledge Key Point:
In an ecosystem, the resident plants and animals interact with each other and the environment in ways that allow each to meet its basic needs. This interaction of living and nonliving things is called interdependence. Ecosystems vary, each including matter and organisms unique to that particular location; for example, a wooded area, desert, and ocean shoreline. (RATIONALE: *To foster and support the balance of an ecosystem, we must first understand the parts of the ecosystem and how they work together.*)

Standards Addressed:
Indiana Science: 5.4.4, 3–4.6.2
Indiana Social Studies: 3.3.5

Inquiries:
• Observe the outdoors. Using your Ecosystem Observation Guide, record examples of living organisms and nonliving elements of the ecosystem. In your Learning Club, make a T-chart of living organisms and nonliving elements you observed. Post your chart in the classroom. Take a Gallery Walk, viewing the T-charts. List five items from the charts, including at least one nonliving element, and analyze how these interact with one another. Share your findings with a partner. (L, BK, LM)
• After receiving your ecosystem materials, sort the materials into two categories: nonliving matter and living organisms. Share your sort with the class. Look at the living organisms and discuss how these work within the system. As a Learning Club, use the procedures for creating an ecosystem to develop a terrarium or an aquarium. Create an Interaction and Interdependence chart with another Learning Club. Display your ecosystem in the Immersion area. (L, BK, S, LM)

Lifelong Guidelines/LIFESKILLS Focus: Effort

Creating a Sense of Belonging Activity:
• Design a nametag
• Who am I?

Town Hall:
• Lifelong Guideline/LIFESKILL focus on "Effort"

• World Map (Leadership, Stewardship, Citizenship), Tony Blair (Leadership, Cooperation, Community), Catalina Island, CA

• Closure – What one word would describe a feeling that you have about today?

Quote of the Day/Week:
"The only place where *success* comes before *work* is in the dictionary."
– Vidal Sassoon

Reading Selection:
• Conceptual Key Point
• Significant Knowledge Key Point

Journal Topic:
What words describe what you know about a system?

Reflection Question:
What is a characteristic of our local region?

Skill Key Point:

Research is a process of discovery that allows a person to find out information about a topic. Information is found through analyzing multiple sources which could include print materials, Internet resources, interviews, and other resources. After finding information, the researcher takes the information gathered and develops his or her own ideas. Once the information has been understood, the researcher is able to share the findings with others.

Standards Addressed:

Indian English Language Arts: 3.4.4, 4.4.6, 4.4.7, 5.2.1, 5.4.1

Inquiries:

• Using the research materials provided, (video, encyclopedia, websites, and recorded interview), find answers to the question provided in your ecosystem/region journal. In your Learning Club, discuss how each of the resources was different but necessary to find key information. (L)

Movement:

• Bodymap
• Observation of outdoors
• Gallery Walk

Collaboration:

• Learning Club Collaboration
• Partner Collaboration

Music:

• Soothing music for reflection time

Graphic Organizers:

• System to Parts chart
• Ecosystem Observation Guide
• Compare/Contrast chart
• T-chart of living and nonliving organisms

Extended Learning Opportunities:

Books to take home for further reading/research about ecosystems and regions

Celebration of Learning (Assessment):

Follow the rubric provided for the assignment(s) given. Compare your Learning Club's part in the class assignment with the expectations listed in the columns.
Can the students report what they have learned about systems to one another?

Social/Political Action Focus:

Arrange an interview with the administrators and teachers about the need for improvement in our school ecosystem. Review the data. Decide the first change you would like to see. How could you make that change?

Reference Resources Used:

• http://www.msnbc.msn.com (Catalina Island, California)
• Systems notebook or journal
• Video from *being there* experience
• Procedure notebooks

Lessons for Which I Will Give Direct Instruction:

• Lifelong Guidelines and LIFESKILLS
• Procedures
• Introduction of Conceptual Key Points (CKP)
• Introduction of CKP Guided Inquiry
• Introduction of Significant Knowledge Key Point (SKKP)

Lessons Using Indirect Instruction:

• CKP Guided Inquiries
• SKKP Independent Inquiries
• *Being there* experience organizer

THOUGHTS ON LESSON PLANNING

3Cs of Assessment

A set of criteria to assess student work used by both students and teachers. The Cs stand for Correct—conforming to fact or truth, free from error, accurate; Complete—having all parts or elements, the assignment is done to the defined specifications; Comprehensive—of large scope, inclusive, extensive mental range or grasp, reflects multiple points of view, thorough.

Absence of Threat/Nurturing Reflective Thinking

The first of the 10 Bodybrain-Compatible Elements of the *HET* (Highly Effective Teaching) model.

Adequate Time

The seventh of 10 Bodybrain-Compatible Elements of the *HET* model.

Age-Appropriate

Concepts and/or facts which are understandable (versus having to be memorized) to students, given the current degree of development of the brain. These biological stages of thinking and learning gained attention through the work of Piaget and continued through in the work of Larry Lowery.

Assessment/Evaluation

A process by which student achievement is assessed. In an *HET* classroom, the expectation is for mastery of key points by all students on an "A/no credit yet" basis.

Being There

The most powerful input to the brain is being in a real world location that activates all 20 senses, thereby significantly increasing learning (pattern identification and program building). Basing curriculum in being there locations is also the second of 10 Bodybrain-Compatible Elements of the *HET* model.

Bloom's Taxonomy

A model by Benjamin Bloom originally designed for enhancing development of questioning strategies for college exams. In the Highly Effective Teaching model, the action verbs characterizing each level of this taxonomy are used to develop inquiries.

Bodybrain-Compatible Elements

Ten conditions that enhance and support powerful learning, the basis for the Highly Effective Teaching *(HET)* model. They are Absence of Threat/Nurturing Reflective Thinking, *Being There* Experiences, Movement to Enhance Learning, Meaningful Content, Enriched Environment, Choices, Adequate Time, Collaboration, Immediate Feedback, and Mastery/Application.

Bodybrain Learning Partnership

One of the five concepts from brain research upon which the Highly Effective Teaching model is based. Includes emotions as the gatekeeper to learning and performance and movement to enhance learning.

Brain-Compatible Learning

Coined by Leslie A. Hart in his book *Human Brain and Human Learning,* it is a key goal of the Kovalik Highly Effective Teaching model. A brain-compatible environment is one that allows the brain to work as it naturally, and thus most powerfully, works. Recent brain research has updated this term to "bodybrain-compatible" learning.

Choices

The sixth of the 10 Bodybrain-Compatible Elements of the *HET* (Highly Effective Teaching) model.

Collaboration

Eighth of the 10 Bodybrain-Compatible Elements of the *HET* model.

Component

An integral structure of the *HET* model based on a being there location. Components are related to the organizing concept of the yearlong theme; based in a being there location; a framework designed for approximately one month of study, broken into topics of typically one to two weeks.

Direct Instruction

The 11 to 16 minutes of teacher presentation of a key point which provides the focus of the classroom activities; direct instruction is only one way of orchestrating key points.

Effective First Teaching

The goal of the *HET* model; a commitment to doing the job right the first time—teaching through ability to apply what is understood and wiring into it long-term memory. Should be the rallying cry for today's school reform efforts. Now possible to do if current brain research is applied to curriculum development and instructional strategies. The ITI/*HET* model is such a vehicle.

Emotion as Gatekeeper to Learning and Performance

One of the two aspects of bodybrain learning partnership, a brain research concept upon which the *HET* model is based.

Enriched Environment

Fifth of the 10 Bodybrain-Compatible Elements of the *HET* model.

Hands-On Experience

A term describing two levels of sensory input: hands-on of the real thing and hands-on of something symbolic or representative of a real thing. Hands-on of symbolic or representational things provides significantly less sensory input, and thus less stimulation of the brain, than does interacting with the real thing.

Group Development, 3 Stages of

In the *HET* model, group development and creating community occurs in three stages: Developing a sense of belonging, creating common ground, and taking action. The end result is a sense of community that increases academic learning as well as enhances personal and social growth.

Highly Effective Teaching (HET) *model, formerly known as ITI (Integrated Thematic Instruction) model*

The name given to a bodybrain-compatible, fully integrated instructional model developed by Susan Kovalik and Associates. It is a comprehensive model that translates the best of what we know about learning from current brain research into effective teaching strategies and meaningful curriculum.

Immediate Feedback

Ninth of the 10 Bodybrain-Compatible Elements of the *HET* model.

Immersion

An environment that simulates as richly as possible the real-life environment being studied, e.g., transforming a classroom into wetlands or a pond or a period of history, allowing students to experience or role-play as if they were actually there.

Input, Types of

(1) Being there, physically being in the real-world environment; (2) Immersion—full simulation of the real-world environment, includes many real-world things; (3) Hands-on of the real thing, (e.g., frog); (4) Hands-on of representation (e.g., plastic model of a frog); (5) Second-hand—pictorial representation, written word (e.g., pictures, videos, or stories about frogs); and (6) Symbolic—mathematics, phonics, grammar (scientific definition of a frog)

Inquiries

A key curriculum development structure in the *HET* model, inquiries are ways for students to understand and apply a key point (concept, significant knowledge, or skill). The primary purpose of inquiries is to enable students to develop mental programs for applying a key point in real-world situations and wiring such knowledge and skills into long-term memory. Inquiries make learning active and memorable.

Inquiry Builder

A chart that organizes the action verbs associated with Bloom's Taxonomy of Cognitive Objectives according to five of Howard Gardner's seven intelligences.

Inseparable Bodybrain Learning Partnership

Current brain research indicates that the limbic system is part of a larger emotional system involving information substances produced and received throughout the body. In other words, the brain talks to the body and the body talks back to the brain. Learning is the result of an inseparable bodybrain partnership.

Instructional Strategies

A variety of instructional strategies are critical to implementing the *HET* (Highly Effective Teaching) model at each stage.

Integrated

As used in the *HET* model, using a physical location to identify and bring together related concepts under the umbrella of an organizing concept. This allows for integration that is natural, not forced, and that is immediately recognizable and understandable by students.

Intelligence as a Function of Experience

One of the four principles from brain research upon which the *HET* model is based.

Key Point

The essential concept, significant knowledge, or skill all students are expected to master (know and be able to use). Key points should be written so they enhance students' ability to detect pattern, i.e., to readily identify the collection of attributes that is essential for understanding the concept, skill, or significant idea of the key point. They also provide a clear focus for the teacher for instructional planning and for orchestration of learning.

Learning, a Two–Step Process

Defined by Leslie Hart as a two-part process: (1) Detecting and understanding patterns — a process through which our brain creates meaning; (2) Developing meaningful mental programs to use what is understood and to store it in long-term memory — the capacity to use what is understood first with assistance and then almost automatically.

Lifelong Guidelines

The parameters for classroom/schoolwide interactions with other students and staff. They are TRUSTWORTHINESS, TRUTHFULNESS, ACTIVE LISTENING, NO PUT-DOWNS, and PERSONAL BEST.

LIFESKILLS

The 19 LIFESKILLS are the day-to-to-day definition of the Lifelong Guideline of Personal Best. The LIFESKILLS are the personal/social parameters for everyone — students and adults. They are: Caring, Common Sense, Cooperation, Courage, Creativity, Curiosity, Effort, Flexibility, Friendship, Initiative, Integrity, Organization, Patience, Perseverance, Pride, Problem Solving, Responsibility, Resourcefulness, and Sense of Humor.

Mastery

The final of 10 Bodybrain-Compatible Elements of the *HET* (Highly Effective Teaching) model. Mastery in the Highly Effective Teaching model means completion of both steps in the new definition of learning; it means being able to apply what is understood in real-world ways and practicing how to use that skill or knowledge until it becomes wired into long-term memory.

Meaningful Content

The fourth of 10 Bodybrain-Compatible Elements of the Highly Effective Teaching model.

Mindmapping

A way to visually represent information, usually as a web or cluster around the main idea with symbols and colors, rather than in traditional outline form.

Movement to Enhance Learning

The third of 10 Bodybrain-Compatible Elements of the Highly Effective Teaching model. Also one of the two aspects of bodybrain learning partnership, a brain research concepts upon which the Highly Effective Teaching model is based.

Multiple Intelligences

Defined by Howard Gardner as "problem-solving or product-producing capabilities." The first seven intelligences identified by Gardner and used in curriculum development in this book are (1) logical-mathematical, (2) linguistic, (3) spatial, (4) bodily-kinesthetic, (5) musical, (6) intraersonal, and (7) interpersonal. Humans are born with all the intelligences but will develop each according to family and cultural preference, demands of one's environment, and the individual's inclinations and experiences. Gardner has subsequently added an eighth intelligence, naturalist. The multiple intelligences are a key ingredient of inquiries.

Organizing Concept

The organizing concept is the central organizer for integrated curriculum in the Highly Effective Teaching model. It is a concept that organizes all the concepts, significant knowledge, and skills to be learned during the theme. It is represented by a kid-grabbing title.

Pattern Seeking

A key concept of bodybrain-compatibility; describes the means by which the brain makes meaning from incoming sensory input. Together with program building, is one of the four concepts from brain research upon which the *HET* model is based.

Procedures, Written

Written procedures are an important classroom leadership strategy in the Highly Effective Teaching model. They state the social and personal behaviors are expected for commonly occurring events, such as entering and leaving the room, lunchroom behaviors, and so forth. By describing what social and personal behaviors are expected, these procedures allow students to be successful.

Program Building

A key concept of brain-compatibility describing how the brain stores and uses what it learns. It is defined as "a personal goal achieved by a sequence of steps or actions" which becomes stored in the brain for later retrieval when an action is required. Every goal we accomplish is due to implementation of a program or programs. Together with pattern seeking, is one of the four concepts from brain research upon which the *HET* model is based.

Social/Political Action

An integral part of the Highly Effective Teaching model which provides students a vehicle for applying what they learn to real-world problems. It assists students in becoming contributing citizens.

Symbolic Input

The most difficult way for the brain to grasp new information such as phonics, grammar, and algebraic equations.

Topics

A curriculum development structure of the Highly Effective Teaching model for dividing each component into important topics or areas of the concept for the component's being there experience.

LIST OF FIGURES

SUSAN J. KOVALIK

Susan J. Kovalik: a lifelong learner. After graduating in 1961 from California State University, San Jose, with a BA in elementary Education, Susan began her teaching career as a sixth-grade elementary teacher followed by time as a science teacher in a K-6 elementary school of 1,200 and a GATE (Gifted and Talented Education) teacher in five schools. In 1984, Susan was awarded the California Gifted and Talented Teacher of the Year. During this time, she also found time to share her love for experiential learning as the community leader of a multi-faceted 4-H club with 50 families and 37 projects.

Building on her own teaching experiences and emerging brain research, Susan developed the ITI (Integrated Thematic Instruction) model, now referred to as the *HET* (Highly Effective Teaching) model. Over the next 25 years, Susan and her remarkably talented associates have trained thousands of teachers in hundreds of schools throughout the United States, Europe, and Asia.

In 1987, the ITI model was selected by the David and Lucile Packard Foundation to support the teaching of science in Monterey County, California. Over 700 teachers participated in the program known as Monterey County Science Improvement Project (MCSIP).

The ITI/*HET* model was one of the 56 programs in the national Comprehensive School Reform Catalog, was selected for inclusion in the college text *Instructional-Design Theories and Models: A New Paradigm of Instructional Theory* by Charles Reigeluth, and selected by the American Youth Policy Forum targeting Service Learning and Educational Reform as one of its 22 models.

Susan has created support materials, publications, and media products for teachers in brain-compatible instruction. Several of her 20 training videos received both the Gold Apple and the Silver Apple awards from the National Educational Film and Video Festival.

A keynoter of national reputation, Susan continues to dedicate herself to improving education and helping others in implementing a bodybrain-compatible learning environment for students and their teachers.

KAREN D. OLSEN

Karen D. Olsen (BS, MA, MEd) brings a wealth of experience to her writing. The product of a one-room school for Grades 1–8 and growing up on a ranch, Karen has retained her insistence that what we learn should be usable in very practical as well as academically rigorous ways. Following doctoral studies at Columbia University Teachers College, she worked for the California State Department of Education for 12 years. Her assignments included planning and development, writing schoolwide planning and quality program review documents and processes, and managing of the consortium support unit serving districts highly committed to school change.

Karen was one of the original founders of the California Institute of School Improvement, a non-profit organization designed to support schools and districts in a wide range of school change issues. As program director, she conducted seminars on a range of topics including implications of recent legislation, schoolwide planning and program quality review processes, and the role of mentor teachers as change agents.

Karen served as Executive Director of the Mid-California Science Improvement Program (MCSIP), a 10-year effort funded by the David and Lucile Packard Foundation to improve science education using the ITI/*HET* model, an experience resulting in the first draft of this book. She also served as Executive Director of the Bay Area Middle School Program, a project to create model middle schools.

Karen is author, co-author, and contributing editor of two dozen books focusing on using brain research to create schoolwide change. Her most recent book is *What Brain Research Can Teach About Cutting School Budgets*, also published by Corwin.

ABC News Prime Time. "Your Child's Brain" with Diane Sawyer. January 25, 1995.

Armstrong, Thomas. *In Their Own Way.* Los Angeles: Tarcher Press, 1987.

Armstrong, Thomas. *7 Kinds of Smart: Identifying and Developing Your Multiple Intelligences.* New York: Penguin Putnam, 1999.

Bell, Nanci. *Visualizing and Verbalizing for Improved Comprehension: A Teacher's Manual.* San Luis Obispo, CA: Gander Educational Publishing, 1991.

Bloom, Benjamin, *Taxonomy of Educational Objectives: The Classification of Educational Goals, Handbook #1: Cognitive Domain.* New York: Longman, Green Publishers, 1956.

Brady, Marion. *What's Worth Teaching? Selecting, Organizing, and Integrating Knowledge.* Covington, WA: Books for Educators, 2004.

Bruner, John. "A Bridge Too Far" article in *Educational Researcher*, August, 1997.

Burz, Helen, and Marshall, Kit. *Performance-Based Curriculum for Science: From Knowing to Showing.* Thousand Oaks, CA: Corwin, 1997.

Caine, Renata and Geoffrey. *Making Connections: Teaching and the Human Brain.* San Francisco, CA: Addison-Wesley, 1994.

Calvin, William. *How Brains Think: Evolving Intelligence, Then and Now.* New York: Basic Books, 1996.

Calvin, William H. *"The Mind's Big Bang and Mirroring,"* unpublished manuscript. Seattle, WA: University of Washington, 2000.

Castelli, Darla, C. H. Hillman, S. M. Buck, and H. E. Erwin, "Physical Fitness and Academic Achievement in Third- and Fifth-Grade Students, *Journal of Sport & Exercise Psychology*, 29, 2007.

Childre, Doc. *Freeze Frame: One Minute Stress Management.* Boulder Creek, CA: Planetary Publications, 1998.

Childre, Doc, and Martin, Howard, with Beech, Donna. *The HeartMath Solution.* San Francisco: Harper, 2000.

Cohen, Elizabeth. *Designing Groupwork: Strategies for the Heterogeneous Classroom*, Second Edition. New York: Teachers College Press, 1994.

Cohen, Isabel and Marcelle Goldsmith. *Hands-On: How to Use Brain Gym in the Classroom.; A Practical Photo Manual for Educators, Parents, and Learners.* Ventura, CA: Edu-Kinesthetics, Inc., 2003.

Csikszentmihalyi, Mihaley. *Flow: The Psychology of Optimal Experience.* New York: Harper Row, 1990.

Damasio, Antonio. *Descartes' Error: Emotion, Reason, and the Human Brain.* New York: G. P. Putnam Sons, 1994.

Damasio, Antonio. *Looking for Spinoza: Joy, Sorrow, and the Feeling Brain.* New York: Harcourt, 2003.

Damasio, Antonio. "Thinking About Emotion." Presentation at Emotional Intelligence, Education, and the Brain: A Symposium. Chicago, IL, December 5, 1997.

Diamond, Marion, and Hopson, Janet. *Magic Trees of the Mind: How to Nurture Your Child's Intelligence, Creativity, and Healthy Emotions From Birth Through Adolescence.* New York: Penguin, 1998.

Gallese, Vittorio, and Goldman, Alvin. "Mirror Neurons and the Simulation Theory of Mind-Reading" in *Trends in Cognitive Sciences*, Vol. 2, 1998.

Gardner, Howard. *Frames of Mind: Theory of Multiple Intelligences.* New York: Basic Books, 2008.

Gardner, Howard. *Intelligence Reframed: Multiple Intelligences for the 21st Century*. New York: Basic Books, 1999.

Gibbs, Jeanne. *TRIBES: A New Way of Learning and Being Together*. Windsor, California: Center-Source Systems, LLC, 2001.

Glasser, William, M.D. *Control Theory in the Classroom*. New York: Perennial Library, 1986.

Goldberg, Elkhonon. *The Executive Brain: Frontal Lobes and the Civilized Mind*. Oxford, UK: University Press, 2001.

Goldberg, Elkhonon. *The Wisdom Paradox: How Your Mind Can Grow Stronger as Your Brain Grows Older*. New York, NY: Gotham Books/Division of Penquin Books, 2005.

Gopnik, A., A. Meltzoff, and Patricia Kuhl. *The Scientist in the Crib: Minds, Brains, and How Children Learn*. New York: William Morrow and Company, 1999.

Gossen, Diane. *It's All About We: Rethinking Discipline Using Restitution*. Saskatoon, SK: Chelsom Consultants Ltd., 2004.

Gossen, Diane. Restitution: *Restructuring School Disclipline*. Chapel Hill, NC: New View Publications, 1996.

Grissom, Jim. "Physical Fitness and Academic Achievement," *Journal of Exercise PhysiologyOnline (JEPonline)*, 8, No. 1 (February 2005).

Grissom, Jim. "California Physical Fitness Test: A Study of the Relationship Between Physical Fitness and Academic Achievement in California Using 2004 Test Results." California State Department of Education, 2004.

Hannaford, Carla. *Playing in the Unified Field: Raising and Becoming Conscious, Creative Human Beings*. Salt Lake City, UT: Great River Books, 2010.

Hannaford, Carla. *Smart Moves: Why Learning Is Not All in Your Head*. Alexander, NC: Great Ocean, 1995.

Hardwired to Connect. A collaborative work by the Commission of Children at Risk. New York: sponsored by YMCA of the USA, Dartmouth Medical School, Institute for American Values, 2003 and the work of Dr. Sigurd Zielke.

Hart, Leslie A. *Human Brain and Human Learning*, 3rd ed. Black Diamond, WA: Books for Educators, 2002.

Hawkins, Jeff, with Sandra Blakeslee. *On Intelligence: How a New Understanding of the Brain Will Lead to the Creation of Truly Intelligent Machines*. New York: Times Books/Henry Holt and Company, 2004.

Healy, Jane. *Different Learners: Identifying, Preventing, and Treating Your Child's Learning Problems*. New York: Simon & Schuster, 2010.

Healy, Jane. *Endangered Minds: Why Children Don't Think — and What We Can Do About It*. New York: Simon & Schuster, 1990.

Healy, Jane. *Failure to Connect: How Computers Affect Our Children's Minds — And What We Can Do About It*. New York: Simon & Schuster, 1998.

Hillman, Charles H., Pontiflex, Matthew B., Raine, Lauren B., Castelli, Darla M., Hall, Eric E., and Kramer, Arthur F. "The Effect of Acute Treadmill Walking on Cognitive Control and Academic Achievement in Preadolescent Children," *Neuroscience* 159 (2009).

Iacoboni, Marco. *Mirroring People: The New Science of How We Connect With Others*. New York: Farrar, Straus and Giroux, 2008.

Kagan, Spencer. *Cooperative Learning*. San Clemente, CA: Kagan, 1994.

Kagan, Spencer. *SmartCards*. San Juan Capistrano, CA: Kagan, 2003.

Keirsey, David. *Please Understand Me II: Temperament Character Intelligence*. Del Mar, CA: Prometheus Nemesis Book Company, 1998.

Kohn, Alfie. *Punished by Rewards: The Trouble With Gold Stars, Incentive Plans, A's, Praise, and Other Bribes*. Boston: Houghton Mifflin, 1993.

Kotulak, Ronald. *Inside the Brain: Revolutionary Discoveries of How the Mind Works*. Kansas City, MO: Andrews McMeel Publishing, 1996.

Kovalik, Susan. *Teach for Success: A Thematic Approach to Teaching Science*. Covington, WA: Susan Kovalik and Associates, 1986.

Kovalik, Susan J., and Olsen, Karen D. *Exceeding Expectations: A User's Guide to Implementing Brain Research in the Classroom*, 5th ed. Federal Way, WA: The Center for Effective Learning, 2010.

Lieberman, Gerald A. and Hoody, Linda I. *Closing the Achievement Gap: Using Environment as an Integrating Context for Learning, Executive Summary*. Poway, CA: Science Wizards, 1998.

LeDoux, Joseph. "The Emotional Brain." Presentation at Emotional Intelligence, Education, and the Brain: A Symposium, Chicago, IL, December 5, 1997.

LeDoux, Joseph E. *The Emotional Brain: The Mysterious Underpinnings of Emotional Life*. New York: Simon and Schuster, 1996.

Lowery, Lawrence F. *Thinking and Learning: Matching Developmental Stages With Curriculum and Instruction*. Kent, WA: Books for Educators, 1996.

McGovern, M. K. "The Effects of Exercise on the Brain." serendip.brynmawr.edu/bb/neuro/neuro05/web2/mmcgovern.html.

Medina, John. *Brain Rules: 12 Principles for Surviving and Thriving at Work, Home, and School*. Seattle, WA: Pear Press, 2008.

Motluk, Alison. "Read My Mind." *New Scientist*, January 27, 2001.

Olsen, Karen D. *Science Continuum of Concepts*, K-6. Black Diamond, WA: Center for the Future of Public Education, 2010.

Olsen, Karen D. *What Brain Research Can Teach About How to Cut School Budgets*. Thousand Oaks, CA: Corwin, 2010.

Olsen, Karen D. *Your Personal Guide to Implementing the* ITI/HET *Model: Stages 1–3*. Federal Way, WA: The Center for Effective Learning, 2010.

Private Universe, A. Cambridge, MA: Harvard-Smithsonian Center for Astrophysics, 1987.

Pearson, Sue. *Tools for Citizenship and Life: Lifelong Guidelines and LIFESKILLS in Your Classroom*, 5th ed. Federal Way, WA: The Center for Effective Learning, 2010.

Pert, Candace. *Molecules of Emotion: Why You Feel the Way You Feel*. New York: Scribner, 1997.

Posner, Michael, and M. K. Rothbart. *Educating the Human Brain*. Washington, DC: American Psychological Association, 2007.

Project 2061. *Atlas of Science Literacy*. Washington, DC: American Association for the Advancement of Science and National Science Teachers Association, 2001.

Project 2061. *Benchmarks for Science Literacy*. American Association for the Advancement of Science and National Science Teachers Association. New York: Oxford University Press, 2009.

Ramachandran, V. S. *Mirror Neurons and Imitation Learning as the Driving Force Behind "The Great Leap Forward" in Human Evolution*. http://www.edge.org/documents/archive/edge69.html

Ratey, John. *Spark: The Revolutionary New Science of Exercise and the Brain*. New York: Little, Brown and Company, 2008.

Ratey, John J. *A User's Guide to the Brain: Perception, Attention, and the Four Theaters of the Brain*. New York: Pantheon Books, 2001.

Restak, Richard. *The New Brain: How the Modern Age Is Rewiring Your Mind*. Emmaus, PA: Rodale, Inc., 2003.

Rivlin, Robert, and Gravelle, Karen. *Deciphering Your Senses*. New York: Simon and Schuster, 1984.

Science Framework for the California Public Schools, Kindergarten Through Grade Twelve, California Department of Education, 1990.

Shaffer, Carolyn, and Anundsen, Kristin. *Creating Community Anywhere: Finding Support and Connection in a Fragmented World*. New York: Putnam's Son, 1993.

Shores, E. F. "Howard Gardner on the Eighth Intelligence: Seeing the Natural World, *Dimensions of Early Childhood*. Summer, 1995.

Simon, Herbert, *The Sciences of the Artificial*. Cambridge, MA: MIT Press, 1996.

Smith, Frank. *Insult to Intelligence: The Bureaucratic Invasion of Our Classrooms*. New York: Arbor House Publishing Company, 1986.

Smith, Frank. *to think*. New York: Teachers College Press, 1990.

Sylwester, Robert. *A Celebration of Neurons: An Educator's Guide to the Human Brain*. Chicago: Zephyr Press, 1995.

Sylwester, Robert. *How to Explain a Brain: An Educator's Handbook of Brain Terms and Cognitive Processes*. Thousand Oaks, CA: Corwin, 2005.

Sylwester, Robert. *A Child's Brain: The Need for Nurture*. Thousand Oaks, CA: Corwin, 2010.

Sylwester, Robert. "The Role of The Arts in Brain Development and Maintenance," 6. Available at http://ode.state.or.us/teachlearn/subjects/arts/resources/rolesbraindevelopment.pdf.

Wolfe, Patricia. *Brain Matters: Translating Research into Classroom Practice*. Alexandria, VA: ASCD, 2001.

Zielke, Dr. Sigurd. "An Introduction to Neurobehavioral-Developmental & Social Classroom Management." Presentation to Susan Kovalik & Associates, January, 20-22, 2005.

Zielke, Sigurd H, and Zielke, Debra L. *Neurobehavioral-Development Behavior Address and Care (NBD): Critical Notions and Science — Addiction and Beyond: A Grounded, Empirical, and Theory-Informed Strategy to Build Civil, Competent, and Moral Behavior in American Children and Youth*. Indianapolis, IN: Fairbanks, 2010.

FRYER, CARR and HARRIS
present

GWEN VERDON
as

Sweet Charity

A New Musical Comedy
with

JOHN McMARTIN

THELMA OLIVER   JAMES LUISI   ARNOLD SOBOLOFF   RUTH BUZZI
SHARON RITCHIE   JOHN WHEELER   BARBARA SHARMA
and

HELEN GALLAGHER

Book by

NEIL SIMON

Music by

CY COLEMAN

Lyrics by

DOROTHY FIELDS

Based upon an original screenplay by
FEDERICO FELLINI, TULLIO PINELLI AND ENNIO FLAIANO

Scenery and Lighting by
ROBERT RANDOLPH

Costumes Designed by
IRENE SHARAFF

Musical Direction and Dance Music Arranged by
FRED WERNER

Orchestrations by
RALPH BURNS

Production Manager   Associate Producer
ROBERT LINDEN   **JOHN BOWAB**

Conceived, Staged and Choreographed by

BOB FOSSE

On the cover: Gwen Verdon, the original Charity
Image used by permission of Nicole Fosse

ISBN-13: 978-1-4234-2967-8
ISBN-10: 1-4234-2967-2

All materials courtesy of Notable Music Co. Inc./The Cy Coleman Office.
For info, visit **www.cycoleman.com** and **www.myspace.com/cycoleman**

HAL•LEONARD®
CORPORATION
7777 W. BLUEMOUND RD. P.O. BOX 13819 MILWAUKEE, WI 53213

INDEXED

Visit Hal Leonard Online at
www.halleonard.com

CY COLEMAN

CY COLEMAN was a musician's composer, classically trained at piano, composition and orchestration at New York City's High School for the Performing Arts and NY College of Music. Mr. Coleman was being groomed to be the next great conductor. Instead he turned his passion to jazz and formed the popular Cy Coleman Trio. Born Seymour Kaufman on June 14, 1929 in the Bronx, he changed his name at age 16 in time to use it on his first compositions with lyricist Joe A. McCarthy ("Why Try to Change Me Now" and "I'm Gonna Laugh You Right Out of My Life"). While still performing in jazz clubs and enjoying a successful recording career, Cy began writing with veteran songwriter Carolyn Leigh. Hits like "Witchcraft" and "The Best Is Yet to Come" were followed by their leap to Broadway with *Wildcat*, starring Lucille Ball ("Hey, Look Me Over") and then *Little Me* ("I've Got Your Number" and "Real Live Girl"). In 1966 Cy, along with legendary lyricist Dorothy Fields, triumphed with the smash hit *Sweet Charity* ("Big Spender" and "If My Friends Could See Me Now"). Cy continued on Broadway and wrote the scores for *Seesaw, I Love My Wife, On the Twentieth Century, Barnum, City of Angels, The Will Rogers Follies,* and *The Life.* In 2004 Cy returned to his roots and revived the Cy Coleman Trio, once again wowing audiences with his amazing skill at the piano. In Mr. Coleman's amazing career he took home three Tony® Awards, two GRAMMY® Awards, three Emmy® Awards, an Academy Award® nomination and countless honors. Cy served on the Board of ASCAP for three decades.

DOROTHY FIELDS

DOROTHY FIELDS wrote some of the most beloved lyrics in all American Popular Song ("I Can't Give You Anything but Love, Baby," "On the Sunny Side of the Street") and some of the most romantic ("Don't Blame Me," and the 1936 Oscar winner, "The Way You Look Tonight.") All were penned before she was 33 years old. She discovered her genius early in life and that youthful output included "I'm in the Mood for Love," "Exactly Like You," "Pick Yourself Up," and "A Fine Romance." But Dorothy remained a star among lyricists for six decades, and wrote successfully for revues, Hollywood films and classic Broadway book musicals. After her collaborations with Jimmy McHugh and Jerome Kern, and still not 40, Dorothy began writing librettos for musical comedies as well as lyrics. Most notably, she collaborated with her brother Herbert on the book for *Annie Get Your Gun* (1946) which starred Ethel Merman and was revived in 1999 with Bernadette Peters (later, Reba McEntire). Dorothy's book-writing experience accounted for dramatically matured lyrics and likely helped define characters in a way not foreseeable in the early review songs. This

evolution is clearly audible in her lyrics for *A Tree Grows in Brooklyn* (1951), set to music by yet another major collaborator, Arthur Schwartz. Dorothy's career continued to flourish right up to the end of her life. Her late scores with Cy Coleman include some of her best known and, arguably, some of her most resourceful efforts, filled with wit, insight and poignancy. When she died in 1974, Dorothy Fields was nearly unique among her peers, the great American songwriters: She had a new work, not a revival, running on Broadway, the musical *Seesaw.* Dorothy's titles and lyrics have become part of our language and have helped establish the character and popularity of American art forms that have endeared our culture to much of the world.

Reviewers gush in a full-page ad in the February 7, 1966 New York Daily News.

Gwen Verdon strikes her famous pose on the cover of the 1966 Broadway cast recording.

A gold ticket for opening night at the Palace Theatre on Broadway, January 27, 1966.

Bob Fosse's choreography for the "Rich Man's Frug" in the 1966 Broadway production.

Gwen Verdon dances the fandango with Helen Gallagher and Thelma Oliver in the 1966 Broadway production.

Gwen Verdon and Sammy Davis, Jr. with a "mysterious" Cy Coleman in the background.

Shirley MacLaine and Sammy Davis, Jr. depicted on the front of the 1969 motion picture soundtrack album.

OVERTURE: (a) Big Spender
(b) It's A Nice Face
(c) Sweet Charity
(d) Where Am I Going?
(e) I'm A Brass Band
MY PERSONAL PROPERTY
BIG SPENDER
THE POMPEII CLUB (Rich Man's Frug)
IF MY FRIENDS COULD SEE
ME NOW
THERE'S GOTTA BE SOMETHING
BETTER THAN THIS

IT'S A NICE FACE
RHYTHM OF LIFE
SWEET CHARITY
I'M A BRASS BAND
I LOVE TO CRY AT WEDDINGS
WHERE AM I GOING?
FINALE: SWEET CHARITY
(Rebirth)

The back cover of the 1969 motion picture soundtrack album, featuring Shirley MacLaine and Sammy Davis, Jr.

Molly Ringwald onstage during the 2006 touring production.

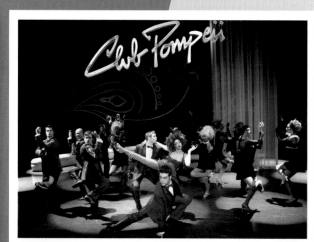

Makin' the scene at the Club Pompeii in the 2005 Broadway revival.